The Quest for Quality

The Quest for Quality
Promising Innovations for Early
Childhood Programs

edited by

Patricia W. Wesley, M.Ed.

and

Virginia Buysse, Ph.D.

FPG Child Development Institute
University of North Carolina at Chapel Hill
Chapel Hill

Baltimore • London • Sydney

Paul H. Brookes Publishing Co.
Post Office Box 10624
Baltimore, Maryland 21285-0624
USA

www.brookespublishing.com

Copyright © 2010 by Paul H. Brookes Publishing Co.
All rights reserved.

"Paul H. Brookes Publishing Co." is a registered trademark of
Paul H. Brookes Publishing Co., Inc.

Typeset by Aptara, Inc., Falls Church, Virginia.
Manufactured in the United States of America by
Sheridan Books, Inc., Chelsea, Michigan.

Library of Congress Cataloging-in-Publication Data

Wesley, Patricia W.
 The quest for quality : promising innovations for early childhood programs /
Patricia W. Wesley, Virginia Buysse.
     p.   cm.
 Includes index.
 ISBN-13: 978-1-59857-086-1
 ISBN-10: 1-59857-086-2
 1. Early childhood education—United States.   2. Child development—United States.
I. Buysse, Virginia. II. Title.
LB1139.25.W47 2010
372.210973—dc22   2010015211

British Library Cataloguing in Publication data are available from the British Library.

2014 2013 2012 2011 2010
10   9   8   7   6   5   4   3   2   1

Contents

About the Editors vii

About the Contributors ix

Foreword   *Anne W. Mitchell* xiii

Preface xvii

1   Changing Times and the Quest for Quality
    Patricia W. Wesley and Virginia Buysse 1

2   Research on Program Quality: The Evidence Base
    Ellen S. Peisner-Feinberg and Noreen Yazejian 21

3   Issues in Measuring Program Quality
    Donna M. Bryant, Martha Zaslow, and Margaret Burchinal 47

4   Early Learning Standards and Quality Improvement
    Initiatives: A Systemic Approach to Supporting Children's
    Learning and Development
    *Catherine Scott-Little, Deborah J. Cassidy,
    Joanna K. Lower, and Sarah J. Ellen* 69

5   Quality Rating and Improvement Systems: Achieving
    the Promise for Programs, Parents, Children, and Early
    Childhood Systems
    Kathryn Tout and Kelly L. Maxwell 91

6   Professional Development and Quality Initiatives: Two
    Essential Components of an Early Childhood System
    Pamela J. Winton 113

7   Rethinking Technical Assistance to Support Quality
    Improvement
    Patricia W. Wesley and Virginia Buysse 131

8   Early Childhood Policy and Implications for Quality Initiatives
    Beth Rous and Kim F. Townley 165

9   Program Quality Through the Lens of Disruptive
    Innovation Theory
    Virginia Buysse and Patricia W. Wesley 183

Index 199

About the Editors

Patricia W. Wesley, M.Ed., is Senior Scientist Emerita at the FPG Child Development Institute at the University of North Carolina at Chapel Hill. Her work has spanned more than three decades and includes directing one of the first inclusive early childhood programs in North Carolina; managing a statewide technical assistance network supporting high-quality inclusion; developing and researching the effectiveness of an on-site consultation model to promote early childhood program quality; and publishing numerous books, chapters, and articles on topics such as technical assistance, communities of practice, and the meaning of evidence-based practice in the early childhood field. Ms. Wesley currently provides professional development across the country on promoting high-quality early childhood education, with a special emphasis on advancing the practice of effective consultation.

Virginia Buysse, Ph.D., is Senior Scientist at the FPG Child Development Institute at the University of North Carolina at Chapel Hill. She directs research and development projects on a variety of topics related to promoting high-quality early childhood programs, including Recognition & Response (R&R)—a response to intervention (RTI) model for prekindergarten, differentiated instructional strategies for dual language learners, and models of professional development focused on creating integrated, cross-sector systems and a decision-making process using principles from evidence-based practice. She serves as President of the Division for Early Childhood (DEC) of the Council of Exceptional Children (CEC). She also serves on the editorial boards of many leading journals, including the *Journal of Early Intervention,* for which she serves as Associate Editor. She has co-authored books on consultation and evidence-based practice and currently is co-editing a volume on effective educational practices for diverse young learners.

About the Contributors

Donna M. Bryant, Ph.D., Senior Scientist, FPG Child Development Institute, The University of North Carolina at Chapel Hill, CB #8180, Chapel Hill, NC 27599-8180

Dr. Bryant recently completed a five-state randomized study of the Partnerships for Inclusion model of quality enhancement for early childhood programs and is coleading the national evaluation of the Bounce Learning Network's Educare programs. She also consults on evaluations of quality indicators and Quality Improvement and Rating Systems.

Margaret Burchinal, Ph.D., Director, Design and Statistical Computing Unit, FPG Child Development Institute, The University of North Carolina at Chapel Hill, and Professor, Department of Education, University of California–Irvine, 226 Sheryl Mar South, 510 South Greensboro, Carrboro, NC 27510

Dr. Burchinal has served as the applied statistician for many large child care studies and has helped demonstrate the use of sophisticated statistical methods to developmental psychologists.

Deborah J. Cassidy, Ph.D., Professsor, Department of Human Development, and Family Studies Professor in the Birth-Kindergarten Licensure Program, The University of North Carolina at Greensboro, School of Human Environmental Sciences UNCG, P.O. Box 26170, Greensboro, NC 27402-6170

Dr. Cassidy is Director of the North Carolina Division of Child Development. She has published extensively in the area of early childhood professional development and policy.

Sarah J. Ellen, M.Ed., Director, Twin Oaks Child Care Center, McLeansville, NC.

Ms. Ellen is a recent graduate of UNC-Greensboro's Birth through Kindergarten Interdisciplinary Studies in Education master's program. As part of her master's degree studies, she completed a review of state-level Quality Improvement and Rating Systems.

Joanna K. Lower, M.S., Ph.D. Candidate, Department of Human Development and Family Studies, The University of North Carolina at Greensboro, Post Office Box 26170, Greensboro, NC 27402

Ms. Lower's research focuses on informing public policy in the best interest of children, families, and society; conceptualizing and assessing early childhood classroom quality; and strengthening and developing the early childhood workforce and profession.

Kelly L. Maxwell, Ph.D., Research Scientist and Associate Director, FPG Child Development Institute, The University of North Carolina at Chapel Hill, CB #8180, Chapel Hill, NC 27599-8180

Dr. Maxwell's research interests include quality rating and improvement systems, school readiness, and evaluation of early childhood initiatives. She has conducted several studies of child care and family child care and has helped states pilot-test and evaluate quality rating and improvement systems.

Ellen S. Peisner-Feinberg, Ph.D., Senior Scientist, FPG Child Development Institute, The University of North Carolina at Chapel Hill, 105 Smith Level Road; Chapel Hill, NC 27516

Dr. Peisner-Feinberg's background is in developmental psychology and public policy, and she has more than 20 years of research experience in early childhood education and program evaluation. Dr. Peisner-Feinberg has conducted numerous statewide and national research studies focused on the quality of early education programs and initiatives; the effects on children, especially dual language learners and children at risk; and quality improvement strategies.

Beth Rous, Ed.D., Associate Professor, Educational Leadership Studies, University of Kentucky, 126 Mineral Industries Bldg. Lexington, KY 40506-0051

Dr. Rous has done extensive research and training related to early childhood systems design and policy implementation at the state and local levels. Her areas of interest include accountability, cross-sector system design, and professional development systems.

Catherine Scott-Little, Ph.D., M.S., B.S.H.E., Associate Professor in Human Development and Family Studies, The University of North Carolina at Greensboro, 248 Stone Building, Greensboro, NC 27402

Dr. Scott-Little teaches in the Birth through Kindergarten Teacher Education program at The University of North Carolina at Greensboro. She has conducted several national studies on early learning standards developed by states and has worked with several states to develop and analyze the content of their early learning standards.

Kathryn Tout, Ph.D., Director of Applied Research in Early Care and Education, Child Trends, 615 First Ave N.E., Suite 225, Minneapolis, MN 55413

Dr. Tout oversees projects in Child Trends's Minnesota office. Her research focuses on policies and programs to improve the quality of early care and education and families' access to quality settings, and programs to improve the quality and effectiveness of the early childhood workforce.

Kim F. Townley, Ph. D., Associate Professor, 229 Taylor Education Building, University of Kentucky, Lexington, Kentucky 40506-0001

Dr. Townley has more than 30 years of experience as a teacher of young children and university students. As Executive Director of the Governor's Office of Early Childhood Development in Kentucky, she led a major, comprehensive early childhood initiative that resulted in implementation or expansion of more than 17 programs to support children reaching their full potential.

Pamela J. Winton, Ph.D., M.A., B.A., Senior Scientist and Director of Outreach, FPG Child Development Institute, The University of North Carolina at Chapel Hill, CB #8185, Chapel Hill, NC 27599

Dr. Winton has been involved in research, outreach, and professional development related to early childhood since the mid-1980s. This includes directing federally funded national centers; publishing books; and being involved with 11 different federally funded early childhood research institutes and projects, including directing (as principal investigator or co–principal investigator) 6 of them.

Noreen Yazejian, Ph.D., M.A., B.A., Investigator, FPG Child Development Institute, The University of North Carolina at Chapel Hill, 105 Smith Level Road, CB #8180, Chapel Hill, NC 27599-8180

Dr. Yazejian is an investigator at the FPG Child Development Institute at The University of North Carolina at Chapel Hill. Dr. Yazejian's research focuses on early childhood program evaluation, including work related to professional development interventions, models of programming for birth to 5 years, quality rating and improvement systems, and early childhood language and literacy.

Martha Zaslow, Ph.D., Director, Office for Policy and Communications, Society for Research in Child Development, Office for Policy and Communications, Society for Research in Child Development, 1313 L Street NW, Suite 140, Washington, DC 20005 and Senior Scholar, Child Trends, 4301 Connecticut Avenue, NW, Suite 250, Washington, DC 20008

Dr. Zaslow is Director of the Office for Policy and Communications of the Society for Research in Child Development. She is also Senior Scholar at Child Trends, a nonpartisan, nonprofit research organization in Washington, D.C., that focuses on research and statistics on children and families in the United States. Dr. Zaslow's research focuses on early childhood development and takes an ecological approach, considering the role of multiple contexts, including the family, early care and education settings, and programs and policies for families with young children. She is especially interested in understanding how to strengthen quality in early care and education settings and in how children's experiences in such settings contribute to school readiness.

Foreword

Many edited volumes of research are essentially a close examination of the bark on the trees, rather than a sweeping view of the forest and its ecology. This book is different. Wesley and Buysse have collected the best thinking of first-rate early childhood researchers, all of whom took up the challenge of looking beyond the bark and trees they know well to the ecology of the early care and education forest. This book is about the early care and education (EC&E) system and its quality.

All of the contributors deserve a round of applause for their courage in taking on the wide-ranging set of issues that affect the quality of the EC&E system. The history of the quality movement and quality research grounds the volume. The chapter on measurement will be especially welcome to policymakers as it identifies the practical issues well and poses helpful questions. Researchers can support the designers and policy makers of quality improvement strategies by focusing on measuring those aspects of practice and conditions that relate to and can predict better child outcomes.

The contributors have done a huge service to early childhood innovators everywhere by focusing clearly on quality improvement and correctly lodging that movement right in the heart of EC&E system building. Improving the current experience, ongoing development and later outcomes of young children is our collective goal. System building is the means to those ends. We have come to realize a system is necessary: addressing each of the parts one at a time does not produce sufficient progress because the parts are interdependent (Stoney, Mitchell, & Warner, 2006).

An effective system is based on aligned standards: standards for programs, for practitioners, and for children's early learning. As pointed out in Chapter 4— standards by themselves do not cause quality improvement. Indeed, an effective system also needs accountability through appropriate means of assessment and monitoring; program and practitioner outreach and support, including training, technical assistance, mentoring and other forms of professional development and program improvement; financing that is intentionally linked to compliance with quality standards; and consumer engagement and outreach so that parents and others are able to effectively use quality information to guide their decision making (Mitchell, 2009).

Beyond documenting the historical and current knowledge base on quality, this book contributes to the discourse on system building by reminding us that affecting day-to-day practice is essential to achieving our ends. Intentional teaching, individualizing, and the preparation and support of practitioners to practice these are consistent themes.

The need for greater investment is mentioned in several chapters but is not a focus of any chapter. Financial investment is clearly necessary and needs to be part of any discussion of EC&E systems, focusing on questions such as What are the fair shares for public and private investment? What is an equitable family contribution? Are there essential elements, such as the infrastructure of support for quality improvement (monitoring, accountability, data systems, professional development, and organizational development) that ought to be publicly funded? What is the right balance between federal, state, and local financial responsibility?

Several chapters recommend national standards. As states have forged ahead on standards development, leading the quality movement in recent years, there is legitimate debate about what functions are best conducted at which levels. The federal role may be to establish benchmarks for quality improvement and track progress of states rather than to establish a single set of national standards.

One emerging and useful system element that is not mentioned here is practitioner registries—these would address many of the issues raised throughout the book about accurately capturing the qualification, credentials and ongoing professional development activities of the workforce. The National Registry Alliance brings together these state information systems and is pioneering unified data definitions, collection and verification procedures among others. For more information, see http://www.registryalliance.org/.

Further, several states are developing robust data systems to support and manage their quality rating improvement system (QRIS). These track the features and conditions of programs in terms of QRIS standards, as well as the quality initiative supports (professional development, technical assistance of all kinds) taken up by the program and the costs of these. Much like the ability to connect teacher to student in education data systems, these data systems connect programs to the practitioners to the technical assistance (TA) and professional development (PD) data (who, when, what, how, and how much) to program quality improvement. Researchers can collaborate with database developers (for QRISs, Practitioner Registries) to ensure the necessary precision and specificity is built into these data systems—that they are accurately capturing factors of duration, intensity, timing, cost, progress benchmarks, and so forth—so that these information systems can serve research as well as policy purposes.

The chapter on TA thoughtfully describes the problems of defining the wide range of activities that are labeled as such, proposes better definitions and does a good job of identifying the challenges that face the quality movement in the early care and education enterprise.

Disruptive innovation is a thought provoking concept introduced by the editors. It raises a host of questions and practical issues. Who disrupts? What needs to be disrupted? At what levels can such innovation occur?

The concepts that underlie the "new governance"—theories about how government really works and how public management and public problem solving occur (Salamon, 2002)—support the changes and recommendations proposed in this book. Governance uses a wide array of tools to carry out broad societal goals, relying on networks of public and private actors, managed through negotiation, persuasion, incentives, and sometimes prohibitions. Discussing the collaborative nature of new governance, Salamon says to utilize government "for what it does best—raising revenue and setting broad societal directions" while empowering networks of public and private actors to implement, deliver and innovate. The Early Childhood Advisory Councils that states are now launching are perfect examples of the networked nature of governance. These Councils bring together the network of public and private actors for collective review, alignment and design of the unified early childhood system.

A final caution: researchers must not let the best be the enemy of the "good enough"—policy evolves and systems and standards are reviewed and revised over time. Children cannot wait for all the research to be in. Genuine demand for quality leads states to proceed with the best knowledge available when the conditions are right to take action. States do it as well as they can. Collaborations among researchers, policymakers, and system designers can be mutually informing. The states are now a natural laboratory on system building—a good deal messier than a treatment–control or planned variation study design for sure—yet nonetheless present golden opportunities to advance knowledge of practice and policy.

A book in which researchers are attempting to answer the questions policymakers are actually asking is a delight to read. These chapters are thoughtful, provocative, and engaging to such an extent the reader will want to have an immediate conversation with the authors.

Anne W. Mitchell
Cofounder, Alliance for Early Childhood Finance
Climax, New York

Preface

The Quest for Quality: Promising Innovations for Early Childhood Programs represents an opportunity for the early childhood community to consider where we have been, where we are now, and where we are headed with respect to a topic that is integral to everything we do on behalf of young children and families. In this volume, we bring together the big ideas and the best thinking around early childhood program quality. This would not be possible, of course, without the contributions of our colleagues, many of whom are leading scholars on research, policy, and the particular dimensions of program quality, such as early learning standards, professional development, quality rating and improvement systems (QRISs), and measurement within quality accountability systems. We are indebted to our colleagues and friends for sharing their collective wisdom and knowledge on this important topic.

Several prominent themes run through all of the chapters. First, the meaning and definition of program quality in the United States continue to evolve, making program quality a moving target in our ongoing efforts to improve and regulate it. At the same time, this volume affirms the need to modify definitions of program quality to reflect the changing demographic landscape and the early educational needs of an increasingly diverse population of young children and families—another important theme in this book.

Just as in the broader field of K–12 education, there is a growing realization in early childhood that we need to customize teaching and learning to ensure that practitioners are equipped to help every child develop to his or her full potential, including those with learning or behavior difficulties, those with identified disabilities, and those from diverse cultural and linguistic backgrounds. The customization of early education will reverberate throughout the system, directly affecting organizational structures and introducing new technologies and approaches related to teaching, intervening, and progress monitoring. We should expect that clearly defined practices aimed at addressing the educational needs of each and every child will result in corresponding changes to the program quality infrastructure that is designed to support and promote these very educational practices.

Another recurrent theme throughout this volume is the need to integrate the various components of program quality into a single, coherent system—a monumental task that lacks consensus from the field about how we will get there. Although this book does not provide a blueprint or lay out concrete steps for reaching this goal, it offers many promising directions for improving program quality in the future across key dimensions, including quality standards, measures, and methods for achieving and supporting quality programming. Further, this volume provides ideas about ways of advancing program quality improvement efforts through future innovations. We maintain that the best ideas for achieving improvements in program quality down the road will come not through increasing program monitoring and accountability efforts but through innovations that fundamentally change the current structures and ways of thinking about program quality. The choice we face as a field is to continue to make slow, steady progress to improve what is currently in place or to move in the direction of innovation to produce fundamental changes in how we conceptualize and support program quality in the future.

CHAPTER 1

Changing Times and the Quest for Quality

Patricia W. Wesley and Virginia Buysse

It is almost impossible to participate in a conversation about early childhood programs these days without mentioning quality. It is on the minds of researchers, state and local administrators, teachers, and families, which is not surprising, given how much we have learned about the importance of early care and education in recent years. Expectations have grown considerably since Belsky and Steinberg's conclusion that center-based programs had neither "salutary nor deleterious effects" on children (1978, p. 929). Not only do we know more about the importance of early experiences for brain development, but substantial research evidence suggests a causal link between the quality of early childhood programs and developmental outcomes in young children. Among the population of children enrolled in early childhood programs, high-quality early care and education offer a strong foundation for school readiness across key domains of learning and set the stage for future school success (Burchinal & Cryer, 2003; Howes, Phillips, & Whitebook, 1992; National Research Council & Institute of Medicine, 2000; Peisner-Feinberg et al., 2001; Vandell, 2004). This is good news for young children and families who are fortunate enough to participate in high-quality early childhood programs and services. Unfortunately, the care and education received by many children in early childhood programs is not of high quality. Research has shown that the quality of most prekindergarten programs for 3- to 5-year-olds is mediocre at best, whereas the quality of infant-toddler programs generally has been characterized as mediocre to poor (Cost, Quality, & Child Outcomes Study Team, 1995; National Association of Child Care Resource and Referral Agencies [NACCRRA], 2006; Peisner-Feinberg & Burchinal, 1997).

The prevalence of low-quality care and the link between quality and child outcomes have spawned a movement to improve program quality in the United States and have prompted calls for consumer advocacy and education on this issue. This chapter provides an overview of the quality improvement movement, its history, key features, and challenges. After reflecting on how the early childhood field has conceptualized program quality and the initiatives that support and sustain it, we identify areas in which change is needed to increase the scope and effectiveness of these efforts. Each of these proposed areas of change are examined more closely in subsequent chapters within this volume.

WHAT IS QUALITY?

As we begin to explore our understanding of quality, it may be helpful to consider that in the United States the meaning of quality resides largely in concepts related to measuring, evaluating, and regulating quality. In the field of early childhood, program quality is generally understood to be necessary for optimal outcomes in children and has become a method for managing people and programs using specific tools to determine their conformity to predetermined norms (see Chapter 3).

Although researchers and policy makers increasingly address issues related to quality, and numerous state and local initiatives promise to improve it, the early childhood field lacks a universally accepted and applied definition of *program quality*. This is true in spite of the fact that much is known about which cognitive, physical, social, emotional, and academic competencies enable children to achieve their potential in development and learning and the conditions that support development in these areas. Numerous sets of standards exist for different sectors that describe expectations for programs, teachers, and now children, but programs may not choose to apply the standards. Moreover, the standards are not aligned with each other sufficiently or coordinated through state or federal policy. For example, many states have early learning standards that describe what young children should know and be able to do at various stages of development, but these standards often are not aligned with a local program's curriculum goals and its methods for documenting child progress and outcomes. Similarly, there is a need to articulate how professional development standards (at both the state and national levels) are related to program standards and early learning standards (see Chapter 4).

Dimensions of Program Quality

Considerable research focusing on measuring program quality suggests that quality comprises multiple dimensions and that these dimensions predict child outcomes differently. The accuracy of our measurement of early childhood program quality varies across these dimensions (Burchinal, 2009). Although the field lacks consensus on a single approach for categorizing factors that define program quality, two broad dimensions are associated with whether early experiences ultimately promote higher rates of learning and development. These dimensions include 1) the quality of the curriculum and intentional teaching (e.g., planning, delivering, and evaluating instruction and relating positively to others) and 2) structural aspects such as the physical environment, child–caregiver ratio, caregiver qualifications, and compensation (Bryant, Maxwell, & Burchinal, 1999; Burchinal & Cryer, 2003; Cryer & Clifford, 2003; Early et al., 2007; National Association for the Education of Young Children [NAEYC], 1995; National Center for Early Development and Learning, 1997). It is important to understand that these dimensions are associated with learning and development for the general population of young children but may not be sufficient for those children with disabilities; therefore they may not reflect dimensions of high-quality inclusion (Buysse & Hollingsworth, 2009). Another significant gap in our ability to both define and measure quality lies in the inability to evaluate the extent to which teachers' practices are of high or low quality, although, as stated above, teachers' instructional practices are at the heart of program quality. The field lacks a valid measure of teachers' ability to plan, organize, and implement instruction for all children as well as their ability to scaffold learning for individual children who require additional supports to learn. Without being able to evaluate the quality of teaching practices, it is impossible to determine whether colleges and universities prepare teachers adequately for their jobs. It is also difficult to plan how to address teachers' ongoing needs for professional development. There are other dimensions of children's experiences in early childhood programs that are widely believed to be important to children's development but that have not been addressed adequately by research—for example, the engagement of the child in various activities and the roles of teaching assistants and peers in the setting.

The discourse on quality has not been without debate on the social and cultural values reflected in various conceptualizations of quality. Lively and rich discussion has encompassed a range of issues, including the organization of classroom environments, the emphasis on health and safety versus learning and development, the role of formal instruction compared to constructivist perspectives that stress following the child's initiative, school readiness, the use of early learning standards with diverse populations, the value of a child's self-expression, the value of social justice teaching with young children, and the nature of relationships with families (see, e.g., Jipson, 1991; Knitzer, 2002; Pelo, 2008; Scott-Little, Kagan, & Frelow, 2006; Spodek & Saracho, 1997; Walsh, 1991). Such ongoing questioning, along with research-driven changes in core knowledge, continue to influence recommended practices and, to some extent, program standards. At the same time, the national dialogue about the measurement, assurance, and improvement of quality in early childhood programs has institutionalized the emphasis on regulation and management and has led to state and local systems of quality ratings and supports. It is important to be aware of how the emphasis on rating quality affects the discussion of quality and to consider that some quality aspects may not be addressed if the goal is for an observer to make a decontextualized and objective statement of quality (Moss & Dahlberg, 2008).

Licensing and Standards as a Framework for Quality

From a public perspective, licensing is often considered a definition of quality. Many early childhood programs are licensed, but licensing represents a relatively low bar and typically focuses on the safety and adequacy of the physical environment, with only a few states requiring minimal caregiver training (NACCRRA, 2006). It should also be pointed out that some states do not require licensing for programs serving five or fewer children, and a few do not require family child care homes of any size to obtain licenses (NACCRRA, 2008).

The more rigorous National Association for the Education of Young Children (NAEYC) Program Standards and Accreditation Criteria (2006) are widely recognized to define global program quality (although other organizations also offer accreditation—for example, for family child care and after-school programs), but program participation is typically voluntary. In fact, less than 10% of nonmilitary programs are accredited (RAND Corporation, 2008). Even if more programs participated in NAEYC's accreditation process, existing standards primarily reflect the needs of the general population of young children, and their guidance in overall program improvement, although important, may not be sufficient to address the needs of children with disabilities and those with diverse learning characteristics, including dual language learners.

It is important to examine how standards are determined, including the nature and scope of participation and input during development and review, and the extent to which standards reflect the best research evidence. Whereas position statements may be informed and shaped by the field's professional wisdom and values, as gathered through public forums and (thanks to Internet technology), the input of thousands, standards may not receive such wide exposure during development.

Recommended Practices

The development of recommended practices or practice guidelines is another way to conceptualize quality, and several frameworks exist to guide early childhood professionals. NAEYC's (2009) position statement titled *Developmentally Appropriate Practice in Early Childhood Programs Serving Children from Birth Through Age 8* describes principles of child development and learning along with guidelines that should inform all levels of decision making about how to meet the needs of young children. This document is intended to complement the organization's other documents on practice, including *Early Learning Standards* (2002); *Early Childhood Curriculum, Assessment, and Program Evaluation* (2003); *NAEYC Early Childhood Program Standards and Accreditation Criteria* (2006); and the *Code of Ethical Conduct* (2005). The 2009 position paper differs significantly from its 1987 and 1997 forerunners in its description of what constitutes developmentally appropriate practice (DAP). The 1987 document (Bredekamp, 1987), which elaborated on NAEYC's accreditation criteria, was designed to discourage the tendency to push down academic curricula and formal instruction designed for elementary grades into early childhood programs. Rooted in Piagetian constructivism and maturationist psychology, DAP emphasized children's construction of their own knowledge and their individual self-expression, creativity, and self-initiated exploration of the environment, with the teachers' role being one of preparing the environment and facilitating the children's discovery. DAP experiences were considered active, concrete, and manipulative. The juxtaposition of examples of appropriate and inappropriate practice in the 1987 guidelines led to a polarized view of educational practice and created a widening gap between preschool and elementary school experiences for most children (Bevilacqua, 2008).

The 1997 revised publication (Bredekamp & Copple, 1997) built on the advances in research over the previous 10 years showing the importance of the early childhood program and its quality to children's development and learning. The 1987 concerns about academic pressures were absent in the newer document, and teachers were reminded about the need for intellectually engaging classrooms and even warned about failing to challenge children adequately. As presented in Dickinson's (2002) description of the early childhood field's changing perspective on literacy, this shifting view of teaching was illustrated clearly in statements from each document about print awareness. The 1987 document described as inappropriate "isolated skill development such as recognizing single letters [and] reciting the alphabet" and "activities designed solely to teach the alphabet, phonics, and penmanship" (p. 55). The 1997 version of *Developmentally Appropriate Practice in Early Childhood Programs* stated that it is appropriate that "children have opportunities to develop print awareness . . . and understanding of the various uses of the written word, while learning particular letter names and letter–sound combinations and recognizing words that are meaningful to them" (p. 131). In contrast to these statements from the early documents, the 2009 edition emphasized the importance of "mastering the alphabet principle—that there is a systematic relationship between letters and sounds, and that all spoken sounds and words can be represented by a limited set of symbols called letters" (NAEYC, 2009, p. 147). This new version urged teachers to "provide help when a child is striving to identify or form letters" and to place "alphabet charts and letters where children can refer to them" (p. 148). It recommended strategies such as "using alphabet books that illustrate letter sounds with pictures of objects, and inviting children to say what letter a word starts with or to say another word that starts with the same letter" (p. 148).

The 2009 position paper reflected the continually evolving knowledge base in early childhood and highlighted three particular concerns: the challenges of reducing learning gaps and increasing achievement in all children, increasing continuity and collaboration between preschool and elementary education, and recognizing teacher knowledge and decision making as vital to educational effectiveness (NAEYC, 2009). Compared with the previous documents, the new position statement described the teacher as the most powerful influence on whether and what children learn and emphasized the importance of "well-grounded intentionality" to guide "real-time decisions" and " moment-to-moment interactions" (p. 8). The document described the need for teachers to draw on a well-developed repertoire of teaching strategies, including modeling, demonstrating, giving directions, and other techniques to scaffold children's learning as they implement a robust curriculum with attention to known learning sequences in various domains. The chart of teaching practices presented in the document described the curriculum scope in greater detail than in previous versions, including sections on physical education and health, language and literacy, mathematics, science, social studies, and creative arts. The importance of integrating assessment, teaching, and curriculum also was stressed.

The Council for Exceptional Children's Division for Early Childhood's (DEC) *Recommended Practices* (Sandall, Hemmeter, Smith, & McLean, 2005) were intended to reflect both the scientific literature on effective practices for young children with disabilities, their families, and the personnel who work with them and the knowledge and experience of those who work with young children and their families. Although the DEC document did not include specific practices related to setting up developmentally appropriate classrooms or general suggestions for high-quality care and education, its use in conjunction with NAEYC's framework would inform quality in inclusive classrooms. The goal of DEC's *Recommended Practices* was to improve services for and outcomes of children with disabilities and their families by identifying the specialized supports and teaching strategies that are required to meet the needs of children with disabilities—those for whom teachers, families, caregivers, and other professionals need to design an individualized learning environment. Although discussions about the best use of quality-improvement funds available through the American Recovery and Reinvestment Act (ARRA) of 2009 have included the possibility of planning links between the early intervention system and early care and education services, there have been no explicit efforts to link DEC's *Recommended Practices* with program quality initiatives or to expand dimensions of program quality to reflect them.

A joint DEC/NAEYC (2009) position statement identified defining features of high-quality early childhood inclusion (access, participation, and supports) and several specific promising practices to help programs conceptualize and implement inclusive practices to achieve these features. These practices included universal design to support access to physical environments and multiple and varied formats for instruction and learning, including embedded interventions, explicit teaching strategies, and tiered instructional approaches that matched instruction to individual needs. According to the DEC/NAEYC position statement on inclusion, an infrastructure of program-level supports undergirds the efforts of individuals and organizations providing high-quality inclusive services to children and families. Such supports included professional development, opportunities for communication and collaboration among key stakeholders (e.g., families, program staff, specialists), a coordinated system of specialized services and therapies that could be integrated with general early care and education services, and fiscal and other incentives to increase access to high-quality inclusive opportunities.

The concept of desired results was also included in the definition of high-quality inclusion described in the DEC/NAEYC (2009) position statement. Goals of early childhood inclusion included learning and development in young children that allowed them to reach their full potential, including the development of a sense of belonging in children and families and of positive relationships with peers. These desired results should be a part of early discussions to plan high-quality inclusion and should be addressed in program evaluation to document the experiences and outcomes of inclusion for young children and families.

As researchers, policy makers, and the public continue to refine definitions of effective programs and practices, a number of federal initiatives have been launched to promote and guide early childhood program improvement. For example, the development of quality rating systems and early learning standards have stimulated and informed state and local efforts to assess, enhance, and monitor program quality. Next we briefly describe federal legislation and state initiatives that are at the heart of the early childhood quality-improvement movement.

THE EARLY CHILDHOOD QUALITY MOVEMENT

Legislation provides a foundation for the important values of affordable, accessible, high-quality early childhood programs that allow parents to work and that promote children's development and learning. Since the 1990s, the Child Care and Development Fund (CCDF) has been a significant resource in helping states invest in improving quality. This fund provides block grant allocations to states to assist low-income families, families receiving temporary public assistance, and parents transitioning from public assistance to obtain child care so that they can work. The fund now supports early childhood services for nearly 2 million children each month (see www.workworld.org). A minimum of 4% of CCDF funds must be used by states to improve the quality of child care and offer additional services to parents, such as resource and referral counseling regarding the selection of appropriate child care providers to meet their child's needs. These funds have supported various activities in many states, including professional development, grants and loans to providers, improved monitoring, and special compensation projects. Native American Tribes may use a portion of their funds to construct child care facilities, provided there is no reduction in the current level of child care services (Administration for Children and Families web site: http://www.acf.hhs.gov). The ARRA of 2009 provides $2 billion for quality improvement, including funds designated for infant and toddler care, $225,186,000 of which is set aside beyond the 4% required minimum for quality enhancement.

The Good Start, Grow Smart initiative of 2002 increased attention on the quality of care by focusing on children's academic achievement and the skills they needed to be ready for and successful in school. Good Start, Grow Smart encouraged states to develop voluntary guidelines to address children's language and literacy skills, and through the years educators and policy makers have expanded the focus to other areas of learning. These guidelines have taken the form of early learning standards in many states. The scrutiny on children entering kindergarten and the emphasis on school readiness have led to increased public funding and accountability of prekindergarten programs, especially for those children at risk of entering school without the necessary social and cognitive skills. These developments are an important foundation for improving early childhood program quality, especially in light of research suggesting that global program quality may be higher in states with more exacting regulations (Phillipson, Burchinal, Howes, & Cryer, 1997).

A Fragmented System

Although quality has been a key focus of discussion and activity across the nation in the early childhood field, little has been done to change the fragmented nature of early childhood services. Programs have different standards, funding sources, eligibility criteria, accountability systems, and professional affiliations. The field continues to struggle to integrate the concepts of child care and early education, as illustrated in the prevalent use of the term *early care and education* to describe programs for young children and the name of the Child Care and Development Fund. In many communities, child care, prekindergarten, and early intervention programs operate in separate worlds, turning to different sources for professional development and interpreting the meaning of program quality in different ways. As the following introductions to quality rating systems and early learning standards suggest, the early childhood field has more work to do to integrate and coordinate these components in the quality movement.

Quality Rating and Improvement Systems

There has been growing momentum at the state and local levels in this country to develop rating systems that would make child care quality transparent and easily communicated. The hope is that such public quality ratings, combined with consumer education about them, will drive the early childhood market to value and compete to provide quality programs. In a quality rating improvement system (QRIS), various components of quality are selected, combined, and weighted to produce an overall quality rating. Typically these components include child–staff ratios, group size, staff training and education, and some assessment of the classroom or learning environment. Some states also address family involvement and national accreditation. The ratings may be stars (or steps), with 1 to 2 stars, for example, indicating low quality and 4 to 5 stars indicating high quality, but the way in which the components are weighted and summed has received little empirical or policy attention.

Propelled by the accountability movement reflected in other fields, such as health and education, the overarching goal of these systems is to improve and link early childhood services and outcomes. Some quality rating systems include a variety of supports, such as feedback, technical assistance, and incentives to motivate and sustain enhanced quality, and these are called quality rating and improvement systems (QRISs). Five common elements are often shared by QRISs: 1) clear quality standards, 2) accountability through assessment and monitoring to meet those standards, 3) program and practitioner outreach and support, 4) financial incentives linked to compliance with standards, and 5) consumer education (see www.acf.hhs.gov for more information). QRISs can be established through agency regulation or statute, and most benefit from private and public support, including financial support (RAND Corporation, 2008). It should be noted that some QRISs are statewide, whereas others are implemented in a locality only—for example, a county or region. Participation in a QRIS is largely voluntary, and in some cases, QRIS standards are applied only to child care programs.

States and localities can have different goals for their QRISs beyond the fundamental quest to identify and improve low quality. Some states hope to use quality ratings to increase subsidy levels or slots for low-income children. Others plan to increase professional development opportunities and compensation for the workforce or begin to incorporate state early learning standards within their child care quality initiative (Mitchell, 2005). There are no federal policies to guide the development of a QRIS and little encouragement for states to aim for consistent QRIS standards or measurements. Given this autonomy, QRIS standards vary widely across the nation.

Notwithstanding the lack of consistency across QRIS initiatives, there are good reasons for families and professionals to be excited about the potential of QRISs to make a difference. In some states, a wide range of early childhood programs participate in QRISs, including center-based and family child care, afterschool, prekindergarten, and Head Start. As an accountability measure for policymakers concerned with results, QRISs can inform decisions about program funding and help gauge the effects of investments. But these are also reasons to develop and implement QRISs cautiously with rigorous scrutiny over how quality is defined and measured. As pointed out earlier, the concept of quality, as it has evolved in the United States, assumes the possibility that it can be defined as a set of indicators against which programs and performance can be assessed. Many QRISs assess quality using environment rating scales, which have been shown through research to be reliable and valid instruments. The feasibility of a local or state system to assess and monitor quality can be affected by logistical and financial constraints, however, and then the message can be misleading and the outcome counterproductive. For example, some QRISs administer only some subscales of environment rating scales, or otherwise combine selected quality components into their own summary measures, without knowing whether their approach to weighting and combining such components is efficacious. The RAND (2008) report of lessons learned from the study of QRISs in five states illuminates this concern. Because the components of quality addressed through QRIS standards are likely selected in a political climate through consensus among diverse stakeholders about what quality means, it is critical to ask hard questions about whether a QRIS measures what it purports to.

Among the different approaches QRISs use to support early childhood programs, professional development in the form of technical assistance (TA) is a primary vehicle for improving quality. The selection of on-site TA as a means of enhancing quality, especially as delivered in the context of several visits over time with a program's administrator or teachers, or both, reflects the common understanding that one-shot workshops rarely effect change. Although there is some evidence that TA services such as on-site consultation can produce significant and lasting changes in program quality when provided in a collaborative and systematic way (Bryant, Wesley, & the QUINCE Study Team, 2009; Palsha & Wesley, 1998; Wesley, 1994), TA activities typically offered in the name of quality enhancement lack a clearly articulated conceptual framework and consistent procedures (Bryant et al., 2009). In general, there has been little research on the effectiveness of various approaches to enhancing quality. Although states have been mandated to implement quality enhancement initiatives, a U.S. General Accounting Office (2002) report found that only three interventions have been evaluated in studies using methodological approaches sufficient to produce conclusive findings, and none of these were TA intervention. In Florida, a study found that more stringent child–staff ratios were related to children's cognitive and social development (see Chapter 7). Two other studies, sponsored by Massachusetts and Washington state, examined the compensation rates, recruitment, and retention of child care providers. The Massachusetts study found that providers with low wages had difficulty recruiting and retaining staff, but the study did not rule out other explanations. The Washington study found no effect of compensation on retention. There is a need for additional research on various quality enhancement strategies, including TA. There also is a need for organized information (as opposed to the informal and unsystematic sharing by states of lessons learned) about the impact of resource allocation in QRISs. (For a more detailed discussion on QRIS, see Chapter 5.)

Early Learning Standards

As a part of national efforts to improve student achievement in the K–12 education system, states have written standards specifying what students are expected to learn. Early learning standards, guidelines that specify what prekindergarten children should know and be able to do prior to kindergarten entry, are increasingly common across the states, with some states also outlining learning expectations for infants and toddlers (Scott-Little, Lesko, Martella, & Milburn, 2007). Efforts to define early learning standards have been prompted in part by research showing the critical importance of brain development in the early years as well as research suggesting that many children enter kindergarten ill prepared to succeed in school (Rimm-Kaufman, Pianta, & Cox, 2000). Undoubtedly, though, it was President Bush's Good Start, Grow Smart initiative of 2002 that was most influential in encouraging states to develop early learning standards that focused on pre-academic skills that aligned with state K–12 standards. Although Good Start, Grow Smart encouraged all states to document their progress in developing early learning guidelines for preschoolers only in language and math, many states also have included other areas, such as social-emotional development and approaches to learning.

The vast majority of states now require prekindergarten programs to use early learning standards, and several are beginning to develop monitoring mechanisms to ensure that standards are applied. With states' promotion of these standards for use in a variety of early childhood programs in addition to prekindergarten (e.g., Head Start, IDEA programs, Even Start), and with voluntary use by those programs on the rise (Scott-Little et al., 2007), learning standards have the potential to synchronize expectations and improve the consistency of experiences for young children across levels and types of early education and schooling. Standards that are well conceived and appropriate also hold potential to build consensus with families and communities with respect to appropriate learning expectations and experiences for young children. Yet, with no national early childhood standards, we can expect wide variability in how states describe desired results, outcomes, and expectations with respect to what children should know and be able to do before entering kindergarten.

Guidelines about what children need to learn should inform standards for early childhood programs and teacher competencies, providing that they reflect goals that predict later school success and are not being confused with performance standards (Kendall, 2003; Neuman & Roskos, 2005). There is concern about the potential negative consequences for children who fail to meet learning standards (e.g., delaying entry into kindergarten), and professionals and families alike question how they will be applied to children with special circumstances such as a home language other than English and disabilities (Scott-Little et al., 2007). As the field continues its quest to identify the program characteristics and teacher knowledge and skills that are essential for all children's optimal development and learning, an undercurrent of debate reminds us that optimal outcomes for children translate into more than school success. Increasingly, policy makers and educators are addressing the importance of supporting social and emotional well-being and positive relationships throughout the early childhood years.

Although the QRIS and early learning standards initiatives attempt to "close in" on quality, to specify what it looks like and reward programs where it is found, the profession's responsibility to promote quality compels us to revisit regularly our collective values and the validity and currency of our knowledge, a point emphasized in NAEYC's (2009) revised position statement on developmentally appropriate practice. Professional development is one of the most critical factors in determining whether early care and education are of high or poor quality and represents a crucial juncture of research and practice. The following section briefly considers the role of professional development in the quality movement.

PROFESSIONAL DEVELOPMENT

Few people would question the importance of having an effective workforce in programs that serve young children and families. Along with a safe and well-equipped learning environment, it is the characteristics and behaviors of the adults themselves that likely contribute most to the quality of the program (Cost, Quality, & Child Outcomes Study Team, 1995; Peisner-Feinberg et al., 2001). Although professional development should reflect this vital connection between the quality of the program and the quality of the early childhood workforce, the field's efforts to ensure that all early childhood practitioners have the essential knowledge and skills they need to be effective have been hampered by numerous factors. These include the disjointed nature of many professional development efforts, the strikingly sparse scientific research indicating which approaches are likely to enhance practice, and, even more unsettling, the lack of a shared understanding of professional development.

The absence of a shared definition of *professional development* in early childhood has contributed to the lack of a common vision for the most effective ways of organizing and implementing professional development. At the same time, there is fairly widespread agreement that professional development is the most viable method for improving the quality of the early childhood workforce by promoting the most effective teaching and intervening practices (Cochran-Smith & Zeichner, 2005). Policy makers, administrators, practitioners, and professional development providers loosely refer to professional development as a process that includes formal and informal learning opportunities such as coursework, training, and mentoring. Existing early childhood professional development efforts are fragmented at best (Winton & McCollum, 2008), with opportunities ranging from a single workshop to a semester-long academic course. These activities are offered by a medley of different professional development providers (with a range of qualifications), and they vary widely with respect to the content and format of the learning experiences provided. Variations in how professional development is organized and implemented frequently lead to uneven, and sometimes incongruent, learning opportunities for both preservice students and practitioners. Practitioners or students who enroll in professional development activities on any number of topics (e.g., instructional strategies to address social-emotional development or early language and literacy, methods for collaborating and communicating with families and professionals) can expect a range of quality in curriculum and instruction, depending on where they reside and the qualifications, experience, and philosophy of their instructor.

In an effort to reach consensus on the meaning of professional development, the National Professional Development Center on Inclusion (NPDCI) developed a definition to guide its work with states related to professional development on inclusion (Buysse, Winton, & Rous, 2009). NPDCI needed a definition and conceptual framework to organize its TA and to facilitate a planning process with states. States needed guidance in their efforts to develop a statewide, cross-agency professional development plan. Consequently, the definition serves as an organizing framework for considering various aspects of professional development for both NPDCI, as the TA provider, and the states, as the recipients of these services. The definition was predicated on certain assumptions—for example, that professional development encompasses both formal and informal teaching and learning opportunities, that the early childhood workforce and the children and families served constitute a widely diverse group, and that the core components of professional development must at a minimum include the characteristics and contexts of the learners (the "who"), the content of professional development (the "what"), and the methods used to organize and facilitate teaching and learning (the "how"). (For the complete definition and conceptual framework, see http://community.fpg.unc.edu/npdci.)

In the NPDCI conceptualization of professional development, the "who," the "what," and the "how" form interlocking circles at the core of an integrated professional development system, whereas key infrastructure supports (i.e., resources, policies, organizational structures, access and outreach, and evaluation) make up the outer circle of the framework. NPDCI recommends that planners consider all of these elements in designing a systematic, comprehensive approach to professional development. Experience in helping states apply this conceptual framework in their efforts to plan integrated professional development systems suggests that it is often easier for planners to consider infrastructure supports such as access and outreach or resources than it is to focus on the "who," the "what," and the "how" components. States may not have information systems in place to describe the characteristics of both professional development providers and learners who make up the early childhood workforce. Nor is there information readily available to help states summarize exactly what constitutes the foundational knowledge, skills, and dispositions that will be the focus of the professional development program (the "what"). Identifying the most effective methods for organizing and facilitating learning experiences (the "how")—for example, approaches such as consultation or coaching to provide guidance and feedback on specific teaching and intervention practices—has proven to be the most challenging component of designing professional development in early childhood.

The Demand for Professional Development

The professional development needs of the early childhood workforce are urgent. Publicly funded preschool is expanding across the nation, as are other types of early childhood programs, to meet the needs of millions of children (NAEYC, 2008). Yet, qualifications of staff in child care centers and homes are declining (Herzenberg, Price, & Bradley, 2005), and annual teacher attrition is an astounding 30%, a rate not likely to improve without increased compensation to lure a more educated workforce (Bellm & Whitebook, 2006).

At the same time, the changing demographics of the early childhood population create a need for professionals to develop knowledge and skills to work with culturally diverse children and families. Approximately 45% of children younger than 5 years of age are racially, ethnically, or linguistically diverse, and increases in this percentage are expected over the next decade (U.S. Census Bureau, 2004). In addition, early childhood programs are serving more children with disabilities than ever before, with 36 of 59 states and territories reporting serving 50% or more of their preschoolers with disabilities in general early education programs (U.S. Department of Education, 2007). Yet, the majority of early childhood personnel, including administrators, teachers, assistants, specialists, and others, are not adequately prepared to educate young children with disabilities (Chang, Early, & Winton, 2005).

Professional Development Systems

To address these and other concerns, most states have put in place at least some components of a statewide professional development system as recommended by the National Child Care Information and Technical Assistance Center (NCCIC). These systems are built around five core elements: 1) knowledge and competencies needed across roles and sectors; 2) access and outreach to ensure a range of professional development options; 3) qualifications, credentials, and career pathways; 4) funding, including financial aid, scholarships, and compensation, and 5) quality assurance, including standards for trainers and content (for more, see the NCCIC web site at http://nccic.acf.hhs.gov). In relation to the NPDCI conceptual definition and conceptual framework for professional development, the NCCIC recommendations address the content or the "what" of professional development in three of its components (#1, #3, #5), and infrastructure supports in two components (#2, #4), but they ignore the methods for facilitating teaching and learning (the "how") and the characteristics and contexts of learners and providers (the "who"). The 2008 reauthorized Higher Education Opportunity Act (PL 110-315) includes a program of state grants to help establish such systems for early education (birth to 5), which, through the opportunity for loans and loan forgiveness, may make it easier for teachers and providers to access professional development. It should be noted, however, that no state has developed an integrated, cross-sector professional development system that includes all the core components.

At least 50% of states have established early childhood competencies for knowledge and skills, but questions remain about how levels of early childhood education should be defined. Should competencies be organized by education degree, stage of career, or by job category? There is wide variation across states in the number of levels and content of each level of competencies and little evidence to drive decisions about what a classroom teacher needs to know and do that is different from, for example, an assistant (National Center for Research on Early Childhood Education, 2008). There is even less evidence to indicate how the combination of specific knowledge and skills tied to degree or role is critical for advancing the quality of early childhood programs. Without sorting out some of these questions and more basic ones about how to map these competencies onto various forms of certification and licensure, it will be difficult to link early childhood education competencies to QRISs or professional development systems. Yet, without such linkages, we do not have a professional development system at all. (For a more detailed discussion on professional development, see Chapter 6.)

POLICY

During the past 70 years, federal early childhood policies have addressed a range of issues, including safety and health, poverty, the needs of working parents for child care, access and affordability, and children's readiness for school. Funding for early childhood programs has fluctuated, and public campaigns have tended to focus on one particular issue at a time—for example, to compensate for disadvantage or to provide protection from abuse and neglect (Cohen, 1996). In the absence of federal policies supporting a unified and comprehensive early childhood approach, services continue to be delivered through a complex maze of programs that typically operate independently of each other, including marketplace child care (both subsidized and nonsubsidized), Head Start, state-sponsored prekindergarten, and a host of miscellaneous programs such as Title I, Even Start, and the Individuals with Disabilities Act (Parts C and B) and its amendments, among others.

The Obama administration's promise to strengthen early childhood education has focused attention on policy as evidenced by the provision of additional funding through the ARRA to Child Care Development Block Grants and Head Start. Continued investment in the CCDF reflects the national attention on raising program quality and increasing options for infants and toddlers. The increase to Head Start demonstrates the longstanding belief that a comprehensive, high-quality program (including nutrition, health-care screening, developmental screening, learning opportunities, and partnerships with families) yields benefits to low-income children and society as a whole. Although these programs need funding to offset years of declining support (based on inflation adjustment), the reality remains that CCDF and Head Start serve only a fraction of the children needing high-quality early care and education programs (National Education Association, 2009).

With increasing evidence that high-quality early childhood programs lead to school success, reduced delinquency and crime, and better job opportunities and productivity, and in the vacuum of federal guidance during previous years, state legislators across the country have developed a number of policies to improve services. Enacted laws have expanded early childhood professional development, advanced quality preschool programs, and linked early childhood services to comprehensive health and social services (RAND Corporation, 2008). However, faced with the overarching problem of inadequate resources, states are constrained in what they can do and face almost impossible tradeoffs in deciding how to allocate resources. For example, in planning how to use CCDF funds, they must choose whether to make families pay more for child care, pay providers less, or serve fewer families. Although increasing funds to prekindergarten programs may seem a promising strategy to prepare 3- and 4-year-olds for school, it may come at a cost to early childhood programs serving working parents whose young children need services from birth.

Early childhood policy makers should use the best available research, and the wisdom and values of professionals and families, to make decisions about allocating limited resources (Wesley & Buysse, 2006). There are many reasons, however, that make it difficult to convert research findings into policy action. Available research may not isolate the relative contributions of different program components to desired outcomes, and it may not address the effects of specific program models on English language learners, children from immigrant families, and children with disabilities. Nonetheless, agreement about key areas that require policy action is reflected in the early childhood literature (see, e.g., Kagan, Kauerz, & Tarrant, 2008) and in testimony to the Committee on Education and Labor during the March 2009 hearings on improving child development policies and practices. These include the need to:

- Unify services to create a comprehensive system of early childhood services that all children can access from birth

- Create common expectations for child outcomes and standards for curriculum and assessment that align with early learning standards

- Establish national standards and expectations for program quality, and

- Set high national standards for professional qualifications and development, including appropriate licensure, certification, and a career lattice linked to compensation.

In the United States, more than 12.4 million children under the age of 6, approximately 60%, are cared for regularly by someone other than their parents (U.S. Department of Education, 2007). To strengthen and coordinate policies to ensure high-quality care and education to support their future happiness and success, we must recognize not only that quality counts but that it also costs, and commit a public funding base for early childhood. (See Chapter 8 for a more detailed discussion on policy.)

THE CALL FOR CHANGE

In recent decades, the early childhood field has witnessed the emergence of new knowledge and innovations designed to promote the quality of early childhood programs and services in the United States. However, the early childhood system remains fragmented in terms of the accountability standards and professional development used to define what is meant by a high-quality program and to promote an effective workforce. As a result, states' efforts to improve quality often proliferate in a haphazard and unproductive way (National Early Childhood Accountability Task Force, 2007). As is the case with any challenging endeavor, resolving complex issues around defining, measuring, and improving program quality will require that the early childhood field engage in a wide range of activities. These activities could include discussions at state and national professional meetings, collective thinking and problem solving through a national task force, and the development and validation of consensus documents to summarize the field's core principles and practices regarding program quality. All these efforts should be directed to addressing the field's most pressing challenges on this topic, which may include the following activities:

1. Reach consensus on the key dimensions of program quality in early childhood. Although there is fairly widespread agreement on some dimensions of program quality (e.g., an effective curriculum and intentional teaching, the quality of the early learning environment, the qualifications of program staff), there is a critical need to operationalize these dimensions to show how they relate to program standards and to define additional dimensions of program quality that respond to the growing diversity of children and families served in these settings (e.g., children with disabilities, children from diverse cultural and linguistic groups, dual language learners). There is an additional need to elaborate dimensions of intentional teaching practices—the ability to plan, organize, and evaluate instruction and interventions—that lie at the heart of high-quality early childhood programs and to incorporate these dimensions into existing definitions and standards of program quality.

2. Align program, professional, early learning standards, and accountability systems. Currently, standards addressing quality and learning goals exist at multiple levels and are promulgated by various types of organizations for different purposes. In most cases, the use of these standards as an index for gauging quality improvement efforts is voluntary, but it could be tied to tangible benefits such as an increase in program resources (e.g., professional compensation, classroom materials) in conjunction with improvements in quality. Broader input from the field, along with additional research, is needed to ensure that current standards represent the most effective teaching and intervening practices and the most appropriate learning goals, those that best predict positive outcomes for children and families. Efforts to align various types of standards should focus both on reducing duplication across these systems as well as ensuring that dimensions of quality specific to working with diverse young learners and their families are reflected. The goal should be to establish a single, coherent system of standards

that can be linked to professional development and accountability efforts. Program and professional standards that define program quality, along with early learning standards, should constitute key content for professional development, addressing what practitioners should know and be able to do to create high-quality early education and intervention services.

3. Provide clear guidelines for developing QRISs. There is wide variability across states with respect to goals and accountability methods related to QRISs. Given the potential for QRISs to assess quality, document quality improvements, and communicate information about program quality to parents and other consumers, states need additional guidance about how to create and maintain these systems. Only a handful of states with approved statewide QRISs include separate standards for children with disabilities and those from diverse cultural and linguistic groups. There is a corresponding need for additional program quality measures that address specific teaching and intervening practices, particularly those that focus on providing targeted interventions for some children who require additional supports to learn. Further, there is a need to integrate early learning standards with state QRISs.

4. Develop an integrated system of professional development. Mirroring the patchwork quilt of early childhood programs and services, professional development also is fragmented and not well integrated across various sectors of the field. Because of the promise it holds for improving the quality of the early childhood workforce by promoting the most effective teaching and intervening practices (and because it frequently takes the form of TA in quality-enhancement efforts), there is an urgent need for states to engage in systematic planning to develop comprehensive and coordinated professional development systems. Reaching consensus on the meaning of professional development and its relationship to TA, and agreeing on the key components of an effective professional development system, would aid states in conducting these planning efforts.

This chapter explored the history and evolution of the movement to improve early childhood program quality in early childhood. We considered how various aspects of the system—definitions of quality, quality standards and accountability systems, professional development, and policies—contribute to our ability to understand and communicate information about the meaning of quality in early childhood. Subsequent chapters explore each of these components in more depth, raise additional challenges related to improving program quality, and point toward promising new directions and innovations for addressing these challenges in the future.

REFERENCES

Bellm, D., & Whitebook, M. (2006). *Roots of decline: How government policy has de-educated teachers of young children.* Berkeley, CA: Center for the Study of Child Care Employment.

Belsky, J., & Steinberg, L.D. (1978). The effects of day care: A critical review. *Child Development, 49,* 929–949.

Bevilacqua, L. (2008) *Developmentally appropriate practice: What have we learned?* Retrieved December 8, 2009, from http://www.coreknowledge.org

Bredekamp, S. (Ed.). (1987). *Developmentally appropriate practice in early childhood programs serving children from birth through age 8.* Washington, DC: National Association for the Education of Young Children (NAEYC).

Bredekamp, S., & Copple, C. (Eds.). (1997). *Developmentally appropriate practice in early childhood programs serving children from birth through age 8* (Rev. ed.). Washington, DC: National Association for the Education of Young Children (NAEYC).

Bryant, D., Maxwell, K., & Burchinal, M. (1999). Effects of a community initiative on the quality of child care. *Early Childhood Research Quarterly, 14*, 449–464.

Bryant, D., Wesley, P.W., & the QUINCE Study Team. (2009, July). *The QUINCE-PFI study: An evaluation of a promising model and delivery approaches for care provider training. Final report to the ACF/Child Care Bureau.*

Burchinal, M.R., & Cryer, D. (2003). Diversity, child care quality, and developmental outcomes. *Early Childhood Research Quarterly, 28*, 401–426.

Buysse, V., & Hollingsworth, H.L. (2009). Program quality and early childhood inclusion: Recommendations for professional development. *Topics in Early Childhood Special Education, 29*, 119–128.

Buysse, V., Winton, P.J., & Rous, B. (2009). Program quality and early childhood inclusion: Recommendations for professional development. *Topics in Early Childhood Special Education, 29*, 119–128.

Chang, F., Early, D., & Winton, P. (2005). Early childhood teacher preparation in special education at 2- and 4-year institutions of higher education. *Journal of Early Intervention, 27*, 110–124.

Cochran-Smith, M., & Zeichner, K. M. (Eds.). (2005). *Studying teacher education: The report of the AERA panel on research and teacher education.* Mahwah, NJ: Lawrence Erlbaum Associates.

Cohen, A.J. (1996). A brief history of federal financing for child care in the United States. *Future of Children, 6*, 26–40.

Cost, Quality, & Child Outcomes Study Team. (1995). *Cost, quality, and child outcomes in child care centers: Final report.* Denver: University of Colorado, Economics Department.

Cryer, D., & Clifford, R.M. (Eds.). (2003). *Early childhood education & care in the USA.* Baltimore: Paul H. Brookes Publishing Co.

DEC/NAEYC. (2009). *Early childhood inclusion: A joint position statement of the Division for Early Childhood (DEC) and the National Association for the Education of Young Children (NAEYC).* Chapel Hill: University of North Carolina, FPG Child Development Institute.

Dickinson, D.K. (2002, January/February). Shifting images of developmentally appropriate practice as seen through different lenses. *Educational Researcher, 26–32.*

Early, D.M., Maxwell, K.L., Burchinal, M., Alva, S., Bender, R.H., Bryant, D., Cai, K., Clifford, R.M., Ebanks, C., Griffin, J.A., Henry, G.T., Howes, C., Iriondo-Perez, J., Jeon, H., Mashburn, A.J., Peisner-Feinberg, E., Pianta, R.C., Vandergrift, N., & Zill, N. (2007). Teachers' education, classroom quality, and young children's academic skills: Results from seven studies of preschool programs. *Child Development, 78*, 558–580.

Good Start, Grow Smart: The Bush administration's early childhood initiative. (2002). Retrieved November 10, 2008, from http://www.whitehouse.gov/infocus/earlychildhood/toc.html

Herzenberg, S., Price, M., & Bradley, D. (2005). *Losing ground in early childhood education: Declining workforce qualifications in an expanding industry, 1979–2004.* Washington, DC: Economic Policy Institute.

Howes, C., Phillips, D.A., & Whitebook, M. (1992). Thresholds of quality: Implications for the social development of children in center-based care. *Child Development, 63*, 449–460.

Howes, C., Pianta, R., Bryant, D., Hamre, B., Downer, J., & Soliday-Hong, S. (2008). *Ensuring effective teaching in early childhood education through linked professional development systems, quality rating systems and state competencies: The role of research in an evidence-driven system.* Report of the 2008 NCRECE Leadership Symposium, Arlington, VA. Retrieved December 8, 2009, from http://www.ncrece.org/wordpress/wp-content/uploads/2008/09/ncrecewhitepaper2008.pdf

Jipson, J. (1991). Developmentally appropriate practice: Culture, curriculum, connections. *Early Education and Development, 2*, 120–136.

Kagan, S.L., Kauerz, K., & Tarrant, K. (2008). *The early care and education teaching workforce at the fulcrum.* New York: Teachers College Press.

Kendall, J.S. (2003). Setting standards in early childhood education. *Educational Leadership, 60*, 64–68.

Knitzer, J. (2002). *Set for success: Building a strong foundation for school readiness based on the social-emotional development of children. Promoting social and emotional readiness for school: Toward a policy agenda.* Kansas City, MO: The Kaufman Foundation.

Mitchell, A.W. (2005). *Stair steps to quality: A guide for states and communities developing quality rating systems for early care and education.* United Way, Success by 6. Retrieved December 8, 2009, from http://nccic.acf.hhs.gov

Moss, P., & Dahlberg, G. (2008). Beyond quality in early childhood education and care—Languages of evaluation. *New Zealand Journal of Teachers' Work, 5,* 3–12.

National Association of Child Care Resource and Referral Agencies (NACCRRA). (2006). *Parents' perceptions of child care in the United States: NACCRRA's national parent poll.* Alexandria, VA: Author.

National Association of Child Care Resource and Referral Agencies (NACCRRA). (2007, June). *Threshold of licensed family child care.* Retrieved December 8, 2009, from http://www.naccrra.org/randd/licensing_training_qr/fcc/threshold.php

National Association for the Education of Young Children (NAEYC). (1995). *Quality, compensation, and affordability: A position statement of the National Association for the Education of Young Children.* Author: Washington, DC.

National Association for the Education of Young Children (NAEYC). (2005). *Code of ethical conduct and statement of commitment.* Retrieved December 8, 2009, from http://www.naeyc.org/dap

National Association for the Education of Young Children (NAEYC). (2006). *NAEYC early childhood program standards and accreditation criteria: The mark of quality in early childhood education.* Washington, DC: Author.

National Association for the Education of Young Children (NAEYC). (2008). *Workforce designs: A policy blueprint for state early childhood professional development systems.* Washington, DC: Author.

National Association for the Education of Young Children (NAEYC). (2009). *Developmentally appropriate practice in early childhood programs serving children from birth through age 8.* (3rd ed.) Washington, DC: Author.

National Association for the Education of Young Children (NAEYC) & National Association of Early Childhood Specialists in State Departments of Education (NAECS/SDE). (2003). *Early childhood curriculum, assessment, and program evaluation: Building an effective, accountable system in programs for children birth through age 8* (Joint Position Statement). Retrieved December 8, 2009, from http://www.naeyc.org/dap

National Association for the Education of Young Children (NAEYC) & National Association of Early Childhood Specialists in State Departments of Education (NAECS/SDE). (2002). *Early learning standards: Creating the conditions for success* (Joint Position Statement). Retrieved December 8, 2009, from http://www.naeyc.org/dap

National Center for Early Development and Learning. (1997). Quality in child care centers. *Early Childhood Research and Policy Brief.* Chapel Hill: University of North Carolina, FPG Child Development Institute.

National Early Childhood Accountability Task Force. (2007). *Taking stock: Assessing and improving early childhood learning and program quality.* Washington, DC: Pew Charitable Trusts.

National Education Association. (n.d.). *Expand and improve early childhood education and children's programs.* Retrieved December 8, 2009, from http://www.nea.org/home/29875.htm

Neuman, S.B., & Roskos, K. (2005). The state of state pre-kindergarten standards. *Early Childhood Research Quarterly, 20,* 125–145.

Palsha, S., & Wesley, P. W. (1998). Improving the quality in early childhood environments through on-site consultation. *Topics in Early Childhood Special Education, 18,* 243–253.

Peisner-Feinberg, E.S., & Burchinal, M.R. (1997). Relations between preschool children's child-care experiences and concurrent development: The cost, quality, and outcomes study. *Merrill-Palmer Quarterly, 43,* 450–477.

Peisner-Feinberg, E.S., Burchinal, M.R., Clifford, R.M., Culkin, M.L., Howes, C., Kagan, S.L., & Yazejian, N. (2001). The relations of preschool childcare quality to children's cognitive and social development through second grade. *Child Development, 72,* 1534–1553.

Pelo, A. (2008, Fall). Embracing a vision of social justice in early childhood education. *Rethinking Schools, 23.*

Phillipsen, L.C., Burchinal, M.R., Howes, C., & Cryer, D. (1997). The prediction of process quality from structural features of child care. *Early Childhood Research Quarterly, 12*(3), 281–303.

RAND Corporation. (2008). *Report on child care quality rating and improvement systems in five pioneer states.* Santa Monica, CA: Author.

Rimm-Kaufman, S.E., Pianta, R.C., & Cox, M.J. (2000). Teachers' judgments of problems in the transition to kindergarten. *Early Childhood Research Quarterly, 15,* 147–166.

Sandall, S., Hemmeter, M.L., Smith, B.J., & McLean, M.E. (2005). *DEC recommended practices: A comprehensive guide for practical application in early intervention/early childhood special education.* Missoula, MT: Division for Early Childhood (DEC) of the Council for Exceptional Children.

Scott-Little, C., Kagan, S.L., & Frelow, V.S. (2006). Conceptualization of readiness and the content of early learning standards: The intersection of policy and research? *Early Childhood Research Quarterly, 21,* 153–173.

Scott-Little, C., Lesko, J., Martella, J., & Milburn, P. (2007). Early learning standards: Results from a national survey to document trends in state-level policies and practices. *Early Childhood Research and Practice, 9.* Retrieved December 8, 2009, from http://ecrp.uiuc.edu/v9nl/little.html.

Shonkoff, J.P., & Phillips, D.A. (Eds.). (2000). *From neurons to neighborhoods: The science of early childhood development.* Washington, DC: National Academies Press.

Spodek, B., & Saracho, O.N. (1997). Evaluation in early childhood education: A look to the future. In B. Spodek & O.N. Saracho (Eds.), *Issues in early childhood educational assessment and evaluation. Yearbook in early childhood education* (Vol. 7, pp. 198–206). New York: Teachers College Press.

U.S. Census Bureau. (2006). *Nation's population one-third minority.* Retrieved May 10, 2009, from http://www.census.gov/

U.S. Department of Education, National Center for Education Statistics. (2007). *National Household Surveys Education Program, Digest of education statistics.* Retrieved December 8, 2009, from http://nces.ed.gov/programs/digest/do7/tables/dt07_042.asp

U.S. General Accounting Office. (2002, September 6). *Child care: States have undertaken a variety of quality improvement initiatives, but more evaluations of effectiveness are needed* (GAO-02-897). Washington, DC: Author.

Vandell, D.L. (2004). Early child care: The known and the unknown. *Merrill-Palmer Quarterly, 50,* 387–414.

Walsh, D.J. (1991). Extending the discourse on developmentally appropriateness: A developmental perspective. *Early Education and Development, 2,* 109–119.

Wesley, P.W. (1994). Providing on-site consultation to promote quality in integrated child care programs. *Journal of Early Intervention, 18,* 391–402.

Wesley, P.W., & Buysse, V. (2006). Making the case for evidence-based policy. In V. Buysse & P.W. Wesley (Eds.), *Evidence-based practice in the early childhood field* (pp. 117–159). Washington, DC: ZERO TO THREE.

Winton, P.J., & McCollum, J. (2008). Preparing and supporting high-quality early childhood practitioners: Issues and evidence. In P.J. Winton, J.A. McCollum, & C. Catlett (Eds.), *Preparing and supporting effective practitioners: Evidence and applications in early childhood and early intervention* (pp. 1–12). Washington, DC: ZERO TO THREE National Center for Infants, Toddlers, and Families.

CHAPTER 2

Research on Program Quality
The Evidence Base

Ellen S. Peisner-Feinberg and Noreen Yazejian

In this chapter, we discuss key issues around the research base on program quality for early childhood care and education programs. We begin with definitions of *program quality* as they have been used in research and program evaluation studies, including the definitional linkages between major practice standards and measurement tools. We then examine the research evidence about program quality, providing a broad historical synopsis and summarizing key findings about factors influencing quality, the existing state of quality, the associations with costs, and the effects on children's outcomes. Finally, based on this review, we offer suggestions of directions for future research and evaluation studies. Our focus in this chapter is on out-of-home care and education programs, primarily center-based programs, although many of these same issues would apply to family child care homes.

DEFINITIONS OF QUALITY IN RESEARCH AND PRACTICE

In the research literature, as well as in applications to practice such as licensing standards and quality-improvement efforts, the measurement of early childhood program quality traditionally has been viewed as having two primary aspects—structural features and process quality. Structural features refer to those aspects of early education programs that can be regulated, tend to be more quantitative in nature, and are readily observable and/or measurable. Some examples of structural features are levels of teacher education and credentials, staff–child ratios, and group size. These types of characteristics are easily adopted for policy and are commonly included in state child care licensing regulations. They are also easily adaptable for use in research, as they can be clearly defined and consistently measured across various types of early education settings. The second aspect, process quality, refers to the direct experiences of children in early childhood programs, is more dynamic and qualitative in nature, and requires more in-depth observation to measure. Some examples of process quality are the ways in which educational activities are implemented (e.g., the types of activities, the ways in which instruction is organized, the roles of children and teachers), the characteristics of interactions among teachers and children or among the children themselves, and the ways in which routine care needs are handled (e.g., meal times, toileting). Some programming features may cross both categories; for example, the number and types of materials available to children in the classroom would be a structural feature, whereas the ways in which they are used for instruction would be an indicator of process quality.

Both structural and process aspects are important to consider with regard to research and program evaluation studies aimed toward examining the quality of care, implementing high-quality practices, and ensuring that policies are effective in promoting high-quality care. Structural features are often related to specifying minimum standards for care, and even in cases where there are tiered standards (i.e., lower and higher levels), these often represent the more basic aspects of quality. Much of the focus of early research efforts was on examining structural features themselves, such as staff–child ratios and group size, and these are still a key component of many studies of program quality. Structural characteristics are measured in research both to provide descriptive information about the context within which studies are conducted and to be used as variables of interest themselves. As the research literature on early education program quality has grown, along with the tools for measuring quality, the focus has moved beyond looking solely at structural features to include the study of levels of process quality. The latter have included descriptive studies of process quality and studies of both the predictors of quality and the outcomes for children's skill development. Many studies have examined the relation of structural features to process quality, viewing the former as covariates (e.g., after controlling for differences in staff–child ratios, what were the differences in the level of quality?), as predictors (e.g., do classrooms with better ratios have higher levels of process quality?), and as moderators of children's experiences (e.g., do classroom practices have an even stronger impact on children's skill development when staff–child ratios are higher?). Many of the earlier studies of process quality examined it as a global construct that represents a summary of various features—such as the types of activities and the nature of interactions—to give an overall score or picture of the level of classroom quality. This view is also consistent with attempts to utilize the measurement of process quality in program standards, which require the designation of a criterion or minimum score for meeting the standards. In recent years, there has been a trend in the research to "unpack quality"—in other words, to examine and measure more specific aspects of process quality, especially the relation of these particular features to children's outcomes. Rather than considering quality as a global construct, these studies have focused in more depth on particular aspects of quality, such as specific domains of learning (e.g., language and literacy practices or math practices), instructional practices (e.g., how teachers organize and facilitate learning), and the nature of social interactions (between teachers and children and among peers).

In examining the historical course of research on program quality, it is important to note that developments in research have not occurred independently from developments in the broader early childhood education field. The definition of quality is inherent in various guidelines and standards for practice and in the measurement tools used in research as well as in monitoring and technical assistance efforts. The way early education program quality has been defined and consequently measured by researchers has informed, and has been informed by, the way it has been defined for practice and for setting standards. In both research and practice, current definitions of quality incorporate both structural and process elements and include both global and domain-specific aspects.

However, research and practice sources are designed for different purposes and represent this information in different ways. The research tools are designed to measure the implementation of various concepts of quality underlying their construction; accordingly, they provide operational definitions of these concepts, but they do not offer comprehensive explanations of the concepts themselves. In contrast, practice statements are primarily designed to provide conceptual definitions of what is meant by quality in early childhood programs and may offer some examples for implementation, but they are not designed to provide information on how to measure the implementation of quality. Program and licensing standards often fall somewhere in between, offering some explicit guidance on implementing high-quality practices as well as conceptual information. The next section illustrates these associations by providing some examples of the primary components defining quality within current guidelines and standards for practice and how these correspond with widely used research tools for measuring quality.

Relations Between Practice Statements and Research Tools

The National Association for the Education of Young Children (NAEYC) position statement on developmentally appropriate practices in early childhood programs represents one of the most well-known definitions of best practice, including information about the underlying concepts as well as examples of how to implement practices designed to promote children's development. The most recent edition of the NAEYC's guidelines, *Developmentally Appropriate Practice in Early Childhood Programs* (Copple & Bredekamp, 2009), describes practices around four key areas of child development—physical, social and emotional, cognitive, and language and literacy—organized by age group (preschool, kindergarten, and primary grades). For the youngest age group, infants and toddlers, the information focuses largely on relationships and interactions, rather than areas of development. The approach taken by these guidelines is consistent with how research tools have measured quality by areas of practice related to key domains of development. Some tools focus more in-depth on practices related to a particular domain of development, such as practices related to language and literacy development as measured by the Early Language and Literacy Classroom Observation Pre-K (ELLCO Pre-K; Smith, Brady, & Anastasopoulos, 2008) or practices related to social and emotional development as measured by the Caregiver Interaction Scale (CIS; Arnett, 1989). Other tools measure global practices across these different domains of development, such as the Early Childhood Environment Rating Scale–Revised (ECERS-R; Harms, Clifford, & Cryer, 2005), the Assessment Profile (Abbott-Shim & Sibley, 1988), the Classroom Assessment Scoring System (CLASS; Pianta, LaParo, & Hamre, 2008), and the Observational Record of Caregiving Environment (ORCE; NICHD Early Child Care Research Network, 1996, 2000a). Further, this definition is consistent with the domains of children's development examined as outcomes of variations in program quality in research studies. It is important to acknowledge that much less attention has been paid in research (as well as in practice) to the domain of physical development in terms of measurement tools and outcomes for children.

The NAEYC (2007) Early Childhood Program Standards, which form the basis for the criteria used for determining program accreditation, define 10 elements considered essential for a high-quality program: relationships, curriculum, teaching, assessment of child progress, health, teachers, families, community relationships, physical environment, and leadership and management. In contrast to the developmentally appropriate practice guidelines, the program standards for accreditation focus on implementation and define specific, observable practices for different age groups, although both are based on the same underlying concept of quality. There are also accompanying tools for self-assessment and external assessment to evaluate the extent to which a program meets the accreditation standards. Many of the specific practices described in the accreditation standards are similar to the descriptors of high-quality practices used in research tools, including both global and domain-specific tools.

The Head Start program, including both Early Head Start for infants and toddlers and Head Start for preschoolers, is the largest federally funded program providing comprehensive early childhood education services to economically disadvantaged children. The Head Start Program Performance Standards (Office of Human Development Services, 2007) incorporate definitions of quality in their guidelines for program operations. The purpose and scope of services are described for several different areas of operations, including health (physical and mental health, safety, and nutrition), education and child development, and family and community involvement, as well as program management and facilities (including materials and equipment). Basic ideas of quality are further defined with the standards; for example, *developmentally appropriate* is defined as "any behavior or experience that is appropriate for the age span of the children and is implemented with attention to the different needs, interests, and developmental levels and cultural backgrounds of individual children" (p. 121). These performance standards provide conceptual definitions of quality for the different key areas but generally do not provide specific exemplars of practice. The key areas and descriptions of services are consistent with those covered in global research tools, although the definitions are generally broader within the Head Start standards. Further, some areas that are important for program performance standards, such as program management and community involvement, are typically excluded or only minimally addressed in research, which tends to focus on aspects of program quality that are more clearly linked to educational practices and children's development.

State Standards

Finally, as the role of states in the prekindergarten world and the number of state-funded prekindergarten programs has grown, it is important to acknowledge that there are definitions of quality incorporated in numerous other sets of program standards related to the guidelines for particular programs, state early learning standards, and child care licensing standards (including quality rating and improvement systems, or QRISs). Many of the same definitional concepts are reflected in these various program standards, which are often based on national standards but also often include greater levels of specificity with regard to practice, as expected, especially for standards with evaluative components (e.g., standards tied to funding or licensing levels). Although it is beyond the scope of this chapter to provide a comprehensive review of all of these different sets of state-level standards, this movement represents yet another facet of the intersection between research and practice. These standards often include the use of measurement tools that are also used in research, albeit for different purposes of monitoring compliance, evaluating performance, and/or improving quality.

HISTORY OF RESEARCH ON QUALITY

Rather than present a detailed historical review of the research on early childhood program quality, this section discusses the major studies published and the broader themes explored in the research literature. (For an earlier review of research on quality in child care programs—in particular, structural aspects of quality—see Hayes, Palmer, & Zaslow, 1990; for a more recent review on early childhood care and education generally, see Phillips, McCartney, & Sussman, 2006.) We have organized the section by decades to facilitate the review. In addition, Table 2.1 presents a summary of the large-scale studies on program quality that have been conducted.

1970s

As women began entering the workforce in greater numbers starting in the 1970s, more families began to rely on some form of child care. Child care thus initially served as a basic employment support for families and as a new worksite for a primarily female, low-wage workforce. The first wave of research on child care was not concerned with quality but rather compared outcomes of children in various arrangements, including full-time center child care, nonparental (e.g., "sitter") care in the home, exclusive parent care, or some combination of arrangements (e.g., Winett, Fuchs, Moffatt, & Nerviano, 1977). A particular focus of research in this era considered whether children attending care were harmed by maternal separations, especially in terms of attachment (e.g., Doyle & Somers, 1978; Farran & Ramey, 1978; Moskowitz, Schwarz, & Corsini, 1977; Vaughn, Gove, & Egeland, 1980). Studies during this time were often limited by analysis techniques that did not consider child or family characteristics as covariates or selection effects (e.g., Winett et al., 1977), potentially obfuscating any effects of care that may have been present. Toward the end of this period, it was recognized that the quality of care was likely more important than the type of care or separations themselves in mediating any impact of child care experiences on children's development (e.g., Suwalksy & Klein, 1980).

When quality of care did become a focus of research at the end of this period, it was structural aspects of care that received the most attention as variables amenable to policy regulation. Results from the well-known National Day Care Study (Ruopp, Travers, Glantz, & Coelen, 1979; Smith & Spence, 1980; Travers, Goodson, Singer, & Connell, 1979) identified three primary structural aspects—group size, caregiver–child ratios, and teacher qualifications—as those most consistently associated with children's experiences in care and their developmental outcomes. Smaller groups, better ratios, and caregivers with specialized training or education in child-related fields were related to more positive learning environments and to higher developmental test scores for children.

While structural aspects of care received the majority of attention, process quality also began to be explored in the research literature toward the end of this time period. For example, descriptive studies examined teacher–child interactions and engagement in classrooms (Sheehan & Abbott, 1979) as well as peer social interactions (Rubenstein & Howes, 1979). In addition, the National Day Care Study (Ruopp et al., 1979) examined teacher and child classroom behaviors, including teacher classroom management behaviors and interactions with children. Analyses examined the effect of the "policy variables" (now more commonly referred to as structural quality variables) on these process variables that describe children's experiences in care.

1980s

During the 1980s, the study of early education program quality was propelled forward by the development of process quality measurement tools. Key among these are the Early Childhood Environment Rating Scale (ECERS; Harms, Clifford, & Cryer, 1980, revised 1998, 2005) and the Assessment Profile (Abbott-Shim & Sibley, 1987, revised 1998), both measures of global process quality, as well as the Early Childhood Classroom Observation Scale (Bredekamp, 1986), the accreditation assessment tool for NAEYC. The ECERS, and its companion tools for infant and toddler classrooms (Infant/Toddler Environment Rating Scale [ITERS]; Harms, Cryer, & Clifford, 1990, revised 2003) and family child care homes (Family Child Care Rating Scale [FCCRS]; Harms & Clifford, 1989, revised 2007) in particular became widely used as measures of process quality. Other measures of quality were focused on teacher–child interactions, such as the Caregiver Interaction Scale (CIS, Arnett, 1989). Studies during this time frame also overcame the flaws of earlier research by considering family characteristics related to early childhood program selection and children's outcomes—such as parent education and family income—and controlling for these confounding variables in analyses (e.g., Holloway & Reichhart-Erickson, 1989; Phillips, McCartney, & Scarr, 1987).

The major study related to early education quality of this time period was the National Child Care Staffing Study (NCCSS; Whitebook, Howes, & Phillips, 1989). A striking finding of the study was that teacher wages were the strongest predictor of structural (ratios) and process (global) quality. The study also highlighted the associations of higher quality with lower teacher turnover as well as quality differences by auspice, with nonprofit centers generally having higher quality programs.

1990s

During this period, research on program quality began to be couched in terms of broader theoretical frameworks. While researchers in the previous period improved upon the study of quality by accounting for family factors, researchers in the 1990s often adopted an ecological perspective (see Bronfenbrenner & Morris, 2006, for a recent specification of this evolving theoretical system). Many of the researchers studying early education program quality during this period recognized that program quality is one aspect of the microsystems in which children develop over time and that systems beyond the microsystem-level also exert influences. For example, the Cost, Quality, and Outcomes in Child Care Centers (CQO) Study (CQO Study Team, 1995) conceptualized process quality as influenced by the structural aspects of both the classroom and the center, with these in turn influenced by center financial and facility variables. At the same time, larger contextual variables—including state (e.g., licensing regulations, political environments) and labor market (e.g., wage structures) factors—were posited to have effects on the structural aspects of care.

The CQO Study was not alone in exploring relations among structural and process quality. During this period, there was a surge in research that examined associations between structural aspects of care and process quality in efforts to identify predictors of quality (e.g., Arnett, 1989; Howes & Norris, 1997; Howes &

Smith, 1995; Phillipsen, Burchinal, Howes, & Cryer, 1997). By identifying predictors of quality, the ultimate goal of this line of research was to provide information to help shape public policy. Cross-national comparisons of quality (e.g., Tietze, Cryer, Bairrão, Palacios, & Wetzel, 1996) and of the association between structural and process quality (e.g., Cryer, Tietze, Burchinal, Leal, & Palacios, 1999) were also conducted during this period.

Besides the CQO Study, the other major study that began during this period was the National Institute of Child Health and Human Development (NICHD) Study of Early Child Care (SECC). One of the many contributions to the literature offered by this study has been the exploration of quality effects in relation to quantity, or the amount of time children spend in care. Although there has been a fairly consistent finding that quantity of care is positively associated with behavior problems (e.g., NICHD ECCRN, 1998), other researchers have found extensive child care to be a risk only for children in low-quality care (Votruba-Drzal, Coley, & Chase-Lansdale, 2004). However, the mechanisms through which time spent in child care poses a risk have yet to be identified.

Finally, by the 1990s the link between quality and child outcomes was becoming well established. In addition, findings from large-scale early intervention programs, including the Abecedarian Study (e.g., Campbell & Ramey, 1994), the Perry Preschool Project (Schweinhart & Weikart, 1998), and the Chicago Child–Parent Centers Study (Reynolds & Temple, 1998), had shown the positive effects of model high-quality programming on the outcomes of children from low-income families. Thus, a particular area of interest in quality research was examining the quality of programs designed for children from low-income families and looking at associations with outcomes (e.g., Caughy, DiPietro, & Strobino, 1994; Phillips, Voran, Kisker, Howes, & Whitebook, 1994). The federal Head Start/Early Head Start programs have been laboratories for much of this work. The longitudinal Head Start Family and Child Experiences Study (FACES; 1997–2010), the consortium of Head Start Quality Research Centers (1995–2000, 2001–2006), and the Early Head Start Research and Evaluation Project (1996 to present) were all tasked with defining, assessing, and verifying the effectiveness of high-quality program practices in Head Start/Early Head Start programs.

2000 to Present

In recent years, the research on program quality has continued to investigate the themes explored in previous research, including structural predictors of process quality (e.g., Dowsett, Huston, Imes, & Gennetian, 2008; Early et al., 2007; Fukkink & Lont, 2007; NICHD ECCRN, 2002b; Torquati, Raikes, & Huddleston-Casas, 2007), relations between quality and quantity of care and effects on children (e.g., NICHD ECCRN, 2003a), and quality and effects of programming for low-income children (e.g., Head Start Impact Study and Follow-up, U.S. Department of Health and Human Services, Administration for Children and Families, 2005). The dramatic increase in public prekindergarten programs during the 1990s has afforded another setting in which to explore these and other topics on program quality, especially for low-income children (e.g., Gilliam & Zigler, 2000).

Throughout the previous decades, quality was often defined and measured globally (e.g., with the ECERS and related instruments or through the creation of quality indexes). More recent measurement tools have attempted to unpack

Table 2.1. Summary of large-scale studies on early childhood program quality

Study name and primary reference(s)	Sample characteristics	Sample size	Types of quality data	Settings	Age groups
National Day Care Study Ruopp et al., 1979 Travers et al., 1979	Urban Low income English speaking	57 programs 140 classrooms 1,383 children	Structural Teacher–child interactions Child engagement	Community centers, some public school and Head Start Mostly nonprofit	3–4 years (small substudy examined quality for birth to 3 years)
National Child Care Staffing Study (NCCSS) Whitebook et al., 1989	Urban/suburban Economically diverse English speaking	227 programs 643 classrooms 255 children	Structural Global Teacher–child interactions	Community centers, some public school and Head Start Mostly nonprofit	Birth to 5 years quality 3–4 years outcomes
Cost, Quality, and Outcomes in Child Care Centers Study (CQO) CQO Study Team, 1995 Peisner-Feinberg et al., 2001	Urban/suburban and rural Economically diverse English speaking	401 programs 749 classrooms 826 children (151 programs, 183 classrooms)	Structural Global Teacher–child interactions Teacher–child relationships	Community centers, some public school and Head Start Half nonprofit	Birth to 5 years quality 3–4 years outcomes
NICHD Study of Early Child Care NICHD Early Child Care Research Network, 1996, 1998, 1999, 2000a, 2000b, 2002a, 2002b, 2003a, 2003b	Urban/suburban and rural Economically diverse English speaking	1,364 children	Structural Global Teacher–child interactions	Various	Birth to 5 years

Study	Sample characteristics	Quality measures	Setting	Age
Family and Child Experiences Study (FACES) Zill et al., 2001 Zill et al., 2006 *Zill, Sorongon, Kim, Clark, & Woolverton, 2006*	Nationally representative of Head Start children and families Urban/suburban and rural Low income English or Spanish speaking	Structural Global Teacher–child interactions	Head Start centers	3–4 years
Early Head Start Research and Evaluation Project (EHSRE) *Kisker, Paulsell, Love, & Raikes, 2002*	Urban/suburban and rural Low income English or Spanish speaking	Structural Global Teacher–child interactions	Early Head Start centers and home based	Birth to 3 years
National Center for Early Development and Learning (NCEDL) Multi-State Study and Statewide Early Education Programs Study (SWEEP) *Clifford et al., 2005* *Early et al., 2005*	Urban/suburban and rural Majority low income English or Spanish speaking	Structural Global Teaching practices Teacher–child relationships	Public prekindergarten in community and school sites	3–4 years
Early Childhood Longitudinal Study–Birth Cohort (ECLS-B) *Flanagan & West, 2004* *Mulligan & Flanagan, 2006*	Nationally representative Urban, suburban, and rural Economically diverse Primarily English and Spanish speaking, but various languages	Structural Global	Various	Birth to 5 years

Sample sizes:
- FACES: 40–60 programs, 2,400–2,800 children
- EHSRE: 3,001 children
- NCEDL/SWEEP: 705 programs, 705 classrooms, 2,800 children
- ECLS-B: 10,700 children

global quality in efforts to define subcomponents that may be more important for outcomes or more amenable to quality improvement. Researchers thus are investigating more fine-grained elements of quality. For example, with the increased emphasis on prereading skills for young children, investigators have explored the quality of environments through the lens of emergent literacy (e.g., Diamond, Gerde, & Powell, 2008; Dickinson & Caswell, 2007; Justice, Mashburn, Hamre, & Pianta, 2008). Other researchers have focused on the quality of the environment for supporting children's math skills (e.g., Clements & Sarama, 2008). In addition, the quality of teacher–child interactions continues to be an area of focus (e.g., Gerber, Whitebook, & Weinstein, 2007; Mashburn et al., 2008).

Because of several decades of documenting program quality and its correlates, there is now a good understanding of the importance of quality for young children in care. Thus the field has shifted from showing this link toward evaluating efforts to improve program quality. A 2002 U.S. General Accounting Office (GAO; 2002) report noted that states were using set-aside funds for a variety of quality initiatives but that evidence of their effectiveness was limited. A search of the Educational Resources Information Center (ERIC) database with the terms *early childhood education or preschool, program evaluation*, and *quality* revealed 13 peer-reviewed journal articles published since 2002 (10 on professional development interventions, 3 related to state-funded prekindergarten programs). There are likely dozens more reports evaluating the effectiveness of quality improvement interventions.

PREDICTORS OF QUALITY

While the previous section presented an overview of the major studies and themes of research on early education program quality, this section further highlights research that has explored the associations between structural characteristics of center-based settings and the process quality of those environments. Illuminating these associations has been a focus of social policy research because governments can readily regulate structural aspects of care in attempts to improve the quality of children's experiences in care, whereas directly measuring and monitoring process quality is more difficult. Accordingly, structural aspects of care have been one focus of QRISs.

Researchers have found clear relations among structural characteristics of center-based settings and quality of care. For example, investigators of the four-state CQO Study found that program quality related to teacher–child ratios, teacher education, and administrator experience (CQO Study Team, 1995). In addition, quality was higher in states with more stringent child care regulations as well as in programs with funding sources linked to more stringent regulations (Phillipsen et al., 1997).

Other researchers have found links between program quality and administrator experience (e.g., Phillips, Scarr, & McCartney, 1987), teacher education (e.g., Barnett, Tarr, Lamy, & Frede, 2001; Howes, 1997; Howes & Smith, 1995; Roach, Adams, Riley, & Edie, 2002; Torquati et al., 2007), teacher training (Arnett, 1989; Fukkink & Lont, 2007; Gerber et al., 2007; Ghazvini & Mullis, 2002; Love, Ryer, Faddis, 1992), teacher–child ratio and group size (Asher & Erickson, 1979; Ghazvini & Mullis, 2002; Howes & Norris, 1997; NICHD ECCRN, 1996), teacher turnover (Whitebook,

Howes, & Phillips, 1998), and teacher wages (Scarr, Eisenberg, & Deater-Deckard, 1994; Torquati et al., 2007; Whitebook et al., 1989). Generally, quality is higher in programs that have administrators with more experience, teachers with more years of formal education and specialized training, classrooms with smaller groups and higher teacher–child ratios, and programs with lower turnover rates and higher teacher wages. However, some researchers have not found relations between quality and teacher–child ratios in particular (Love et al., 1992; Scarr et al., 1994).

The seemingly clear relation between teacher education and quality was challenged by a recent secondary analysis of seven large-scale studies, which found few or contradictory associations between teacher educational attainment and quality for center-based programs for 4-year-olds (Early et al., 2007). These results highlight the fact that teacher educational attainment is part of a larger complex system that cannot be reduced to a dichotomous variable (e.g., presence/absence of a bachelor of arts degree). To understand the relation between quality and teacher education, more comprehensive information is needed about teachers' specific experiences with professional development—including preservice, supervised practica, and in-service training experiences—as well as other supports, such as supervision, coaching, consultation, and mentoring.

WHAT DOES QUALITY LOOK LIKE?

Examining the research on early education program quality in the United States over the past 20 years reveals a slight upward trend in quality over time but also exposes absolute levels of care that are marginal to satisfactory; children generally are not attending programs characterized by high quality. The evidence for this comes from a limited number of large national studies. Although the older studies from this time frame might be considered somewhat dated, along with the more recent studies they provide a broad picture of program quality trends and the best indication available of the level of early childhood program quality experienced by children today.

The study of early education program quality has corresponded directly to how programs are organized, especially in terms of age groups. This chapter focuses on the quality of center-based programs and therefore specifically addresses the quality of preschool and infant-toddler classrooms as separate areas of research (as opposed to family child care or kith-and-kin care, which tend to be mixed-age settings). In addition, programs can be categorized by whether they provide an inclusive setting (e.g., serve children with special needs); therefore we discuss what little information is known about program quality for inclusive programs.

Quality of Preschool Classrooms

What we know nationally about the levels of quality of preschool classrooms comes primarily from five large-scale studies: the National Child Care Staffing Study (NCCSS), the CQO Study, the NICHD SECC, the Head Start Family and Child Experiences Study (FACES), and the National Center for Early Development and Learning (NCEDL) 11-state study of prekindergarten. Research has shown that the quality of care and education programs for preschoolers in our country is generally in the mediocre range (CQO Study Team, 1995; Whitebook et al., 1989), adequate to meeting the basic health and safety needs of children but not sufficient to enhance children's development. Evidence generally suggests that quality of care in community early education programs may be relatively lower than care in government-sponsored programs, such as federally funded programs for at-risk children (e.g., Head Start). For example, ECERS-R scores in the FACES samples have averaged approximately 4.8 (on a 7-point scale) for the 1997, 2000, and 2003 studies, reflecting good quality classroom practices (Zill et al., 2006). In contrast, care in community programs as measured by ECERS has averaged 4.0 (CQO Study Team, 1995), reflecting more mediocre care. The quality of care in state-funded prekindergarten programs has generally been in line with the mediocre quality of community programs. In a national study of 11 states, the quality of care in state-funded prekindergarten programs was 3.8 (Early et al., 2005) as measured by the ECERS-R, although other studies of individual state's prekindergarten programs have revealed higher quality (e.g., Layzer, Goodson, & Moss, 1993; Peisner-Feinberg & Schaaf, 2008a). Further, when different factors have been examined in these large-scale studies, the quality of teaching and interactions generally has been rated higher than the quality of activities or provisions for learning (CQO Study Team, 1995; Early et al., 2005; Whitebook et al., 1989).

Quality of Infant-Toddler Classrooms

Our knowledge of the quality of infant-toddler classrooms nationally comes primarily from five large-scale studies: NCCSS, CQO, SECC, the Early Head Start Research and Evaluation Project (EHSRE), and the Early Childhood Longitudinal Study–Birth Cohort (ECLS-B). For three of these studies (NCCSS, CQO, EHSRE), quality data were gathered and reported at the classroom or program level, whereas for the other two (SECC, ELCS-B), the data were collected and reported at the child level. Generally, the quality of programming for infants and toddlers has been lower than that reported for preschool-age children (CQO Study Team, 1995; Whitebook et al., 1989). For example, in the community centers included in the CQO study, the Appropriate Caregiving subscale of the Environment Rating Scales (ITERS and ECERS) was significantly lower for infants and toddlers than for preschoolers, with averages of 3.6 and 4.4, respectively. Similarly to preschool-age children, infants and toddlers attending federally funded programs for children from low-income families tend to experience higher quality environments. For example, the average ITERS score for Early Head Start programs was 5.3 (Kisker, Paulsell, Love, & Raikes, 2002). However, recent studies suggest that the majority of infants and toddlers in the United States are not enrolled in high-quality settings. Results from the ECLS-B suggest that of the children in center-based care, 9% are in low-quality settings (ITERS-R scores of 1 to <3), 66% are in medium-quality settings (ITERS-R scores of 3 to <5), and 24% are in high-quality care (ITERS-R scores of 5–7) (Mulligan & Flanagan, 2006). This represents an improvement from the findings of the CQO study conducted in the 1990s, in which 40% of infant-toddler classrooms were low quality, and only 8% were high-quality environments (CQO Study Team, 1995). However, children living below the poverty threshold are even more likely to be in lower quality settings, with 15% of those in center-based care attending programs with ITERS-R scores below 3 (Mulligan & Flanagan, 2006). Using data from the NICHD Study of Early Child Care and extrapolating to all American children, researchers determined that 61% of American toddlers (children ages 1–3 years) did not experience positive caregiving (NICHD ECCRN, 2000a).

Quality of Inclusive Programs

Generally, the quality of center-based inclusive programs—those that serve children with special needs—has been found to be higher than the quality of non-inclusive programs (Buysse, Wesley, Bryant, & Gardner, 1999; Hestenes, Cassidy, Shim, & Hegde, 2008). Typically this finding has been true for children in preschool classrooms as well as infant-toddler classrooms (Hestenes, Cassidy, Hegde, & Lower, 2007), although some research has found that infant–toddler classrooms do not vary in quality based on inclusion status (Knoche, Peterson, Edwards, & Jeon, 2006). Neither ratings of perceived severity of children's disabilities (Hestenes et al., 2008) nor the number of children with disabilities (Hestenes et al., 2007) have been found to relate to measures of classroom quality. The studies conducted in this area have been relatively small, with restricted samples in some cases. More research is needed to fully understand issues related to quality in inclusive settings, including further examination of the associations between quality in inclusive settings and outcomes for children with special needs.

INPUTS AND OUTPUTS: THE COST OF QUALITY AND ITS IMPACT ON CHILDREN

A substantial body of research has been amassed looking at the inputs to and the outputs of variations in program quality. In economic parlance, at the input side, the focus is on the production or operating costs of early childhood programs and how different levels of quality relate to different levels of cost. On the output side, the focus is on the relation of the level of program quality to the amount of growth in children's skills across various domains of learning and development (language and literacy, cognitive, and social-emotional). A third area, known as the throughputs in economic terms, is the predictors or mediators of quality, which were addressed in a previous section. In sum, the findings related to inputs and outputs are not surprising—that higher quality is generally related to higher operating costs and to better outcomes for children. In other words, it costs more to generate higher quality programs, and children are likely to derive greater educational benefits from higher quality care and education experiences. In the next two sections, we take a closer look at the research evidence linking program quality to costs at the input side and to children's outcomes at the output side.

The Costs of Quality

A few multi-state studies have been conducted looking at issues around the cost and quality of early childhood programs. One of the first major studies to examine this issue was the National Child Care Staffing Study (NCCSS), which found positive associations between teacher wages and program quality, including both structural and process measures (Whitebook et al., 1989), and other multi-state or national studies have since found similar associations (e.g., Goelman et al., 2006; Scarr et al., 1994; Torquati et al., 2007).

The CQO Study was unique at the time in bringing together early childhood researchers and economists to gather detailed information about both cost and quality in center-based programs in four states (CQO Study Team, 1995). The results from that study still offer one of the best pictures of the intersection between the operational costs of early childhood programs and the resulting quality. One of the key findings of the CQO Study, simply stated, is that good quality costs more to produce than lower quality. Further, as the level of quality increases (from low to medium to high), it costs proportionally more to generate. The costs involved in creating good-quality programs are related to a variety of operational characteristics, including labor costs (e.g., staff wages and benefits), occupancy costs (e.g., facilities, utilities), food costs, and other operating expenses. Although different types of programs may expend different proportions of their total costs on these categories (e.g., nonprofit centers spent proportionally more on labor and less on occupancy costs than for-profit centers), higher total expenditures were related to higher quality. Labor costs accounted for the majority of the operating costs of child care centers (70% on average), and staff wages were one of the strongest discriminators related to quality, with higher wages associated with better quality. Yet, teacher wages are low compared to what individuals with similar education and experience could earn in other occupations. One of the seminal findings of this study entailed examination of the full program costs by including the concept of foregone wages, the idea that programs would cost much more to operate if teachers were paid wages similar to other fields. In looking at costs from another perspective of the costs to families, higher quality was also related to higher revenue, with the majority of the revenue being generated by parent fees (71% on average).

The Effects on Children

On the output side, research has focused on the extent to which variations in program quality are associated with differences in children's outcomes, as well as the extent to which the effects of program quality vary for children with different characteristics (such as level of risk). A number of large-scale studies have found positive associations, although generally in the small to moderate range, between program quality and child outcomes, with better learning and developmental outcomes found for children who attended higher quality early childhood programs (Committee on Family and Work Policies, 2003; Vandell, 2004). Although there have been some exceptions to these findings, most of the larger studies have consistently found these associations across a number of different measures of both program quality and children's outcomes, whereas some smaller studies may not have had sufficient variation in the levels of program quality or large enough sample sizes to detect these associations. The CQO Study was one of the first multi-site studies to examine children's longitudinal outcomes in elementary school in relation to the quality of child care they experienced prior to school entry (Peisner-Feinberg & Burchinal, 1997; Peisner-Feinberg, et al., 1999, Peisner-Feinberg et al., 2001). Children who attended higher quality preschool classrooms, both in terms of classroom practices and teacher–child relationships, had better language, cognitive, and social skills. Not only were these differences evident at the end of preschool, but these effects lasted through kindergarten and even into second grade for many skills. Moreover, an important contribution from this study was the examination of whether quality mattered more for some children than others. The results indicated that the effects of program quality were even stronger for children at greater risk (as measured by lower levels of maternal education), suggesting that these children have more to gain from high quality experiences but potentially more to lose from low-quality ones.

The NICHD SECC has examined the longitudinal associations between child care experiences and children's outcomes from infancy through early childhood. In a series of studies, this project has found that better program quality, including measures of both structural and process quality, is associated with better outcomes for children. In studies examining structural characteristics of quality, children attending centers with better adult–child ratios had fewer behavior problems and more positive social behaviors (NICHD ECCRN, 1999); children attending centers with smaller group sizes had better academic achievement and better cognitive development (NICHD ECCRN & Duncan, 2003); and children attending centers that met more recommended standards had fewer behavior problems and better school readiness and language skills (NICHD ECCRN, 1999). In looking at process quality, children attending higher quality settings consistently had better cognitive and language skills at various ages (15, 24, 36, and 54 months) from toddlerhood through preschool (NICHD ECCRN, 2000b; 2002a; 2003b).

As the number of state- and federally funded prekindergarten programs for children in the year before kindergarten has grown, it has become of interest to examine how the quality of these programs relates to children's school readiness skills. In general, the findings from large-scale studies suggest that global measures of program quality are not as strongly associated with children's skill development in these programs as in broader samples of child care programs (as described above). The NCEDL's Multi-state Study and the Statewide Early Education Programs Study (SWEEP) specifically examined state-funded prekindergarten programs in 11 states. The findings from this set of studies indicated that children had better academic and language skills at the end of prekindergarten when they attended higher quality classrooms as measured by teachers' emotional and instructional interactions with children, but there was little relation to broader measures of program quality (Howes et al., 2008; Mashburn et al., 2008). Another major early childhood program that has been studied is Head Start, a federally funded preschool program specifically for children from economically disadvantaged families. The Head Start Family and Child Experiences Survey study (FACES) has studied the quality and effects of Head Start in nationally representative samples of Head Start programs, classrooms, teachers, parents, and children. The findings from these studies have been mixed, with some indications that children attending classrooms with higher ratings on specific aspects of program quality, such as having richer language learning opportunities, performed better (Zill et al., 2001), whereas other analyses of more recent samples have indicated that there were few associations between classroom quality and children's outcomes (Zill et al., 2006).

RESEARCH IN RELATION TO EARLY CHILDHOOD PROGRAM STANDARDS

One area that has demonstrated the intersections among research, policy, and practice is that of the relations between early childhood program standards and program quality. There are two primary types of program standards associated with required compliance: those related to specific types of programs such as Head Start or public prekindergarten programs and those related to state licensing regulations for child care. These two types of standards have different purposes and, accordingly, are often intended to achieve different minimum levels of quality. The standards related to the operations of specific programs are tied to particular sources of funding, and typically the intent of these standards is to ensure that these types of programs maintain higher levels of quality. In contrast, state licensing standards are designed to ensure that programs are meeting at least a minimum level of quality so that children are not endangered. Although many states have moved toward tiered systems of licensing, with standards for higher licensing levels tied to indicators of higher levels of quality (and often to higher reimbursement rates or other resources), the minimum required level typically focuses on basic health and safety issues, representing standards for what would be considered a low level of process quality. A third type of program standard involves voluntary compliance, such as with national accreditation standards, and these are designed specifically to ensure high program quality.

Research examining the relation of program standards to level of quality has generally found that higher standards are associated with higher levels of process quality. Although this conclusion may seem obvious, many of the requirements contained in the standards often represent indicators or mediators of process quality, such as structural characteristics (e.g., staff–child ratios, teacher qualifications, materials), rather than direct measures of process quality itself. However, there has been a trend in recent years to incorporate direct indicators of process quality in some program standards, often through required observations of classroom operations using tools designed to measure process quality.

One large-scale study that examined the broad effects of program standards on classroom quality was the CQO Study. This study found that child care centers in states with more stringent licensing standards (i.e., standards requiring higher levels of structural quality) were of higher quality than those in states with more lax standards (CQO Study Team, 1995; Phillipsen et al., 1997). The CQO Study also found that programs that comply with additional standards, such as nationally accredited programs or those with public funding sources tied to higher standards, had higher levels of process quality. Moreover, these centers often had extra resources (donations or outside funding) that they were able to use to increase the level of quality of their programs. A lasting contribution of this work is that it helped spawn the QRIS movement throughout the country, beginning with one of the first multi-tiered, statewide licensing systems in one of the study's states, North Carolina, in 1999 (the North Carolina Star-Rated License).

A number of other studies have examined the relative level of quality in programs meeting a known set of high standards, such as state-funded prekindergarten programs. In general, these studies have found that quality is generally higher in these programs. For example, a series of studies has been conducted of the North Carolina More at Four Pre-kindergarten Program, a state-funded program for at-risk children. These studies have found that quality has remained relatively high over time even as the program has engaged in major expansion and scale-up, with the maintenance of quality attributed to compliance with the program standards that require high levels of both structural and process quality indicators (Peisner-Feinberg & Schaaf, 2007, 2008a, 2008b). Several studies have also found that children who attended state-funded prekindergarten programs, which have these higher quality standards in place, have positive outcomes with regard to school readiness skills (Gormley, Gayer, Phillips, & Dawson, 2005; Peisner-Feinberg & Schaaf, 2007, 2008a, 2008b; Wong, Cook, Barnett, & Jung, 2008).

However, a few studies have not found these same associations between program standards, process quality, and children's development. The NCEDL Multistate Study, which examined state prekindergarten programs in six states, found that process quality was not as high as would be expected given structural program characteristics (Clifford et al., 2005). One possible explanation for this different set of findings was the large number of part-day (as opposed to full-day) programs in this particular sample, which result in fewer daily opportunities for achieving the variety of learning activities expected for high-quality programs. Further, as research has begun to look at how specific aspects of standards relate to quality and child outcomes, some contradictory findings have emerged. A secondary analysis of seven major studies of early care and education programs found that teacher education was not generally associated with classroom quality or children's academic gains (Early et al., 2007). In sum, this research suggests that although higher program standards are a step in the right direction, neither the standards as specified nor specific structural characteristics as measured completely predict the quality of a classroom. There are clearly other factors that need to be considered that have not been as consistently or adequately measured in research studies and that may not be easily defined for purposes of program standards. As a field, we need to conduct further work to figure out how to measure and monitor such critical factors. One area that has been receiving attention in this regard is the quality of instruction for individual children across the spectrum of learners, including the extent to which teachers scaffold instruction for children who need additional supports to learn as well as adjust strategies for advanced learners. Other factors that merit attention with regard to research that will inform both policy and practice include examination of the quality of teacher preparation (as opposed to just examining attainment of degrees or credentials), characteristics related to organizational climate of the program, and the quality of administrative leadership.

Although the growing movement toward evidence-based decision making in early childhood policy and practice is laudable, these findings suggest the need for further discussion of how to set standards based on research, as well as how to measure and monitor their implementation. Although the definitions of quality are consistent between research and practice, they do not always lend themselves easily to the determination of standards. Moreover, the types of measurement tools used in research are not always feasible for use in monitoring the implementation of standards, given the intensive training and knowledge that is often required for their use. Program standards need to be designed in a way that enables them to be readily measured and regulated, given their key purpose of ensuring that sites meet the minimum requirements for achieving broader program goals. Program standards typically also need to be accessible for widespread implementation across a range of settings. However, the greater the range, the greater the likelihood that the interpretation of the standards will result in variations in the degree to which they are implemented as intended (i.e., the fidelity of implementation) and/or result in the highest possible level of quality as opposed to the lowest permissible level based on the standards. Moreover, there are implications for the system of professional development needed so that the standards are implemented in a way that reflects best practice based on the research evidence. Professional development efforts need to incorporate training related to both the implementation and the measurement of program standards to ensure fidelity and promote quality control.

CONCLUSIONS AND FUTURE DIRECTIONS

There is a wide body of research at this point related to studies of early care and education programs, and we have learned a great deal about the quality of these programs, the factors predicting quality, the associations between quality and cost, and the effects of variations in program quality on children's developmental outcomes. Although there have been a limited number of large-scale national research efforts, the numerous studies that have been and continue to be conducted in this field indicate the high level of interest for both research and practice. Although we have made many gains over the past several decades in our knowledge about program quality, the findings from research studies have not always been directly applicable to practice. Unfortunately, the quality of care for children in our country remains below a level that would ensure that children have the cognitive and language stimulation and supportive relationships that are necessary for optimal development. Given the evidence regarding the links between children's experiences in care and their developmental outcomes, it is imperative that the field continues to work to explore ways to improve care and raise the bar on quality. We have come a long way in the research field—from initial questions about whether child care is harmful to what the key features of program quality are and how we can measure it, what factors predict quality, and what its effects on children are. As our knowledge has grown about the importance of program quality for children's growth and development, the focus has shifted to issues around improving program quality and understanding factors influencing its effects. Key topics being addressed through research include intervention studies that ask what the most effective practices are, studies of professional development that ask what the best approaches for changing practice and improving quality are, and studies of moderating factors that ask what the effects of program quality for children with different characteristics are (such as risk level or language proficiency). Even though there are general consistencies in the definitions of quality between research and practice, we still do not know how best to improve practice and optimize the outcomes for children. Further study is needed to determine the most essential and effective elements for quality improvement interventions, including both the instructional practices and the professional development content and delivery methods. And although there is still much more exploratory work to be done, there are some promising trends in the program quality literature that inform discussion about future research directions.

One important area is to continue research directed toward disaggregating aspects of quality. To date, the majority of research on program quality has examined quality as a global construct; recent efforts, however, have begun to look at specific components of quality. Quality is a complex construct with many interrelated aspects, and efforts to understand it require approaches that reflect those nuances. By teasing apart components of quality, researchers will be able to identify aspects of care that are most predictive of outcomes; help guide the design of interventions to improve quality, including professional development initiatives; and help refine quality rating and improvement systems by better specifying the most critical aspects of quality. A recent report on complementary secondary and meta-analyses of data from large-scale studies suggests that measures of the quality of specific practices are better predictors of outcomes for children than are global quality measures (Burchinal et al., 2009).

The disaggregation of quality applies to both structural and process aspects of care. For example, even though teacher education has been shown to be an important component for quality programming, it may not be simply the attainment of a bachelor's degree that matters. Rather, teacher education must be considered as a multifaceted construct and viewed within the context of a larger system of factors that predict quality. For process quality, the current movement toward documenting the quality of care by specific domains, such as language and literacy or math, is a step in the right direction. However, research should begin to look at even more fine-grained aspects of care and education, including specific processes that occur in classrooms that reflect teacher responsivity and sensitivity, cognitive and language stimulation, and social interactions among adults and peers. For example, some work underway to develop a coding scheme for interactions seems to offer promise in this realm (Atwater, Montagna, Reynolds, & Tapia, 2007).

Further, in thinking about new ways to measure and improve the quality of early care and education programs, we need to consider evidence about the impact on children. Although there is substantial research in this area, the results indicate that the measurement of program quality and children's outcomes are not always closely aligned. This is partially a measurement issue, where perhaps we have not figured out how to capture the key dimensions of practice that are most strongly related to children's learning. It is also an indication of the plasticity of children's development, where the same experiences in early childhood programs will not necessarily affect all children in the same way; similarly, we do not yet fully know how to specify or measure all of the moderating factors determining these effects. One promising approach entails consideration of the associations between quality and outcomes in a somewhat different way, looking for evidence of the most effective instructional strategies based on those that best meet children's educational needs and achieve the greatest learning outcomes. In the early childhood field we typically have not looked at children's outcomes themselves as an indicator of quality, but rather as a product. As the broader educational system has directed more efforts toward measuring children's learning and achievement in regard to issues of accountability and quality improvement, there may be some useful considerations for the education of younger children. One new direction in research is the emerging work on applications of response to intervention (RTI) principles to early childhood education, such as the Recognition & Response model (Recognition & Response Implementation Guide, 2008), as well as other tiered approaches for instruction of young children (e.g., Barnett et al., 2006; Brown, Odom, & Conroy, 2001; Greenwood, Walker, Carta,

& Higgins, 2006; Hemmeter, Ostrosky, & Fox, 2006; Sandall & Schwartz, 2008; VanDerHeyden & Snyder, 2006). One of the key components of such models is using the assessment of individual children's progress to inform the decisions teachers make about the level of intensity of instruction needed to promote learning goals. A number of research studies are underway in this area, and there is some preliminary evidence indicating the effectiveness of such approaches as well as the feasibility of implementation by early childhood teachers (e.g., Buysse & Peisner-Feinberg, 2009).

Another important direction for future research is to continue to evaluate the effectiveness of quality improvement initiatives to inform the identification of program features that successfully raise quality and improve outcomes for children. We know from previous research that quality is generally poor, and we have some ideas about what constitutes good quality care, but we know relatively less about what it takes to improve quality and even less still about how quality improvements can be sustained over time. Research is needed at multiple levels of practice, including at the system level, such as evaluations of quality rating and improvement systems; at the program level, such as studies of professional development initiative for directors; and at the individual teacher level, such as discrete intervention studies of specific classroom practices.

In sum, our field is at a crossroads. We know from research that there are important and potentially long-lasting links between children's experiences in early childhood programs and their developmental outcomes. We also know from both research and practice that the quality of these experiences is often far from optimal for promoting children's learning. However, what we do not yet know is the best and most effective ways for improving quality. Both the research and the practice fields recognize that this is one of the most critical educational issues in our country, as evidenced by the attention given to this topic in studies of quality improvement interventions, policies reflecting an emphasis on quality through program standards and licensing regulations, and the variety of professional development efforts underway. The good news is that there is strong agreement between researchers and practitioners in terms of what constitutes good quality, and together we can achieve the goal of ensuring that the early care and educational experiences of young children are as beneficial as possible.

REFERENCES

Abbott-Shim, M., & Sibley, A. (1987). *Assessment profile*. Atlanta: Quality Assist.

Abbott-Shim, M., & Sibley, A. (1998). *Assessment profile, research edition II*. Atlanta: Quality Assist.

Arnett, J. (1989). Caregivers in day-care centers: Does training matter? *Journal of Applied Developmental Psychology, 10*, 541–552.

Asher, K.N., & Erickson, M.T. (1979). Effects of varying child–teacher ratio and group size on day care children's and teachers' behavior. *American Journal of Orthopsychiatry, 49*, 518–521.

Atwater, J., Montagna, D., Reynolds, L.H., & Tapia, Y. (2007). *Classroom CIRCLE: Classroom code for interactive recording of children's learning environments*. Kansas City: Juniper Gardens Children's Project, University of Kansas.

Barnett, D.W., Elliott, N., Wolsing, L., Bunger, C.E., Haski, H., McKissick, C., & Vander Meer, C.D. (2006). Response to Intervention for young children with extremely challenging behaviors: What it might look like. *School Psychology Review, 35*(4), 568–582.

Barnett, W.S., Tarr, J., Lamy, C., & Frede, E. (2001). *Fragile lives, shattered dreams: A report on implementation of preschool education in New Jersey's Abbott districts.* New Brunswick, NJ: National Institute for Early Education Research, Rutgers University.

Bredekamp, S. (1986). The reliability and validity of the Early Childhood Classroom Observation Scale for accrediting early childhood programs. *Early Childhood Research Quarterly, 1,* 103–118.

Bronfenbrenner, U., & Morris, P.A. (2006). The bioecological model of human development. In R.M. Lerner (Ed.), *Handbook of child psychology: Vol. 1. Theoretical models of human development* (6th ed., pp. 793–828). New York: Wiley.

Brown, W.H., Odom, S.L., & Conroy, M.A. (2001). An intervention hierarchy for promoting young children's peer interactions in natural environments. *Topics in Early Childhood Special Education, 21*(3), 162–175.

Burchinal, M., Kainz, K., Cai, K., Tout, K., Zaslow, M., Martinez-Beck, I., & Rathgeb, C. (2009). *Early care and education quality and child outcomes.* Research to Policy, Research to Practice Brief #2009-15. Washington, DC: Office of Planning, Research and Evaluation, Administration for Children and Families, U.S. Department of Health and Human Services and Child Trends.

Buysse, V., & Peisner-Feinberg, E. (2009, July). *Recognition & Response: Results from an implementation study.* Presentation at the 9th National Early Childhood Inclusion Institute, Chapel Hill, NC.

Buysse, V., Wesley, P.W., Bryant, D., & Gardner, D. (1999). Quality of early childhood programs in inclusive and noninclusive settings. *Exceptional Children, 65,* 301–314.

Campbell, F.A., & Ramey, C.T. (1994). Effects of early intervention on intellectual and academic achievement: A follow-up study of children from low-income families. *Child Development, 65,* 684–698.

Caughy, M.O., DiPietro, J.A., & Strobino, D.M. (1994). Day-care participation as a projective factor in cognitive development of low-income children. *Child Development, 65,* 457–471.

Clements, D.H., & Sarama, J. (2008). Experimental evaluation of the effects of a research-based preschool mathematics curriculum. *American Educational Research Journal, 45,* 443–494.

Clifford, R.M., Barbarin, O., Chang, F., Early, D., Bryant, D., Howes, C., Burchinal, M., & Pianta, R. (2005). What is pre-kindergarten? Characteristics of public pre-kindergarten programs. *Applied Developmental Science, 9*(3), 126–143.

Committee on Family and Work Policies. (2003). *Working families and growing kids: Caring for children and adolescents.* Washington, DC: National Academies Press.

Copple, C., & Bredekamp, S. (2009). *Developmentally appropriate practice in early childhood programs.* Washington, DC: National Association for the Education of Young Children.

CQO Study Team. (1995). *Cost, quality, and child outcomes in child care centers* [Technical report]. Denver: Department of Economics, Center for Research in Economic and Social Policy, University of Colorado at Denver.

Cryer, D., Tietze, W., Burchinal, M., Leal, T., & Palacios, J. (1999). Predicting process quality from structural quality in preschool programs: A cross-country comparison. *Early Childhood Research Quarterly, 14,* 339–361.

Diamond, K.E., Gerde, H.K., & Powell, D.R. (2008). Development in early literacy skills during the pre-kindergarten year in Head Start: Relations between growth in children's writing and understanding of letters. *Early Childhood Research Quarterly, 23,* 467–478.

Dickinson, D.K., & Caswell, L. (2007). Building support for language and early literacy in preschool classrooms through in-service professional development: Effects of the Literacy Environment Enrichment Program (LEEP). *Early Childhood Research Quarterly, 22,* 243–260

Dowsett, C.J., Huston, A.C., Imes, A.E., & Gennetian, L. (2008). Structural and process features in three types of child care for children from high and low income families. *Early Childhood Research Quarterly, 23,* 69–93.

Doyle, A., & Somers, K. (1978). The effects of group and family day care on infant attachment. *Canadian Journal of Behavioral Science, 10,* 38–45.

Early, D.M., Barbarin, O., Bryant, D., Burchinal, M., Chang, F., Clifford, R., Crawford, G., Weaver, W., Howes, C., Ritchie, S., Kraft-Sayre, M., Pianta, R., & Barnett, W.S. (2005). *Pre-kindergarten in eleven states: NCEDL's multi-state study of pre-kindergarten & study of*

State-Wide Early Education Programs (SWEEP), preliminary descriptive report. Chapel Hill, NC: FPG Child Development Institute, University of North Carolina.

Early, D.M., Maxwell, K.L., Burchinal, M., Alva, S., Bender, R.H., Bryant, D., Cai, K., Clifford, R.M., Ebanks, C., Griffin, J.A., Henry, G.T., Howes, C., Iriondo-Perez, J., Jeon, H., Mashburn, A.J., Peisner-Feinberg, E., Pianta, R.C., Vandergrift, N., & Zill, N. (2007). Teachers' education, classroom quality, and young children's academic skills: Results from seven studies of preschool programs. *Child Development, 78,* 558–580.

Farran, D.C., & Ramey, C.T. (1978). Infant day care and attachment behaviors toward mothers and teachers. *Annual Progress in Child Psychiatry & Child Development,* 310–318.

Flanagan, K.D., & West, J. (2004). *Children born in 2001: First results from the Early Childhood Longitudinal Study–Birth Cohort (ECLS-B).* Washington, DC: U.S. Department of Education, National Center for Education Statistics.

Fukkink, R.G., & Lont, A. (2007). Does training matter? A meta-analysis and review of caregiver training studies. *Early Childhood Research Quarterly, 22,* 294–311.

Gerber, E.B., Whitebook, M., & Weinstein, R.S. (2007). At the heart of child care: Predictors of teacher sensitivity in center-based child care. *Early Childhood Research Quarterly, 22,* 327–346.

Ghazvini, A., & Mullis, R.L. (2002). Center-based care for young children: Examining predictors of quality. *Journal of Genetic Psychology, 163,* 112–125.

Gilliam, W.S., & Zigler, E.F. (2000). A critical meta-analysis of all evaluations of state-funded preschool from 1977 to 1988: Implications for policy, service delivery and program evaluation. *Early Childhood Research Quarterly, 15,* 441–473.

Goelman, H., Forer, B., Kershaw, P., Doherty, G., Lero, D., & LaGrange, A. (2006). Towards a predictive model of quality in Canadian child care centers. *Early Childhood Research Quarterly, 21,* 280–295.

Gormley, W.T., Gayer, T., Phillips, D., & Dawson, B. (2005). The effects of universal pre-K on cognitive development. *Developmental Psychology, 41*(6), 872–884.

Greenwood, C.R., Walker, D., Carta, J.J., & Higgins, S.K. (2006). Developing a general outcome measure of growth in cognitive abilities of children 1 to 4 years old: The early problem-solving indicator. *School Psychology Review, 35*(4), 535–551.

Harms, T., & Clifford, R.M. (1989). *The Family Day Care Rating Scale.* New York: Teachers College Press.

Harms, T., & Clifford, R.M. (2007). *The Family Child Care Environment Rating Scale-Revised Edition.* New York: Teacher College Press.

Harms, T., Clifford, R.M., & Cryer, D.R. (1980). *The Early Childhood Environment Rating Scale.* New York: Teachers College Press.

Harms, T., Clifford, R.M., & Cryer, D.R. (1998, 2005). *The Early Childhood Environment Rating Scale–Revised Edition.* New York: Teachers College Press.

Harms, T., Cryer, D.R., & Clifford, R.M. (1990). *The Infant/Toddler Environment Rating Scale.* New York: Teachers College Press.

Harms, T., Cryer, D.R., & Clifford, R.M. (2003). *The Infant/Toddler Environment Rating Scale–Revised Edition.* New York: Teachers College Press.

Hayes, C.D., Palmer, J.L., & Zaslow, M.J. (Eds.). (1990). *Who cares for America's children? Child care policy for the 1990s.* Washington, DC: National Academies Press.

Hemmeter, M.L., Ostrosky, M., & Fox, L. (2006). Social and emotional foundations for early learning: A conceptual model for intervention. *School Psychology Review, 35*(4), 583–601.

Hestenes, L.L., Cassidy, D.J., Hegde, A.V., & Lower, J.K. (2007). Quality in inclusive and noninclusive infant and toddler classrooms. *Journal of Research in Childhood Education, 22,* 69–84.

Hestenes, L.L., Cassidy, D.J., Shim, J., & Hegde, A.V. (2008). Quality in inclusive preschool classrooms. *Early Education and Development, 19,* 519–540.

Holloway, S., & Reichhart-Erickson, M. (1989). Child-care quality, family structure, and maternal expectations: Relationship to preschool children's peer relations. *Journal of Applied Developmental Psychology, 10,* 281–298.

Howes, C. (1997). Children's experiences in center-based child care as a function of teacher background and adult:child ratio. *Merrill-Palmer Quarterly, 43,* 404–425.

Howes, C., Burchinal, M., Pianta, R., Bryant, D., Early, D., Clifford, R.M., & Barbarin, O. (2008). Ready to learn? Children's pre-academic achievement in pre-kindergarten programs. *Early Childhood Research Quarterly, 23*(1), 27–50.

Howes, C., & Norris, D.J. (1997). Adding two school age children: Does it change quality in family child care? *Early Childhood Research Quarterly, 12,* 327-342.

Howes, C., & Smith., E.W. (1995). Relations among child care quality, teacher behavior, children's play activities, emotional security, and cognitive activity in child care. *Early Childhood Research Quarterly, 10,* 381–404.

Justice, L.M., Mashburn, A.J., Hamre, B.K., & Pianta, R.C. (2008). Quality of language and literacy instruction in preschool classrooms serving at-risk pupils. *Early Childhood Research Quarterly, 23,* 51–68.

Kisker, E.E., Paulsell, D., Love, J.M., & Raikes, H. (2002). *Early Head Start research: Pathways to quality and full implementation in Early Head Start programs.* Washington, DC: U.S. Department of Health and Human Services, Administration of Children, Youth, and Families.

Knoche, L., Peterson, C.A., Edwards, C.P., & Jeon, H.J. (2006). Child care for children with and without disabilities: The provider, observer, and parent perspectives. *Early Childhood Research Quarterly, 21,* 93–109.

Layzer, J., Goodson., B., & Moss, M. (1993). *Final report volume 1: Life in preschool.* Cambridge, MA: Abt Associates.

Love, J.M., Ryer, P., & Faddis, B. (1992). *Caring environments: Program quality in California's publicly funded child development programs.* Portsmouth, NH: RMC Research.

Mashburn, A.J., Pianta, R.C., Hamre, B.K., Downer, J.T., Barbarin, O.A., Bryant, D., Burchinal, M., Early, D.M., & Howes, C. (2008). Measures of classroom quality in prekindergarten and children's development of academic, language, and social skills. *Child Development, 79*(3), 732–749.

Moskowitz, D.S., Schwarz, J.C., & Corsini, D.A. (1977). Initiating day care at three years of age: Effects on attachment. *Child Development, 48,* 1271–1276.

Mulligan, G.M., & Flanagan, F.D. (2006). *Age 2: Findings from the 2-year-old follow-up of the Early Childhood Longitudinal Study–Birth Cohort (ELCS-B).* E.D. Tab 2006-043. Washington DC: U.S. Department of Education, National Center for Education Statistics.

National Association for the Education of Young Children. (2007). *NAEYC early education program standards and accreditation criteria.* Washington, DC: Author.

NICHD Early Child Care Research Network. (1996). Characteristics of infant child care: Factors contributing to positive caregiving. *Early Childhood Research Quarterly, 11,* 269–306.

NICHD Early Child Care Research Network. (1998). Relations between family predictors and child outcomes: Are they weaker for children in child care? *Developmental Psychology, 43,* 1119–1128.

NICHD Early Child Care Research Network. (1999). Child outcomes when child care center classes meet recommended standards for quality. *American Journal of Public Health, 89*(7), 1072–1077.

NICHD Early Child Care Research Network. (2000a). Characteristics and quality of child care for toddlers and preschoolers. *Applied Developmental Science, 4,* 116–135.

NICHD Early Child Care Research Network. (2000b). The relation of child care to cognitive and language development. *Child Development, 71*(4), 960–680.

NICHD Early Child Care Research Network. (2002a). Early child care and children's development prior to school entry. *American Educational Research Journal, 39*(1), 133–164.

NICHD Early Child Care Research Network. (2002b). Structure > process > outcome: Direct and indirect effects of caregiving quality on young children's development. *Psychological Science, 13,* 199–206.

NICHD Early Child Care Research Network. (2003a). Does amount of time spent in child care predict socioemotional adjustment during the transition to kindergarten? *Child Development, 74,* 976–1005.

NICHD Early Child Care Research Network. (2003b). Does quality of child care affect child outcomes at age 4-1/2? *Developmental Psychology, 39,* 451–469.

NICHD Early Child Care Research Network & Duncan, G.J. (2003). Modeling the impacts of child care quality on children's preschool cognitive development. *Child Development, 74,* 1485–1506.

Office of Human Development Services. (2007). *Head Start program performance standards.* Title 45, Chapter XIII, Part 1304 (10/1/07 Edition). Retrieved April 1, 2009, from http://eclkc.ohs.acf.hhs.gov/hslc/Program%20Design%20and%20Management/Fiscal/

Legislation%20&%20Regulations/Head%20Start%20Program%20Performance%20 Standards/fiscal_pps_00244_093005.html

Peisner-Feinberg, E.S., & Burchinal, M.R. (1997). Relations between preschool children's child-care experiences and concurrent development: The Cost, Quality, and Outcomes Study. *Merrill-Palmer Quarterly, 43,* 451–477.

Peisner-Feinberg, E.S., Burchinal, M.R., Clifford, R.M., Culkin, M., Howes, C., Kagan, S.L., Yazejian, N., Byler, P., Rustici, J., & Zelazo, J. (1999). *The children of the Cost, Quality, & Outcomes Study go to school: Technical report.* Chapel Hill, NC: Frank Porter Graham Child Development Center, University of North Carolina at Chapel Hill.

Peisner-Feinberg, E.S., Burchinal, M.R., Clifford, R.M., Culkin, M.L., Howes, C., Kagan, S.L., & Yazejian, N. (2001). The relation of preschool child care quality to children's cognitive and social developmental trajectories through second grade. *Child Development, 72*(5), 1534–1553.

Peisner-Feinberg, E.S., & Schaaf, J.S. (2007). *Evaluation of the North Carolina More at Four Pre-kindergarten Program: Year 5 (2005–2006): Children's outcomes and program quality in the fifth year.* Chapel Hill, NC: FPG Child Development Institute, University of North Carolina at Chapel Hill.

Peisner-Feinberg, E.S. & Schaaf, J.M. (2008a). *Evaluation of the North Carolina More at Four Pre-kindergarten Program: Children's longitudinal outcomes and program quality over time (2003–2007).* Chapel Hill, NC: FPG Child Development Institute.

Peisner-Feinberg, E.S., & Schaaf, J.M. (2008b). *Evaluation of the North Carolina More at Four Pre-kindergarten Program: Performance and progress in the seventh year (2007–2008).* Chapel Hill, NC: FPG Child Development Institute.

Phillips, D., McCartney, K., & Scarr, S. (1987). Child-care quality and children's social development. *Developmental Psychology, 23,* 537–543.

Phillips, D., McCartney, K., & Sussman, A. (2006). Child care and early development. In K. McCartney & D. Phillips (Eds.), *The handbook of early child development* (pp. 471–489). Oxford: Blackwell.

Phillips, D.A., Scarr, S., & McCartney, D. (1987). Dimensions and effects of child care quality: The Bermuda study. In D.A. Phillips (Ed.), *Quality in child care: What does research tell us?* (pp. 43–46). Washington, DC: National Association for the Education of Young Children.

Phillips, D.A., Voran, M., Kisker, E., Howes, C., & Whitebook, M. (1994). Child care for children in poverty: Opportunity or inequity? *Child Development, 65,* 472–492.

Phillipsen, L.C., Burchinal, M.R., Howes, C., & Cryer, D. (1997). The prediction of process quality from structural features of child care. *Early Childhood Research Quarterly, 12,* 281–303.

Pianta, R.C., LaParo, K.M., & Hamre, B.K. (2008). *Classroom Assessment Scoring System (CLASS).* Baltimore: Paul H. Brookes Publishing Co.

Recognition & Response implementation guide. (2008). Chapel Hill, NC: University of North Carolina, FPG Child Development Institute.

Reynolds, A.J., & Temple, J.A. (1998). Extended early childhood intervention and school achievement: Age thirteen findings from the Chicago Longitudinal Study. *Child Development, 69,* 231–246.

Roach, M., Adams, D., Riley, D., & Edie, D. (2002). *What characteristics relate to child care quality?* (Wisconsin Child Care Research Partnership Issue Brief #8). Madison: University of Wisconsin–Extension.

Rubenstein, J.L., & Howes, C. (1979). Caregiving and infant behavior in day care and in homes. *Developmental Psychology, 15,* 1–24.

Ruopp, R., Travers, J., Glantz, F., & Coelen, C. (1979). *Final report of the National Day Care Study Vol. I: Children at the center.* Cambridge, MA: Abt Associates.

Sandall, S.R., & Schwartz, I.S. (2008). *Building blocks for teaching preschoolers with special needs* (2nd ed.). Baltimore: Paul H. Brookes Publishing Co.

Scarr, S., Eisenberg, M., & Deater-Deckard, K. (1994). Measurement of quality in child care centers. *Early Childhood Research Quarterly, 9,* 131–151.

Schweinhart, L.J., & Weikart, D.P. (1998). High/Scope Perry Preschool Program effects at age twenty-seven. In J. Crane (Ed.), *Social programs that work* (pp. 148–162). New York: Russell Sage Foundation.

Sheehan, A.M., & Abbott, M.S. (1979). A descriptive study of day care characteristics. *Child Care Quarterly, 8,* 206–219.

Smith, A.N., & Spence, C.M. (2008). National Day Care Study: Optimizing the day care environment. *American Journal of Orthopsychiatry, 50,* 718–721.

Smith, M.W., Brady, J.P., & Anastasopoulos, L. (2008). *Early Language and Literacy Classroom Observation Tool, Pre-K (ELLCO Pre-K).* Baltimore: Paul H. Brookes Publishing Co.

Suwalksy, J.T., & Klein, R.P. (1980). Effects of naturally-occurring nontraumatic separations from mother. *Infant Mental Health Journal, 1,* 196–201.

Tietze, W., Cryer, D., Bairrão, J., Palacios, J., & Wetzel, G. (1996). Comparisons of observed process quality in early child care and education programs in five countries. *Early Childhood Research Quarterly, 11,* 447–475.

Torquati, J.C., Raikes, H., & Huddleston-Casas, C.A. (2007). Teacher education, motivation, compensation, workplace support, and links to quality of center-based child care and teachers' intention to stay in the early childhood profession. *Early Childhood Research Quarterly, 22,* 261–275.

Travers, J., Goodson, B.D., Singer, J.D., & Connell, D.B. (1979). *Final report of the National Day Care Study, Vol. II: Research results of the National Day Care Study.* Cambridge, MA: Abt Associates.

U.S. Department of Health and Human Services, Administration for Children and Families. (2005, May). *Head Start impact study: First year findings.* Washington, DC: Author.

U.S. General Accounting Office. (2002). *Child care: States have undertaken a variety of quality improvement initiatives, but more evaluations of effectiveness are needed.* GAO-02-897. Washington, DC: Author.

Vandell, D.L. (2004). Early child care: The known and the unknown. *Merrill-Palmer Quarterly, 50*(3), 387–414.

VanDerHeyden, A.M., & Snyder, P. (2006). Integrating frameworks from early childhood intervention and school psychology to accelerate growth for all young children. *School Psychology Review, 35*(4), 519–534.

Vaughn, B.E., Gove, F.L., & Egeland, B. (1980). The relationship between out-of-home care and the quality of infant-mother attachment in an economically disadvantaged population. *Child Development, 51,* 1203–1214.

Votruba-Drzal, E., Coley, R.L., & Chase-Lansdale, P.L. (2004). Child care and low-income children's development: Direct and moderated effects. *Child Development, 75,* 296–312.

Whitebook, M., Howes, C., & Phillips, D. (1989). *Who cares? Child care teachers and the quality of care in America.* Oakland, CA: Child Care Employee Project.

Whitebook, M., Howes, C., & Phillips, D. (1998). *Worthy work, unlivable wages: The National Child Care Staffing Study, 1988–97.* Washington, DC: Center for the Child Care Workforce.

Winett, R.A., Fuchs, W.L., Moffatt, S.A., & Nerviano, V.J. (1977). A cross-sectional study of children and their families in different child care environments: Some data and conclusions. *Journal of Community Psychology, 5,* 149–159.

Wong, V.C., Cook, T.D., Barnett, W.S., & Jung, K. (2008). An effectiveness-based evaluation of five state pre-kindergarten programs. *Journal of Policy Analysis and Management, 27*(1), 122–154.

Zill, N., Resnick, G., Kim, K., McKey, R.H., Clark, C., Pai-Samant, S., Connell, D., Vaden-Kiernan, M., O'Brien, R., & D'Elio, M.A. (2001). *Head Start FACES (1997): Longitudinal findings on program performance, third progress report.* Washington, DC: U.S. Department of Health and Human Services, Administration for Children and Families.

Zill, N., Resnick, G., Kim, K., O'Donnell,K., Sorongon, A., Ziv, Y., Alva, S., McKey, R.H., Pai-Samant, S., Clark, C., O'Brien, R., & D'Elio, M.A. (2006). *Head Start Performance Measures Center, Family and Child Experiences Survey (FACES 2000): Technical report, February 2006.* Washington, DC: U.S. Department of Health and Human Services, Administration for Children and Families.

Zill, N., Sorongon, A., Kim, K., Clark, C., & Woolverton, M. (2006). *FACES 2003 research brief: Children's outcomes and program quality in Head Start.* Washington, DC: U.S. Department of Health and Human Services, Administration for Children and Families.

CHAPTER 3

Issues in Measuring Program Quality

Donna M. Bryant, Martha Zaslow, and Margaret Burchinal

Researchers have focused on measuring the quality of children's early care and education environments to identify the factors in the child care environment that enhance or deter children's development. One of the most consistent findings is that children who attend higher quality child care are more likely to start school with better cognitive, academic, and social skills, according to the extensive child care research literature (Lamb, 1998; National Institute of Child Health and Human Development [NICHD] Early Child Care Research Network [ECCRN], 2006; Peisner-Feinberg et al., 2001; Vandell, 2004). For this reason, parents and policy makers have focused on improving the quality of child care to increase children's school readiness, especially children from low-income families (Barnett, Hustedt, Hawkinson, & Robin, 2007).

With this focus on improving the quality of early care and education, many policy makers and practitioners have used quality measures in efforts to improve the quality of care. Quality measures have been used by some early care and education practitioners as self-assessment tools as they engage in quality improvement activities (Buysse & Wesley, 2005; Mashburn, Pianta, Downer, & Hamre, 2007; South Carolina ECERS Quality Study Team, 2006; Smith, Sarkar, Perry-Manning, & Schmalzreid, 2006). In such programs, quality is an important outcome measure. Measurement of quality can also be used by states to rate and label the quality of settings in an effort to help parents make early care and education decisions. States and the federal government have also used quality to gain an understanding of the quality of publicly funded programs, such as Head Start, and to evaluate the effectiveness of quality improvement efforts. Recently, quality measures have taken on a new role in early childhood policies as observational assessments are being used in state systems of child care licensing, tiered reimbursement, and quality rating and improvement systems (QRISs; National Child Care Information Center [NCCIC], 2009; Tout, Zaslow, & Halle, 2009; Zaslow, Tout, & Martinez-Beck, 2010). In these systems, significant consequences may be attached to the scores on a quality measure.

Measurement of the quality of children's early education environments has thus become central to many policy, programmatic, and research endeavors. This chapter will describe the research on quality measurements and links to children's development, highlight some key issues concerning quality measurement, and suggest several areas in which quality measurement could be improved.

DEFINITION AND MEASUREMENT OF QUALITY AND LINKS TO CHILD DEVELOPMENT

It is important to define early care and education quality before discussing the measurement of that quality. All major reviews of the child care research (e.g., Vandell & Wolfe, 2000; Committee on Family and Work Policies of the National Research Council, 2003) and reviews of the psychometric properties of existing quality measures (Friedman & Amadeo, 1999; Halle & Vick, 2007) distinguish between structural and process quality. *Process quality* is believed to describe the actual processes that directly affect children and their early development. It includes the caregiver's interactions with children and the degree to which the caregiver structures the environment to ensure emotionally responsive and stimulating care. It also includes the practices that promote the health and safety of the children. *Structural quality* is believed to include the characteristics of caregivers and the child care environment that promote or enable caregivers to create high-quality child care environments but are believed to indirectly impact—via process quality—children's development. Structural quality includes "regulable" features of the environment that can increase the likelihood of positive process quality through limits on group size and ratio and requirements for staff pre- and in-service professional development. Both process and structural quality, considered in more detail next, are measured in both center-based care (including child care centers, prekindergarten, preschools, and Head Start), and home-based care (including licensed family child care and family, friend, and neighbor care). Nevertheless, the particular ways in which both process and structural quality are manifested and measured differ by setting as well as by age of child (infants and toddlers; preschool-age children).

Policy and practice statements of such national organizations as the National Association for the Education of Young Children (NAEYC) and the American Academy of Pediatrics also provide guidelines to promote high-quality care. NAEYC's standards for program accreditation reflect the distinction between process and structural aspects of quality: Some standards focus on children's immediate experiences in the early childhood setting (e.g., standard for relationships), while others focus on the support structure for programs (e.g., standard for leadership and management).

Structural Quality

Structural characteristics are thought to promote the likelihood that caregivers will provide high-quality care to individual children but are indirect assessments of quality (Vandell, 2004). Structural characteristics are often included in licensing criteria or QRISs, because they are believed to be essential to the welfare of young children or have been shown to predict process quality and child outcomes (Lamb, 1998). Structural characteristics are generally easier to assess reliably than are children's experiences in the caregiving setting. Child–caregiver ratios and caregiver education are the most widely studied structural measures. Child–caregiver ratios have tended to be modest but significant predictors of child outcomes in large child care studies (Howes, 1997; NICHD ECCRN, 1999, 2000b;

Phillipsen, Burchinal, Howes, & Cryer, 1997; Pianta et al., 2005) and have also been shown to predict observed interactions in two major child care studies (NICHD ECCRN, 2002b; Phillipsen, et al., 1997).

Caregiver education appears to be a stronger predictor of observed quality and child outcomes in home-based care (Burchinal, Howes, & Kontos, 2002; Clarke-Stewart, Vandell, Burchinal, O'Brien, & McCartney, 2002) and a modest to moderate predictor in center-based care (Lamb, 1998; NICHD ECCRN, 2000a, Phillipsen et al., 1997). Improving caregiver education was frequently touted as the route to ensuring high-quality care. However, a recent reanalysis of data from seven large studies of center-based preschool care (Early et al., 2007) has indicated that while caregiver education level or a teaching certificate modestly predicted better outcomes in community child care, caregiver education or certification was not related to either observed quality or child outcomes in publicly funded Head Start or prekindergarten programs. Vu and colleagues (2009) suggested that this may be in part because of supports, supervision, and monitoring that are in place to a greater extent in the publicly funded settings, therefore making the background of the educator/provider relatively less important. Education may help to predict how much an educator/child care provider will respond to a quality improvement approach. This possibility is raised by suggestive evidence in the National Early Reading First Evaluation (Jackson et al., 2007).

Other caregiver characteristics show a mixed pattern of association with child outcomes. Caregivers with more recent training also have been shown to have children with better outcomes in some studies (Burchinal, Cryer, Clifford, & Howes, 2002; Clarke-Stewart et al., 2002; Howes, 1997; NICHD ECCRN, 1999) and in a recent meta-analysis (Fukkink & Lont, 2007), but recent training was not related to observed quality in at least two large studies (Phillipsen et al., 1997; Pianta et al., 2005). Years of prior experience working with young children was positively related to observed quality in two studies of prekindergarten (Phillips, Gormley, & Lowenstein, 2009; Pianta et al., 2005), but negatively related in a study of community child care (Phillipsen et al., 1997). More distal measures such as wages and turnover have been implicated in a few studies (Helburn, 1995; Howes, 1997; Pianta et al., 2005) but have not been tested as predictors of child outcomes in the large studies.

Structural quality may be measured by self-report of staff or documented onsite, as when observers record group size or ratio directly in the classroom or home-based care setting. The possibility of difficulty with recall (e.g., with respect to number of training hours in the past year) or respondent report bias (e.g., reporting a group size or ratio within licensing regulations) have resulted in discussions about verification of all or some self-report data provided as part of quality rating and improvement systems. Early childhood professional development registries provide one approach for periodic recording of the education and training components of structural quality, with verification of training or coursework done on an ongoing basis.

In summary, only a few classroom and caregiver background characteristics show consistent modest associations with child outcomes, and these associations are believed to be through their impact on process quality measures (NICHD ECCRN, 2002b). Evidence suggests that observations of the caregiving environment tend to provide better prediction of child outcomes than do classroom or caregiver background characteristics. We consider observational measures of quality next.

Process Quality

Direct observation of the child care environment is required for most process quality measures. These measures quantify the aspects of child care that are believed to be essential for promoting child outcomes—both physical features of the environment and interactions between caregivers/educators and children that the children experience immediately. Typically, these instruments entail observations of the child care setting to determine whether the caregiver is providing the children with the kinds of experiences that are believed to enhance young children's development. Table 3.1 summarizes the domains covered by 11 widely used classroom research observation tools, as well as specific data-collection procedures and applicable age range for each measure (Bryant, 2010). No measure covers all domains, but each measure typically includes several domains of classroom experience. These include frequent and warm interactions between teachers and children, rich language use, extending children's knowledge through elaboration and contingent responsiveness, a variety of activities that encourage reasoning and problem solving and are culturally appropriate, opportunities for children to be with others in large and small groups and alone, consistent and positive use of behavior management strategies, safe and healthy daily routines, and good planning and time management.

The typical procedure is that a rater trained on the measure will record data about the child care setting using a time-sampled coding scheme to describe the

Table 3.1. Early childhood classroom observation measures for global quality or dimensions of quality

Measure	Domains observed	Observation procedure[a]	Age range	Key references
CIS: Caregiver Interaction Scale[b]	Emotional tone, discipline style, and responsiveness of teachers	45 minutes; rating of 26 items; 4-point scale	Toddlers–kindergarten	Arnett, 1989
CLASS: Classroom Assessment Scoring System	Teacher–child interactions in three domains: instructional support, emotional support, and classroom organization	2–3 hours; 30-minute cycles of observe/code; 10 items; 7-point scale	Pre-K and K–3 versions; toddler soon	Pianta, LaParo, & Hamre, 2007
ECCOM: Early Childhood Classroom Observation Measure	Quality of instruction, management, social climate, cultural sensitivity, and resources	3 hours; time sample of specific behaviors	Ages 4–7	Stipek & Byler, 2004
ECERS-R: Early Childhood Environment Rating Scale–Rev.	Global quality and seven subscales: space and furnishings, personal care, language and reasoning, activities, interactions, program structure, and parents/staff	3 hours + 20-minute interview; 43 items; 7-point scale	Ages 2.5–5	Harms, Clifford, & Cryer, 1998
ECERS-E: ECERS, Extension	Developed to supplement the ECERS-R with more focus on academic achievement: literacy, math, science, and diversity; reflects the British national preKindergarten curriculum	2 hours + 5-minute interview; 18 items; 7-point scale	Ages 4–6	Sylva, Siraj-Blatchford, & Taggart, 2003

Table 3.1. (*continued*)

Measure	Domains observed	Observation procedure[a]	Age range	Key references
ELLCO: Early Language and Literacy Classroom Observation Pre-K and K–3 Tools	Two parts: 1) classroom observation of 18–19 dimensions of literacy and 2) teacher interview	3.5 hours+; 18–19 checklist items on a 5-point scale	Ages pre-K to K and K to third grade	Smith, Brady, & Anastasopoulos, 2008; Smith, Brady, & Clark-Chiarelli, 2008
ITERS-R: Infant/Toddler Environment Rating Scale–Rev.	Global quality and seven subscales: space and furnishings, personal care, listening and talking, activities, interactions, program structure, and parents/staff	3 hours+ 20-minute interview; 39 items; 7-point scale	Ages birth to 3 years	Harms, Cryer, & Clifford, 2003
ORCE: Observational Record of the Caregiving Environment	Focuses on an individual child's interactions with adults; sensitive, warm, and responsive caregiving; several discrete behaviors and five qualitative ratings	2 observation cycles of 44 minutes; discrete behaviors and global ratings	Ages 6–54 months	NICHD ECCRN, 1996 & 2001
PQA: Preschool Program Quality Assessment, 2nd edition	Three observed domains: learning environment, daily routines, and adult–child interaction; four domains via interview: curriculum planning and assessment, parent involvement, staff qualifications and program management	2–3 hours+ teacher interview; 63 items; 5-point scale	Ages 3–5	High/Scope Educational Research Foundation, 1989 & 2003
Profile: Assessment Profile for Early Childhood Programs	Five subscales: learning environment, scheduling, curriculum, individualizing, interacting	2–3 hrs; 60-item checklist; Yes/No response	Ages 3–7	Abbott-Shim & Sibley, 1998 (the research version)
Snapshot: Emerging Academics Snapshot[b]	Child's exposure to instruction and engagement in six academic activity settings, 11 content areas, and six levels of teacher responsivity	2–4 hours; time sample of specific settings and behaviors	Ages 1–8	Ritchie, Howes, Kraft-Sayre, & Weiser, 2001

[a]Minimum observation time recommended; number of items on measure; and type of rating scale
[b]Measure can also be used with caregivers in family child care homes.

time spent in various activities or types of interaction. Alternatively, the rater observes and scores on a rating scale several items that describe the overall quantity and quality of the activities and the caregiver's interactions with the children. Not surprisingly, even given the issues with self-report noted above, it is more difficult to measure process quality accurately than structural quality.

Each of the measures considered here has shown adequate validity, meaning that it captures the construct of quality that it was designed to assess. Many of the global quality measures have been shown to be highly correlated with each other. Bryant (2010) summarized eight studies that each used two different quality measures, with typical correlations between global quality measures in the .60–.85 range.

Quality improvement programs and policy makers frequently want to know whether one classroom observational measure does a better job than others in measuring "good practice." The relatively high correlations among these measures suggest that the choice of measure should be based primarily on the specific domain(s) of information needed. The quality measures differ in the detail they provide on specific domains, such as stimulation for language and literacy development. Beyond that, concerns such as ease of training or effort needed to maintain reliability should be considered. A few observational measures focus on an individual child's experience rather than the classroom or home-based setting as a whole. These measures will be most appropriate if the aim is to understand the quality of a particular child's experiences in the early childhood setting.

Quality Links to Children's Outcomes

Evidence from many studies using the observational measures in Table 3.1 shows all of them to have been positively related to aspects of children's development; some measures have been related to several outcomes in several studies (see reviews by Friedman & Amedeo, 1999; Halle & Vick, 2007; and Vandell, 2004). This is the primary reason that observational quality measures have achieved such widespread use—the research data lead us to believe that higher quality scores will be related to better language, math, and socio-emotional outcomes for children. However, now that financial consequences may be tied to different quality assessments—for example, when they are made part of a state's QRIS—questions arise about the necessary evidence base for the quality–child outcomes linkage. In addition, in some states, key stakeholders are explicit that the goal is for higher quality levels within the ratings system to provide stronger supports for children's school readiness. An underlying assumption is that quality should provide a strong basis for predicting to children's developmental outcomes (Tout et al., 2009).

While the relationship between quality and child outcomes is found quite consistently, studies indicate that the relationship is not generally large or even moderate in magnitude. Careful analyses with the NICHD data, using different approaches to controlling for background characteristics of the children and families, concluded that the relationship was modest, especially when the most rigorous statistical approaches were used. In a comprehensive examination of this issue, Burchinal and colleagues (2009) conducted both a meta-analysis, looking at the findings across individual early childhood studies, and coordinated secondary analyses with multiple large-scale early childhood datasets. Both research approaches resulted in the conclusion that measures of process quality consistently predicted to children's cognitive, language, and social outcomes, but that the strength of the relationship is modest.

One possible interpretation of this finding concerns measurement quality: It is likely that current measures of quality do not provide sufficient detail on the all aspects of quality most closely related to particular child outcomes (Forry et al., 2009). For example, a measure carefully developed by experts in the field to describe the responsiveness and sensitivity of caregivers (the Observational Record of the Caregiving Environment, ORCE) only shows modest prediction to children's cognitive skills (NICHD ECCRN & Duncan, 2003). It may be important to provide a more detailed description of such specific activities as introducing more complex vocabulary words or math concepts in early childhood settings. Indeed, caregiver spontaneous discussion of mathematics concepts in early childhood settings has been related to fall-to-spring gains in early mathematics achievement test scores (Klibanoff, Levine, Huttenlocher, Vasilyeva, & Hedges, 2006). The development of stronger measures has now become a focus, in part because of a new body of work involving experimental evaluations of approaches to improving quality in early childhood settings (Zaslow, Tout, Halle, Vick, & Lavelle, under review). It is also a focus because new evidence by the NICHD Study of Early Child Care and Youth Development (Vandell, Belsky, Burchinal, Steinberg, & NICHD ECCRN, 2009) suggests that quality in early childhood settings predicts cognitive and social outcomes all the way through adolescence. This suggests that even modest associations during early childhood may have long-term effects, and stronger measures may provide even stronger longer-term prediction. Further, it raises the possibility that even if efforts to strengthen measurement do not produce stronger associations with child outcomes, a small effect that is extremely consistent across studies and persistent over years of development may nevertheless be of importance.

Better alignment of measures with specific outcomes It would be unexpected for any single measure to be the best predictor of school readiness, because we have so many different desired outcomes for children. Increased interest is being focused on measuring specific components of quality (teaching instructional style, language/scaffolding, literacy activities, cultural appropriateness) that might better predict specific domains of children's outcomes. Targeted and content-specific measures often show a stronger association with child outcomes in the particular area they are targeting than do the global measures (e.g., Dickinson & Smith, 1994; Dickinson & Tabors, 2001; Jackson et al., 2007; Sarama & Clements, 2004). For example, Sarama and Clements (2004) reported a much stronger association between the quality of math instruction and math skills when they use aligned measures than is typically seen when global quality and outcome measures are used. Similarly, Whitehurst and Lonigan (1998) and Dickinson and Smith (1994) documented that language and reading skills were improved when Head Start teachers engaged in highly interactive book reading using both careful observation of the book reading interactions as well as overall observations of the child care literacy environment. Observations of literacy activities provided an explanation, along with global measures of quality, for why the federal program Early Reading First improved letter and print knowledge but not language or phonemic skills (Jackson et al., 2007).

In all of these studies, careful measurement of specific instructional activities was critical in establishing how early academic interventions or curricula appeared to improve children's academic skills through specific hypothesized changes in instruction. Accordingly, the combined use of both the specific and global quality measures has proved useful in large-scale evaluations (Howes et al., 2008; Jackson et al., 2007). Some state QRISs are also now including both global and more specific and instructionally focused measures of quality (Tout et al., 2009). It is clear that selection of the most appropriate measure depends on the alignment between characteristics of the instrument and the purpose for which the instrument is being selected. Identification of appropriate measures for particular domains may need to await further development work. However, it is clear that such work is in process (Zaslow, Martinez-Beck, Tout, & Halle, in press). While a 2007 compendium profiled the characteristics, implementation requirements, and reliability and validity information for 34 measures of quality in early childhood settings, a 2010 update will already include 11 new measures and updates on 8 (Halle, Vick Whittaker, Anderson, 2010).

KEY ISSUES CONCERNING QUALITY MEASUREMENT

The use of quality measures in large-scale quality initiatives within states and communities is resulting in a reexamination of our measures of quality (Zaslow et al., 2010). When measures of quality are used throughout a state or community, it becomes particularly important to ask questions such as these: How does the measurement strategy align with current policy goals? Is the policy goal a positive overall experience for children or providing a foundation for children's school readiness? Is the content covered in the measure appropriate for this goal? What logistics issues must be considered when using observational measures? These questions are considered in this section.

Importance of Aligning Measures with Program Goals

Program leaders, policy makers, and researchers alike wonder whether some dimensions of quality are more important than others. Do some measures better assess the important variations in child care environments that lead to better child outcomes? Some researchers urge a stronger focus on teacher–child interactions, setting aside physical features of the environment (Pianta, 2006); others emphasize language and literacy preparation (Dickinson, 2002). Although early childhood research is making some progress in linking specific components of quality to specific child outcomes (Burchinal et al., 2009), currently, measures that reflect multiple and broad dimensions tend to predominate in QRISs and program improvement efforts, sometimes being supplemented by measures with more specific focus. States that have developed QRISs have started the process of development by drawing together a group of stakeholders to discuss the goals of their program, the aspects of quality they will emphasize, and the core components they will include in distinguishing different levels of quality (Mitchell, 2005). A central task then is to select measures that map appropriately onto stakeholders' priorities and view of quality.

Until researchers make more progress in linking specific dimensions of quality to specific domains of child outcomes, we should heed Lambert's (2003) advice that the choice of a measure should reflect the purpose of its use. For example, a measure that emphasizes environmental stimulation for language and literacy development in early childhood classrooms may be most appropriate if the purpose is to assess a policy initiative focusing on improving young children's early literacy. The way in which a measure is implemented also differs by purpose. For example, when a quality measure is completed by someone providing technical assistance in order to set quality improvement goals, there may already be a working relationship between the person giving technical assistance and the child care provider. In contrast, when the quality measure is completed in order to examine whether a quality initiative has been effective, the quality measure must be carried out by someone without a prior relationship with the provider and trained to the highest standards of reliability (see Zaslow, Tout, Halle, & Forry, 2009). Thus, both the selection of the measure and process for implementation are linked to purpose for measurement. All of the measures in Table 3.1 originated in research, but many have now been used for the purposes of self-assessment, program improvement, program evaluation, accreditation, or licensing.

Measures Adopted by States for Quality Rating Systems

Quality rating systems originated in part out of a desire to provide "rungs on the ladder" between the bottom and top rungs of licensing and accreditation. Mitchell

(2005) noted that states with tiered reimbursement policies—policies that involve providing higher reimbursement rates to providers who were accredited—sometimes found that fewer early childhood settings than anticipated were accredited and therefore eligible. These states felt a need to provide recognition for levels of quality above licensing yet below accreditation.

It is central to QRISs that they define these intermediate rungs. Though most states include accreditation in their rating systems, they do so in varying ways (Friedman, 2007). They also include providers both within and outside of the subsidy system.

The process for defining the rungs in a quality rating system is a new focus for discussion and research. What evidence suffices to indicate that levels differ enough to merit incentives or consequences? The environmental rating scales include evaluative labels distinguishing among levels of quality. Yet these are based primarily on an understanding of developmentally appropriate practice. We have few studies validating the distinctions that are being made between levels of quality in QRISs (see FPG UNC-CH Smart Start Evaluation Team, 2001, for an example of one such study). Early work was accomplished in two meetings (Child Trends, 2006, 2007), but research is needed in providing evidence for where we should be differentiating among levels of quality (Tout et al., 2009).

While most states include an observational measure as a core element of their quality ratings, other components are also included—for example, structural aspects of quality such as child–adult ratios, group size, staff education and professional development, use of a curriculum, and administration and management practices (NCCIC, 2007, 2008). A key emerging issue is how to weight these components in a summary rating. Should the observational measure be given the greatest weight? Should the total for group size and ratio be used, or an indicator of whether these met certain thresholds? States vary substantially in how each dimension is scored and then how multiple dimensions are combined into a summary rating. Research is needed providing guidance on approaches to scoring and combining components in summary ratings, as well as examining whether components and summary ratings are related to differences in children's experiences and development (Tout et al., 2009; Weber & Wolfe, 2003; Zaslow et al., 2010).

States have created financial incentives for higher quality programs according to their QRISs, so it is important to examine the validity of these rating systems. These systems can be improved if the measurement of quality is improved. It may be that continued work to strengthen the measurement of quality, building on the new body of experimental studies in early childhood, and using more rigorous empirical approaches to measures development will indeed result in finding a stronger association between quality and child outcomes. However, it is possible that such efforts will not improve the strength of the association or improve it only modestly. If that is indeed the case, then we will need to consider whether financial incentives and consequences should be based on modest association between quality and child outcomes—especially when many of these systems include other aspects of structural quality that show even more limited associations with child outcomes.

Sensitivity of Quality Measures to Interventions to Improve Quality

Witte and Queralt (2004) showed that the simple act of putting observational ratings data on a public web site has small but significant effects on the overall quality of programs. What about specific interventions designed to enhance quality, such as training and consultation? Are our observational measures sensitive to change? Numerous studies of professional development have shown changes in the ECERS or Infant/Toddler Environment Rating Scale (ITERS) as a result of training, technical assistance, or consultation (Palsha & Wesley, 1998; Sakai, Whitebook, Wishard, & Howes, 2003; Wesley, 1994; Whitebook, Sakai, & Howes, 1997; see summary in Zaslow et al., 2010). Some quality enhancement interventions used the ECERS or ITERS as the basis for developing action plans to address areas of weakness, and indeed the endpoint observations (made by independent observers) showed improvement. A Heads Up Reading intervention, where mentors focused on weak ELLCO (Smith & Dickinson, 2002) items, found classroom improvements on the ELLCO but also, unexpectedly, on the ECERS-R (Jackson et al., 2006). All five subscales of the Assessment Profile for Early Childhood Programs showed treatment group differences in the K–3 Head Start Transition demonstration classes (Ramey et al., 2000). Quality factors of the Classroom Assessment Scoring System (CLASS; Pianta, LaParo, Hamre, 2007) showed treatment effects in a study of web-based consultation based on CLASS domains (Pianta, Mashburn, Downer, Hamre, & Justice, 2008). These studies show that we have many observational measures that can reflect significant change in classroom practices as a result of technical assistance. Close alignment of the measure to the type of intervention can ensure adequate assessment of improvement.

Logistics Issues in Quality Measure Data Collection

Training, reliability, and frequency are issues for any program using one or more quality observation measures to consider. Some specific standards have been adopted by researchers over the years, but now that professional development, state licensing, and QRISs are incorporating observational measures of quality into their procedures, one wonders whether these standards are sufficient. Questions concern who can collect the quality data, how they should be trained to a level of reliability, how many classrooms need be observed to obtain an adequate sample of a program, and how frequently programs should be assessed.

Who collects the data? This is one of the most important points of consideration for directors of PD programs and policy makers considering observations for QRISs. Ideally, observers have some background in early childhood education and the ability to code accurately according to the specific measure. As observations have become part of QRIS and licensing systems, some states have separated the observer role from the state rating or licensing agency (e.g., via contract) to allow observers to focus solely on data collection and maintain their independence. An independent observer is also required for PD programs where consultants collect rating scale data and use them as the basis of program enhancement. Consultants' observation accuracy depends on their level of training. Reliable consultants may be able to collect valid data at the beginning of a consultation, but after a period of working with a provider, a consultant is surely too invested in the program and her work with the staff to be considered a reliable and unbiased collector of post-consultation quality data. The bottom line is that for valid data, the observer in any type of evaluation or ratings system must be independent of the program (Bryant, 2010; Zaslow et al., 2009).

How reliable do observers need to be? The standard of reliability to some extent depends on the intended use of the data. For quality improvement programs or distinguishing between high and low quality, a within-one-item standard of accuracy is probably sufficient; for research or licensing with consequences, our goal for reliability should be higher. Although no rule mandates a certain percentage of visits to be reliability visits, in research, interrater reliability is typically documented about every 10th visit. Even well-trained observers can drift in their interpretations of item scoring, especially if one sees mainly very-poor-quality programs and another collects data in very-high-quality programs. Budgeting time and travel for these joint visits is a cost of collection that must be considered.

How much data are needed? A major question for practitioners or evaluators involves whether it is necessary to use all items or scales on a measure of the quality of the early care and education setting. They wish to avoid additional costs associated with training raters to be reliable and in collecting data on items or scales that may not be used. The answer to the question varies with the purpose of the evaluation, as with any design questions. The use of rating systems for self-study likely requires little or no training, and the practitioners should focus on whatever is of particular interest to them. An evaluator might select scales that reflect the focus on a professional development program to pinpoint whether the program changed the targeted practices. An evaluator for a QRIS may need to administer the entire scale if mandated by the state system to ensure that all centers or child care homes within the system are being evaluated in a comparable and comprehensive manner.

How many classrooms in a center should be observed? Our measures of quality were generally developed to rate quality and components of quality at the level of the classroom or home-based group. In research, aggregating ratings of quality has generally meant asking what the average level of quality is across a sample of classrooms or home-based care settings. Yet in the new policy initiatives, quality is assigned to a program. This is raising new questions about measurement. Do all classrooms in a center need to be observed to reach a fair rating of overall quality? If it is appropriate to sample, what proportion of classrooms need to be observed? Should sampling be conducted from all classrooms, or from among those in particular age ranges? For example, should half of all classrooms be randomly selected, or half of all infant-toddler classrooms and half of all preschool-age classrooms? A small body of research is beginning to emerge on this issue. In a recent study in Missouri, researchers found that selecting half of the classrooms in a center for an ECERS or ITERS observation produced a better "match" with the average quality of all classrooms than selecting one-third of the classrooms (Mauzy & Thornburg, 2007). Further work may need to examine the extent to which measuring up to half the classrooms is necessary to determine whether the center meets a quality criterion as defined by a cutoff score on a quality rating scale. More research of this kind will be needed to guide the widespread implementation of quality measurement in as efficient a manner as possible while still obtaining reliable and valid data.

Should the measure focus on one child or all children? Most quality assessments describe the types of activities available to and the caregiver's interactions with all children in her care (e.g., ECERS-R, ITERS, FDCRS, CIS, CLASS, ELLCO). Using these measures, the data collector rates the classroom environment and the teacher or the family child care provider as she interacts with all children in the classroom or family child care home. Because two children in the same classroom might have very different experiences, a few measures (e.g., Snapshot, ORCE) describe the setting from the point of view of a specific child and what he or she is experiencing. The CLASS has also been adapted for child-focused observations of engagement for each child or selected children (La Paro, Pianta, & Stuhlman, 2004).

It is not clear whether focusing on the caregiver's interactions with all children or with a specific child or selected children provides better measurement of the quality of child care experiences, because only a few studies have included both types of measures and directly contrasted the extent to which classroom-level and child-level measures of quality predict child outcomes. Each has suggested that *both* levels of observation are related to children's outcomes.

For example, the 11-state evaluation of prekindergarten programs found modest associations between children's gain scores during the prekindergarten year and classroom-level ratings of intentional instruction and the quality of teacher–child interactions (including child-specific observations of time spent in certain academic interactions and the type of teacher–child interactions) (Howes et al., 2008).

The purpose of the quality assessment is likely the key factor in deciding between the different types of measures. If the purpose is to describe classrooms or family child care homes broadly (e.g., for licensing or program evaluation)—that is, for the average child on a typical day—then measures that use all observed interactions and activities would be chosen. If the purpose is to document the quality experienced by specific children—say, those in a particular language intervention—then a child-focused measure would be appropriate.

How frequently should programs be observed? As with many questions, the frequency answer depends, in part, on the purpose of the measurement. Correlations of same-classroom observations made in the fall and spring are typically relatively high (Bryant, 2010)—if the classroom has not experienced major changes such as being assigned a new teacher. However, if a quality intervention or professional development of some sort has taken place and quality is intended to be affected, then clearly an observation after the intervention would be expected.

In NAEYC's accreditation system, on-site observations are made every 5 years. In some state QRISs, on-site observations are made once a year (e.g., Colorado), whereas for others, 3 years is the time frame (e.g., North Carolina). The cost of annual or even biannual measurement is high, and policy makers in states making such observations want to know whether the observers could collect data less frequently. Research is needed to answer this question. Reasonably, one might expect that as long as conditions remain the same (same location, same director, most of the same staff), a center's quality rating score would remain relatively the same year to year, but is a 3-year gap acceptable or too long? Perhaps a few years could pass between reassessments if the policy contained guidelines that certain changes after the first year post-assessment would trigger a reassessment—for example, if the mean education level of the teaching staff dropped some percentage below where it was on the last observation visit or if a serious complaint were lodged about the program. Unfortunately, at this point we do not have data to answer the question of frequency.

IMPROVING QUALITY MEASUREMENT

In this final section we suggest several directions of new research and ways in which quality measurement could be improved.

Improved Measures for Home-Based Child Care Quality

Too little attention has been paid to measuring quality of home-based care despite the frequent use of this type of setting, especially for infants and toddlers (see Goodson & Layzer, 2010). Reassuring evidence indicates that child outcomes have been predicted modestly from the only across-setting quality measure, the ORCE (Clarke-Stewart et al., 2002; NICHD ECCRN, 2003), and the only widely used setting-specific quality measure for home-based settings, the FDCRS (Bryant et al., 2010; Kontos, Howes, Shinn, & Galinsky, 1995).

Better Measures of Curriculum Use and Professional Development

It is widely believed that curricula matter, but the recent Preschool Curriculum Evaluation Research Consortium (2008) findings were "underwhelming." Programs in the PCERC study were randomly assigned to a group that received training on 1 of 14 different preschool curricula or to a group that continued to use their typical curriculum. The curricula in the study were focused on literacy, numeracy, or socio-emotional development, and some sites implemented a comprehensive curriculum. Impacts were assessed on classroom-level outcomes (quality, teacher–child interactions, and instruction) and child-level outcomes (reading, phonological awareness, language, math, and behavior). Only half of the curricula showed any significant effect on teaching, and 10 curricula showed no statistically significant effects on any of the child outcome measures. Four curricula showed significant effects on some child measures, including both math curricula that were used.

Is the glass half full or half empty? Some curricula seemed to improve children's outcomes, but certainly not all. Why were some effective and others not effective? Each curriculum study had different levels of implementation data to enable better understanding of what actually happened in the classrooms but not sufficient to unpack the outcomes that were or were not achieved. In addition, these studies were not just studies of curricula—all programs received extensive professional development to learn their new curriculum (e.g., 50 hours for one of the math curricula [Clements & Sarama, 2008]). In any study, the combination of curriculum content and professional development duration, type, and features results in variations that we need to measure more accurately in order to better link these presumably important aspects of early childhood programs to children's outcomes. Yet we lack measures focusing directly on the process of professional development—for example, how coaching is actually carried out (Sheridan, Edwards, Marvin, & Knoche, in press). To understand when a curriculum is or is not effective, we need to have ways to assess not only the content of a curriculum but also the adequacy of the professional development for its implementation. Thus, the measurement of quality in early childhood settings may need to be extended to encompass the quality of professional development, involving direct observation of professional development as it is occurring.

The Roles of Other Children and Adults in the Classroom

There is evidence that the peers in the child care setting may affect learning as much as the caregiver (Henry & Rickman, 2007; McCartney et al., in press), and inclusion of information on peers in future studies could make it possible to examine this issue further. The extent to which other children in the classroom setting have behavior or learning problems or conversely are brighter and better behaved appears to predict target children's academic and social development (Henry & Rickman, 2007). Barbarin and colleagues (2006) found that the quality of peer interactions is an aspect of quality in prekindergarten settings to which parents are attuned. Careful examination of the conditions under which peers positively or negatively influence development is needed.

Similarly, it is clear that assistant teachers play an important role in child care centers and larger family child care homes with multiple caregivers. Some quality measures focus solely on the lead teacher, and others require the observer to take into account the language and actions of all adults in the environment. More research is needed to know the extent to which the interactions between assistant teachers and children have an impact on learning separate from that of the lead teacher. Further, these assistants are often playing a much more visible role with the huge increase in dual language learners (DLLs) in child care. They are often the only adults in the setting who speak the first language of the DLL child. Much more work is needed to understand how to assess their impact on the DLL child's development, especially when much of the academic instruction tends to be provided by the lead teacher.

Assessing Quality in Multicultural Classrooms

Whether the existing quality measures are appropriate for children from different backgrounds has been debated. Further work is needed to determine whether the existing and emerging quality measures adequately describe the quality of child care experiences, especially for DLLs. It has been argued that DLL children may require different types of instruction, but little empirical evidence has been collected to address this question regarding the extent to which child care quality measures are appropriate for them. In one recent study, Downer, Booren, Lima, Luckner, and Pianta (under review) asked whether the CLASS functions similarly in classrooms with larger or smaller proportions of children learning English in terms of the way items within the measure group together. They concluded that there was no evidence of differences by proportion of children learning English. Further work of this kind is needed. As the United States becomes increasingly diverse, classroom-quality observation data would be more useful programmatically and more accurate descriptively if these measures would reflect a program's ability to provide culturally appropriate care and reinforce cultural values and heritage (Maher, 2007). Studies of cross-cultural validity exist for only one measure. Using data from two large studies that focused on children from English-speaking homes, Burchinal and Cryer (2003) showed that in the cultural variations found in the United States, quality, as measured by the ECERS, was a good predictor of child outcomes regardless of family income or ethnicity. Studies in Western Europe (Clifford, 2005) and even in Bangladesh (Aboud, 2006) have demonstrated the relation between the ECERS and child outcomes. The CLASS, ECERS-E, ELLCO, Program Quality Assessment, and Profile have items that address cultural sensitivity, but more thorough cross-cultural studies are needed. The lack of cross-cultural validity does not preclude use of measures other than the ECERS but suggests doing so with an awareness of a shortcoming. Meanwhile, new measures that focus solely on cultural sensitivity in early childhood settings are being developed.

Psychometrically Created Measures of Quality

One of the reasons that the association between quality and child outcomes is modest in most studies could be that the true association is underestimated if the assessment tools are not sufficiently sensitive or have limited reliability (Burchinal et al., 2008). Most preschool child outcomes have good reliability and validity, especially the standardized tests of language and academic achievement. It seems unlikely that poor measurement of child outcomes accounts for the modest associations. In contrast, the early childhood quality measures tend to be global and were developed conceptually but not psychometrically. Each has good reliability and some validity, but many different sources of error exist—it may not be possible to assess all potential components of quality within a reasonable amount of time (e.g., it might take a very long time to obtain a representative sample of the caregiver's behavior in the classroom), the instrument may not score the selected items in the best manner (e.g., it might equally weight items that are really important and not very important for predicting child outcomes), or the instrument may not measure all of the relevant dimensions of child care quality (e.g., the measure may gauge sensitivity well but not intentional instruction). The different sources of error contribute both to the observed score and to the variability of that score (Lord & Novick, 1968) and thereby reduce the association between that instrument's scores and other measures.

It appears that we may need more specific and aligned measures, and especially more careful psychometric development of instruments based on a wider set of items and advanced psychometric methods. This should increase reliability of measurement and, accordingly, associations between the scores from that instrument and other measures. This is an important area for new research that might provide better measures to use in monitoring and improving children's experiences in early care and education.

SUMMARY AND CONCLUSION

While we have a strong set of traditions and resources for measuring quality in early childhood settings, as the measurement of quality has been scaled up in quality initiatives that are communitywide or statewide, we are seeing a growing awareness of issues pertaining to the measurement of quality. There is heightened awareness of some longstanding issues when quality is measured throughout a community or state, and new issues also emerge.

Among the issues receiving heightened attention are the need for close alignment between the measure of quality selected and the underlying purpose, the need for independence in measurement, and highly reliable measurement. New issues include the need for development of best practice guidelines on the number of classrooms that need to be observed, and how often, to calculate reliable overall ratings of a center's quality; how differing components should be combined and weighted to arrive at summary ratings of quality; and what the strength of prediction to child outcomes should be for summary ratings of quality to be linked with incentives and consequences.

We are in a very intensive period of new-measures development aimed at providing greater detail on specific facets of quality. This renewed focus on the content of our measures of quality needs to be matched with focus on the empirical basis for measurement. It will be critical to assess whether a new generation of quality measures, providing in-depth focus on particular quality measures, shows strengthened prediction to child outcomes. With a new set of in-depth measures capturing specific facets of quality, an important challenge will be how to create summary or global measures of quality building on them.

REFERENCES

Aboud, F.E. (2006). Evaluation of an early childhood preschool program in rural Bangladesh. *Early Childhood Research Quarterly, 21,* 46–60.

Abbott-Shim, M., & Sibley, A. (1998). *Assessment Profile for Early Childhood Programs: Research Edition II.* Atlanta, GA: Quality Counts, Inc.

Arnett, J. (1989). Caregivers in day-care centers: Does training matter? *Journal of Applied Developmental Psychology, 10,* 541–552.

Barbarin, O.A., McCandies, T., Early, D., Clifford, R.M., Bryant, D., Burchinal, M., Howes, C., & Pianta, R. (2006) Quality of pre-kindergarten: What families are looking for in public sponsored programs. *Early Education and Development, 17,* 619–642.

Barnett, W.S., Hustedt, J.T., Hawkinson, L., & Robin, K.B. (2007). *The state of preschool: 2006 state preschool yearbook.* New Brunswick, NJ: NIEER.

Bryant, D. (2010). *Observational measures of quality in center-based early care and education programs.* Washington, DC: Prepared for the Office of Planning, Research and Evaluation, Administration for Children and Families, U.S. Department of Health and Human Services. Available at www.childtrends.org (OPRE Issue Brief). Washington, DC: U.S. Department of Health and Human Services, Administration for Children and Families, Office of Planning, Research and Evaluation, and Child Trends.

Bryant, D., Wesley, P., Burchinal, P., Sideris, J., Taylor, K., Fenson, C., et al. (2009, September). *The QUINCE-PFI Study: An evaluation of a promising model for child care provider training* [Final report of grant # 90YE0056]. Washington, DC: Child Care Bureau, Administration on Children, Youth, and Families, U.S. Department of Health and Human Services.

Burchinal, M.R., & Cryer, D. (2003). Diversity, child care quality, and developmental outcomes. *Early Childhood Research Quarterly, 18,* 401–426.

Burchinal, M.R., Cryer, D., Clifford, R.M., & Howes, C. (2002). Caregiver training and classroom quality in child care centers. *Applied Developmental Sciences, 6,* 2–11.

Burchinal, M.R., Howes, C., & Kontos, S, (2002). Structural predictors of child care quality in child care homes. *Early Childhood Research Quarterly, 17,* 87–105.

Burchinal, M.R., Howes, C., Pianta, R., Bryant, D., Early, D., Clifford, R., & Barbarin, O. (2008). Predicting child outcomes at the end of kindergarten from the quality of pre-kindergarten teacher–child interactions and instruction. *Applied Developmental Science, 12*(3), 140–153.

Burchinal, M.R., Kainz, K., Cai, K., Tout, K., Zaslow, M., Martinez-Beck, I., et al. (2009, May). *Early care and education quality and child outcomes.* Washington, DC: U.S. Department of Health and Human Services, Administration for Children and Families, Office of Planning, Research and Evaluation, and Child Trends.

Buysse, V., & Wesley, P.W. (2005). *Consultation practice in early childhood settings.* Baltimore: Paul H. Brookes Publishing Co.

Child Trends. (2006, December). *Roundtable on measuring quality in early childhood and school-age settings: At the junction of research, policy and practice: Executive summary.* Washington, DC: U.S. Department of Health and Human Services, Administration for Children and Families, Office of Planning, Research and Evaluation. Retrieved May 30, 2008, from http://www.childcareresearch.org/SendPdf?resourceId=12699

Child Trends. (2007, July). *Roundtable on measuring quality in early childhood and school-age settings: At the junction of research, policy and practice: Meeting summary.* Washington, DC: U.S. Department of Health and Human Services, Administration for Children and Families, Office of Planning, Research and Evaluation. Retrieved May 30, 2008, from http://www.researchconnections.org/SendPdf?resourceId=12621

Clarke-Stewart, K.A., Vandell, D.L., Burchinal, M., O'Brien, M., & McCartney, K. (2002). Do regulable features of child-care homes affect children's development? *Early Childhood Research Quarterly, 17,* 52–86.

Clements, D.H., & Sarama, J. (2008). Experimental evaluation of the effects of a research-based preschool mathematics curriculum. *American Educational Research Journal, 45,* 443–494.

Clifford, R. (2005). Structure and stability of the Early Childhood Environment Rating Scale. In H. Schohenfeid, S. O'Brien, & T. Walsh (Eds.), *Questions of quality.* Dublin, Ireland: Center for Early Childhood Development and Education, St. Patrick's College.

Committee on Family and Work Policies of the National Research Council. (2003). In E. Smolensky & J.A. Gootman (Eds.), *Working families and growing kids: Caring for children and adolescents.* Washington, DC: National Academies Press.

Dickinson, D.K. (2002). Shifting images of developmentally appropriate practice as seen through different lenses. *Educational Researcher, 31*(1), 26–32.

Dickinson, D.K., & Smith, M.W. (1994). Long-term effects of preschool teachers' book readings on low-income children's vocabulary and story comprehension. *Reading Research Quarterly, 29,* 104–122.

Dickinson, D.K., & Tabors, P.O. (Eds.). (2001). *Beginning language with literacy: Young children learning at home and school.* Baltimore: Paul H. Brookes Publishing Co.

Downer, J.T., Booren, L.M., Lima, O.K., Luckner, A.E., & Pianta, R.C. (2010). The Individualized Classroom Assessment Scoring System (inCLASS): Reliability and validity of a system for observing preschoolers' competence in classroom interactions. *Early Childhood Research Quarterly, 25*(1), 1–16.

Early, D.M., Maxwell, K.L., Burchinal, M., Alva, S., Bender, R.H., Bryant, D., et al. (2007). Teachers' education, classroom quality, and young children's academic skills: Results from seven studies of preschool programs. *Child Development, 78*(2), 558–580.

Forry, N., Vick, J., & Halle, T. (2009, May). *Evaluating, developing and enhancing domain-specific measures of child care quality* (OPRE Issue Brief #2). Washington, DC: U.S. Department of Health and Human Services, Administration for Children and Families, Office of Planning, Research and Evaluation, and Child Trends.

FPG UNC-CH Smart Start Evaluation Team. (2001). *Validating North Carolina's 5-star child care licensing system. Smart Start.* Chapel Hill, NC: Frank Porter Graham Child Development Center. Retrieved Feb. 11, 2010, from http://www.fpg.unc.edu/smartstart/reports/validating_licensing_septem_brochure.pdf

Friedman, D.E. (2007). *Quality rating systems—The experiences of center directors.* Retrieved June 5, 2008, from Child Care Exchange: http://www.childcareexchange.com/catalog/product_info.php?products_id=5017306&search=&category=

Friedman, S.L., & Amadeo, J. (1999). The child-care environment: Conceptualizations, assessments, and issues. In S.L. Friedman & T.D. Wachs (Eds.), *Measuring environment across the life span: Emerging methods and concepts* (pp.127–165). Washington, DC: American Psychological Association.

Fukkink, F., & Lont, A. (2007). Does training matter? A meta-analysis and review of caregiver training studies. *Early Childhood Research Quarterly, 22*(3), 294–311.

Goodson, B.D., & Layzer, J.I. (2010). *Defining and measuring quality in home-based care settings.* Washington, DC: Prepared for the Office of Planning, Research and Evaluation, Administration for Children and Families, U.S. Department of Health and Human Services. Available at: www.childtrends.org (OPRE Issue Brief). Washington, DC: Office of Planning, Research and Evaluation, Administration for Children and Families, U.S. Department of Health and Human Services, and Child Trends.

Halle, T., & Vick, J.E. (2007). *Quality in early childhood care and education settings: A compendium of measures*. Washington, DC: U.S. Department of Health and Human Services, Administration for Children and Families, Office of Planning, Research and Evaluation. Retrieved from http://www.childtrends.org

Halle, T., Vick Whittaker, J. E., & Anderson, R. (2010). *Quality in early childhood care and education setting: A compendium of measures* (2nd ed.). Washington, DC: Prepared by Child Trends for the U.S. Department of Health and Human Services, Administration for Children and Families, Office of Planning, Research and Evaluation.

Harms, T., Clifford, R., & Cryer, D. (1998). *Early Childhood Environment Rating Scale–Revised*. New York: Teachers College Press.

Harms, T., Cryer D., & Clifford, R. (2003). *Infant/Toddler Environment Rating Scale–Revised*. New York: Teachers College Press.

Helburn, S. (1995). *Cost, quality and child outcomes in child care centers*. Denver: University of Colorado, Department of Economics, Center for Research in Economic and Social Policy.

Henry, G., & Rickman, D. (2007). Do peers influence children's development in preschool? *Economics of Education Review, 26*(1), 100–112.

High/Scope Educational Research Foundation. (1989). *High/Scope program quality assessment: PQA preschool version*. Ypsilanti, MI: High/Scope Press.

High/Scope Educational Research Foundation. (2003). *Preschool Program Quality Assessment, 2nd Edition (PQA) administration manual*. Ypsilanti, MI: High/Scope Press.

Howes, C. (1997). Children's experiences in center-based child care as a function of teacher background and adult:child ratio. *Merrill Palmer Quarterly, 43*(3), 404–425.

Howes, C., Burchinal, M., Pianta, R., Bryant, D., Early, D.M., & Clifford, R. (2008). Ready to learn? Children's pre-academic achievement in pre-kindergarten programs. *Early Childhood Research Quarterly, 23*, 27–50.

Jackson, B., Larzelere, R., Clair, L.S., Corr, M., Fichter, C., & Egertson, H. (2006). The impact of Heads Up! reading on early childhood educators' literacy practices and preschool children's literacy skills. *Early Childhood Research Quarterly, 21*(2), 213–226.

Jackson, R., McCoy, A., Pistorino, A., Wilkinson, A., Burghardt, J., Clark, M., et al. (2007). *National evaluation of Early Reading First* [Final report]. Washington, DC: Institute of Educational Science. Available at: http://ies.ed.gov/ncee/pubs/20074007/index.asp

Klibanoff, R.S., Levine, S.C., Huttenlocher, J., Vasilyeva, M., & Hedges, L.V. (2006). Preschool children's mathematical knowledge: The effect of teacher "math talk." *Development Psychology, 42*, 59–69.

Kontos, S., Howes, C., Shinn, M., & Galinsky, E. (1995). *Quality in family child care and relative care*. New York: Teachers College Press.

La Paro, K., Pianta, R., & Stuhlman, M. (2004). Classroom Assessment Scoring System (CLASS): Findings from the pre-K year. *Elementary School Journal., Vol. 104,* 409–426.

Lamb, M. (1998). Nonparental child care: Context, quality, correlates, and consequences. In W. Damon, I.E. Sigel, & K.A. Renninger (Eds.), *Handbook of child psychology, Vol. 4: Child psychology in practice* (pp. 77–133). New York: Wiley.

Lambert, R. (2003). Considering purpose and intended use when making evaluations of assessments: A response to Dickinson. *Educational Researcher, 32*(4), 23–26.

Lord, F.M., & Novick, M.R. (1968). *Statistical theories of mental test scores*. Reading MA: Addison-Wesley.

Maher, E. (2007). *Measuring quality in family, friend, and neighbor child care: Conceptual and practical issues* (Research-to-Policy Connections, No. 6). New York: Child Care & Early Education Research Connections.

Mashburn, A.J., Pianta, R.C., Downer, J., & Hamre, B.K. (2007, March). *My teaching partner: Effects of a Web-based intervention to improve teacher quality*. Poster session presented at the biennial meeting of the Society for Research in Child Development, Boston.

Mauzy, D., & Thornburg, K.R. (2007, March). *Developing a state quality rating system based on research*. Presentation at the NAEYC Public Policy Forum, Washington, DC.

McCartney, K., Burchinal, M., Clarke-Stewart, A., Bub, K.L., Owen, M.T., Belsky, J., & NICHD Early Child Care Research Network. (2010). Testing a series of casual propositions relating time in child care to children's externalizing behavior. *Developmental Psychology, 46,* 1–17.

Mitchell, A.W. (2005). *Stair steps to quality: A guide for states and communities developing quality rating systems for early care and education*. Retrieved May 30, 2008, from United Way of

America, Success by 6: http://www.unitedway.org/sb6/upload/StairStepstoQualityGuidebook_FINALforWEB.pdf

National Child Care Information Center. (2009, March). *Common categories of QRS quality standards. Quick facts: Quality rating systems.* Fairfax, VA: Prepared by the National Child Care Information Center for the Child Care Bureau, Administration for Children and Families, U.S. Department of Health and Human Services. Retrieved from http://nccic.acf.hhs.gov/pubs/qrs-comcat.html

National Child Care Information Center. (2007, Winter/Spring). Focus on QRS. *Child Care Bulletin, Issue 32.* Fairfax, VA: Prepared by the National Child Care Information Center for the Child Care Bureau, Administration for Children and Families, U.S. Department of Health and Human Services.

NICHD Early Child Care Research Network. (1996). Characteristics of infant child care: Factors contributing to positive caregiving. *Early Childhood Research Quarterly, 11,* 269–306.

NICHD Early Child Care Research Network. (1999). Child outcomes when child care center classes meet recommended standards for quality. *American Journal of Public Health, 89,* 1072–1077.

NICHD Early Child Care Research Network. (2000a). Characteristics and quality of child care for toddlers and preschoolers. *Applied Developmental Sciences, 4,* 116–135.

NICHD Early Child Care Research Network. (2000b). The relation of child care to cognitive and language development. *Child Development, 71,* 958–978.

NICHD Early Child Care Research Network. (2001). Nonmaternal care and family factors in early development: An overview of the NICHD Study of Early Child Care. *Journal of Applied Developmental Psychology, 22,* 457–492.

NICHD Early Child Care Research Network. (2002a). Child-care structure→Process→Outcome: Direct and indirect effects of child-care quality on young children's development. *Psychological Science, 13*(3), 199–206.

NICHD Early Child Care Research Network. (2002b). Early child care and children's development prior to school entry: Results from the NICHD Study of Early Child Care. *American Educational Research Journal, 39*(1), 133–164.

NICHD Early Child Care Research Network. (2003). Does quality of child care affect child outcomes at age 4½? *Developmental Psychology, 39,* 451–469.

NICHD Early Child Care Research Network. (2006). Child care effect sizes for the NICHD Study of Early Child Care and Youth Development. *American Psychologist, 61*(2), 99–116.

NICHD Early Child Care Research Network & Duncan, G.J. (2003). Modeling the impacts of child care quality on children's preschool cognitive development. *Child Development, 74*(5), 1454–1475.

Palsha, S.A., & Wesley, P.W. (1998). Improving quality in early childhood environments through on-site consultation. *Topics in Early Childhood Special Education, 18*(4), 243–253.

Peisner-Feinberg, E.S., Burchinal, M.R., Clifford, R.M., Culkin, M.L., Howes, C., Kagan, S.L., et al. (2001). The relation of preschool child-care quality to children's cognitive and social developmental trajectories through second grade. *Child Development, 72*(5), 1534–1553.

Phillips, D.A., Gormley, W.T., & Lowenstein, A.E. (2009). Inside the pre-kindergarten door: Classroom climate and instructional time allocation in Tulsa's pre-K programs. *Early Childhood Research Quarterly, 24*(3), 213–228.

Phillipsen, L., Burchinal, M., Howes, C., & Cryer, D. (1997). The prediction of process quality from structural features of child care. *Early Childhood Research Quarterly, 12,* 281–304.

Pianta, R.C. (2006). Standardized observation and PD: A focus on individualized implementation and practices. In M. Zaslow & I. Martinez-Beck (Eds.), *Critical issues in early childhood PD* (pp. 231–254). Baltimore: Paul H. Brookes Publishing Co.

Pianta, R., Howes, C., Burchinal, M., Bryant, D., Clifford, R., Early, D., et al. (2005). Features of pre-kindergarten programs, classrooms, and teachers: Do they predict observed classroom quality and child–teacher interactions? *Applied Developmental Science, 9*(3), 144–159.

Pianta, R.C., LaParo, K.M., & Hamre, B.K. (2007). *Classroom Assessment Scoring System (CLASS).* Baltimore: Paul H. Brookes Publishing Co.

Pianta, R.C., Mashburn, A.J., Downer, J.T., Hamre, B., & Justice, L.M. (2008). Effects of web-mediated PD resources on teacher–child interactions in pre-kindergarten classrooms. *Early Childhood Research Quarterly, 23*(4), 431–451.

Preschool Curriculum Evaluation Research Consortium. (2008, July). *Effects of preschool curriculum programs on school readiness: Report from the Preschool Curriculum Evaluation Research Initiative.* Retrieved from http://ies.ed.gov/pubsearch/pubsinfo.asp?pubid=NCER20082009rev

Ramey, S.L., Ramey, C.T., Phillips, M.M., Lanzi, R.G., Brezausek, C.M., Katholi, C.R., et al. (2000). *Head Start children's entry into public school: A report on the National Head Start/Public School Early Childhood Transition Demonstration Study: Executive summary.* Birmingham: University of Alabama at Birmingham.

Ritchie, S., Howes, C., Kraft-Sayre, M., & Weiser, B. (2001). *Emergent Academic Snapshot Scale.* Unpublished instrument, UCLA.

Sakai, L.M., Whitebook, M., Wishard, A., & Howes, C. (2003). Evaluating the Early Childhood Environment Rating Scale (ECERS): Assessing differences between the first and revised edition. *Early Childhood Research Quarterly, 18,* 427–445.

Sarama, J., & Clements, D. (2004). Building blocks for early childhood mathematics. *Early Childhood Research Quarterly, 19,* 181–189.

Sheridan, S., Edwards, C.P., Marvin, C.A., & Knoche, L.L. (in press). Professional development in early childhood programs: Process issues and research needs. *Early Education and Development.*

Smith, L.K., Sarkar, M., Perry-Manning, S., & Schmalzreid, B. (2006, November). *NACCRRA's National Survey of Child Care Resource and Referral Training: Building a training system for the childcare workforce.* Washington, DC: National Association of Child Care Resource and Referral Agencies.

Smith, M.W., Brady, J.P., & Anastasopoulos, L. (2008). *Early Language and Literacy Classroom Observation Tool, Pre-K (ELLCO Pre-K).* Baltimore: Paul H. Brookes Publishing Co.

Smith, M.W., Brady, J.P., & Clark-Chiarelli, N. (2008). *Early Language and Literacy Classroom Observation Tool, K–3 (ELLCO K–3, Research ed.).* Baltimore: Paul H. Brookes Publishing Co.

Smith, M.W., & Dickinson, D.K. (with Sangeorge, A., & Anastasopoulos, L.). (2002). *Early Language and Literacy Classroom Observation Toolkit (Research ed.).* Baltimore: Paul H. Brookes Publishing Co.

South Carolina ECERS Quality Study Team. (2006, March). *Analyses of ECERS-R data and teachers' attitudes toward the ECERS-R process.* Final report. The South Carolina Classroom Quality Research Project. Greensboro, NC: SERVE Center at the University of North Carolina at Greensboro.

Stipek, D., & Byler, P. (2004). The early childhood classroom observation measure. *Early Childhood Research Quarterly, 19,* 375–397.

Sylva, K., Siraj-Blatchford, I., Melhuish, E., Sammons, P., Taggart, B., Evans, E., et al. (1999). *Characteristics of the centres in the EPPE sample: Observational profiles. Technical Paper 6.* London: Institute of Education.

Tout, K., Zaslow, M., Halle, T., & Forry, N. (2009, May). *Issues for the next decade of quality rating and improvement systems* (OPRE Issue Brief #3). Washington, DC: U.S. Department of Health and Human Services, Administration for Children and Families, Office of Planning, Research and Evaluation, and Child Trends.

Vandell, D. (2004). Early child care: The known and the unknown. *Merrill-Palmer Quarterly, 50,* 387–414.

Vandell, D., Belsky, J., Burchinal, M., Steinberg, L., & NICHD Early Child Care Research Network (2009, April). *Do effects of early child care extend to age 15 years? Results from the NICHD Study of Early Child Care.* Presentation at the biennial meeting of the Society for Research in Child Development, Denver.

Vandell, D.L., & Wolf, B. (2000). *Child care quality: Does it matter and does it need to be improved? A report for the Office of the Assistant Secretary for Planning and Evaluation, U.S. Department of Health and Human Services.* Washington, DC: U.S. Department of Health and Human Services.

Vu, J.A., Jeon, H., & Howes, C. (2008). Formal education, credential, or both: Early childhood program classroom practices. *Early Education and Development, 19*(3), 479–504.

Weber, R.J., & Wolfe, J. (2003). Improving child care: Providing comparative information on child care facilities to parents and the community. *Child Care Policy Research Issue Brief.* Retrieved May 30, 2008, from Oregon Child Care Research Partnership, Oregon State University: http://www.hhs.oregonstate.edu/familypolicy/occrp/publications/2003-Improving-ChildCare.pdf

Wesley, P.W. (1994). Providing on-site consultation to promote quality in integrated child care programs. *Journal of Early Intervention, 18*(4), 391–402.

Whitebook, M., Sakai, L., & Howes, C. (1997). *NAEYC accreditation as a strategy for improving child care quality: An assessment by the National Center for the Early Childhood Work Force.* Washington, DC: NCECW.

Whitehurst, G.J., & Lonigan, C.J. (1998). Child development and emergent literacy. *Child Development, 69,* 848–872.

Witte, A.D., & Queralt, M. (2004). *What happens when child care inspections and complaints are made available on the Internet?* (NBER Working Paper No. 10227). Cambridge, MA: National Bureau of Economic Research.

Zaslow, M., Martinez-Beck, I., Tout, K., & Halle, T. (in press). *Measuring quality in early childhood settings.* Baltimore: Paul H. Brookes Publishing Co.

Zaslow, M., Tout, K., Halle, T., & Forry, N. (2009). *Multiple purposes for measuring quality in early childhood settings: Implications for collecting and communicating information on quality* (OPRE Issue Brief #2). Washington, DC: U.S. Department of Health and Human Services, Administration for Children and Families, Office of Planning, Research and Evaluation, and Child Trends.

Zaslow, M., Tout, K., Halle, T., Vick, J., & Lavelle, B. (under review). *Towards the identification of features of effective professional development for early childhood educators: A review of the literature.* Washington, DC: Child Trends.

Zaslow, M., Tout, K., & Martinez-Beck, I. (2010). Measuring the quality of early care and education programs at the intersection of research, policy and practice (OPRE Issue Brief). *Child Development Perspectives.* Washington, DC: U.S. Department of Health and Human Services, Administration for Children and Families, Office of Planning, Research, Evaluation, and Child Trends.

CHAPTER 4

Early Learning Standards and Quality Improvement Initiatives
A Systemic Approach to Supporting Children's Learning and Development

Catherine Scott-Little, Deborah J. Cassidy, Joanna K. Lower, and Sarah J. Ellen

The early care and education field has specified a variety of standards in an effort to establish high-quality programs. For example, we have developed program standards to define how programs should provide services and early learning standards to define the knowledge, skills, and characteristics programs should seek to help children develop. Standards are a starting point to promoting quality programming—the foundation upon which quality programming is built. Early learning standards, along with other types of standards, are the building blocks to ensure high-quality programming across the wide variety of early care and education programs (Ackerman & Barnett, 2006; Bodrova, Leong, & Shore, 2004; National Association for the Education of Young Children & National Association of Early Childhood Specialists in State Departments of Education [NAEYC/NAECSSDE], 2002). Yet, as Wesley and Buysse argue in Chapter 1, the field remains fragmented, with different standards, requirements, and funding sources for different programs.

By defining what children should learn, state agencies that have developed early learning standards (ELS) aimed at improving the quality of early care and education programs in a number of ways. Among the goals for ELS, states intend to improve teachers' knowledge of child development, engender more intentional teaching practices, and improve the quality of professional development offered to teachers. Although ELS are a relatively new development within the field, state agencies have invested significant resources in writing and implementing the documents. In this chapter, we suggest that ELS be integrated into the various systems and quality improvement efforts to produce a more coherent approach to early care and education. Although the use of ELS would not eliminate fragmentation among systems and programs, starting from a common set of goals for children's learning and development can promote consistency across different program requirements.

We argue that individual states have made progress toward using the ELS to improve the quality of programs by developing professional development based

---

The authors of this chapter are grateful to Tom Schultz, Harriet Egertson, and members of the CCSSO ECEA SCASS for their leadership in the field and for sharing an early draft of a paper reporting their most recent survey of state specialists regarding the use of early learning standards and assessments.

on the ELS, developing and revising professional competencies based on ELS, and selecting curricula and assessments that are aligned or consistent with the content of ELS. We think, however, that a more systemic approach is needed to infuse ELS into all requirements for programs and truly capitalize on the potential benefits of ELS. We present a model that aligns ELS with the typical components of quality rating and improvement systems (QRISs) and that creates a mechanism for implementing quality improvement efforts that are aligned with the content of ELS. By "aligned" we mean consistent with or supportive of the ELS, rather than the traditional definition of alignment that connotes a more literal match between standards and another document. We believe that even absent the traditional type of alignment, that requirements that are generally consistent with ELS can promote quality programs for children.

In short, we suggest that program improvement efforts, program standards, and the use of ELS should go hand in hand, and when they are consistent or aligned with one another, the efforts to improve programs are strengthened and children and families are better served. We understand, however, that there are challenges that need to be addressed for this to be an effective model. Following a brief introduction to ELS—how they have been developed and what content they address—we will discuss how ELS documents are being used in quality improvement efforts, address common challenges state agencies may face when using ELS as part of program improvement efforts, present a model for a QRIS that builds on ELS, and outline several systems-level challenges to this type of aligned approach to quality improvements in early childhood care and education programs.

THE DEVELOPMENT AND CONTENT OF EARLY LEARNING STANDARDS

Bolstered by the standards-based education movement in the K–12 education system, states began to develop ELS for prekindergarten-age children shortly after the turn of the century, and the momentum of the ELS movement has increased over recent years. Furthermore, the momentum for ELS has spread from prekindergarten to programs serving infants and toddlers. In this section, we discuss when and how ELS were developed and the content that has been addressed in ELS.

Prekindergarten ELS

In 2002, 27 states had published ELS documents to define what prekindergarten-age children should know and be able to do, and 12 states were in the process of developing ELS (Scott-Little, Kagan, & Frelow, 2003a). By 2008, all 50 states had published ELS and 12 states had recently revised or were in the process of revising their ELS documents (Council of Chief State School Officers [CCSSO], 2009). In the majority of states (85%), the preschool ELS were developed and implemented by the state's department of education or the state agency responsible for the state-funded prekindergarten program (Scott-Little, Kagan, & Frelow, 2003b). Typically the same agency is responsible for implementation of the ELS, and the state's prekindergarten program is the primary target audience. In fact, 23 of 39 states (59%) that responded to a survey in 2005 indicated that their state's prekindergarten program was required by regulation or law to use the ELS. The remaining states either expected their state's prekindergarten program to use the ELS but did not have an official requirement or did not have a prekindergarten program. Clearly the departments of education took the lead in the ELS movement among programs serving preschool-age children, developing and implementing the documents and requiring prekindergarten programs to use them.

Content analyses conducted on ELS documents published as of January 2005 indicated that there was considerable variability in ELS published by states. Scott-Little, Kagan, and Frelow (2006) found that the number of ELS items included in 46 ELS documents ranged from 42 to 434, with a mean of 154.3 and a standard deviation of 84.5. Overall, the preschool ELS emphasized children's cognition and general knowledge and language and communication development far more than the physical, social-emotional, and approaches toward learning domains. Furthermore, ELS developed by a department of education emphasized children's social-emotional development and approaches toward learning significantly less than ELS developed by other agencies. States have invested significant resources in developing ELS, and the content addressed within the documents varies from state to state.

Infant-Toddler ELS

The standards-based education movement did not stop with preschool programs. ELS documents that define what infants and toddlers should know and skills they should develop—most often called Early Learning Guidelines—have become increasingly common over the past 5 years. Although in 2002 only 4 states had infant-toddler ELS, in 2005 there were 14 states; 22 states had published infant-toddler ELS in 2008, and 10 more were in the process of developing such documents (CCSSO, 2009). Roughly half of the infant-toddler ELS have been developed by the state's department of education and the other half by the state's department of human resources/human services.

Not surprisingly, the content of infant-toddler ELS seems to differ from the content of preschool ELS. In a content analysis conducted on 21 infant-toddler ELS documents published as of July 2007, Scott-Little, Kagan, and Frelow (2008) learned that the content of infant-toddler ELS is relatively balanced across four domains of development. The percentage of ELS written to address the physical, social-emotional, language, and cognitive development domains was relatively equal, ranging from 22% to 25% for the four domains. One domain, approaches toward learning, has been addressed far less often, accounting for only 5.6% of the infant-toddler ELS items. Furthermore, the content of ELS written for the youngest babies (birth through 18 months) differed from the content written for toddlers, with ELS written for the youngest age group emphasizing physical and social-emotional development and ELS written for toddlers emphasizing language and cognitive development. There appears to be considerable momentum for the development of infant-toddler ELS, and the content of the documents, as one might expect, differs with each age for which the standards are written.

Why States Have Developed ELS

State agencies have developed ELS as part of their effort to promote quality early education programming for all children. Data from a survey of state representatives indicate that the developers and implementers of ELS have a number of different purposes in mind for their ELS documents (i.e., the ELS plus other supplemental materials published along with their ELS), all of which are related to improvements in program quality. Scott-Little, Lesko, Martella, and Milburn (2007) surveyed all 50 states and the District of Columbia to document how each intends for its ELS to be used. Representatives from 41 states and the District of Columbia participated in the survey. All respondents indicated that their state intends for the ELS document to be a resource that can improve the quality of instruction or curriculum in early childhood classrooms. By articulating goals for children's learning and development, the state agencies intend to improve the quality of teaching and learning. The next most commonly cited purpose for creating the ELS was to improve professional development (36 states). State agencies viewed the ELS document as a resource to educate teachers about child development and about intentional teaching practices to support the child outcomes described in the ELS. Respondents from 32 states indicated that their state also intends for the ELS documents to be used to educate parents on child development. Respondents from 30 states indicated that a purpose of their ELS was to guide decisions related to child assessments. Responses from 11 states indicated that their state intends for the ELS to play a role in program evaluation, and respondents from 14 states indicated that their state plans for the ELS to be a part of an accountability system. ELS are intended to improve program quality by promoting intentional teaching practices, improving the professional development offered to teachers, serving as a basis for how programs assess children, and providing a guidepost in efforts to evaluate programs.

ELS AND QUALITY IMPROVEMENT EFFORTS

Although the advent of ELS in the field of early childhood education is a relatively new development, the documents are being used in a variety of quality improvement efforts. Given that the ELS define what the state would like for children to learn and be able to do, they have implications for what teachers should know and be able to teach, the content of the professional development teachers receive, and the curricula and assessments used in early childhood programs. In the following section we describe why ELS are important in each of these areas and provide examples of how states are using their ELS in each of these quality improvement strategies.

Early Childhood Educator Professional Competencies

Following the lead of the K–12 education system, many states have defined specific content that early childhood educators should know and be able to do in order to teach young children. Known as Early Childhood Educator Professional Competencies (ECEPC), early childhood competencies, core competencies, or teacher licensing standards, these documents specify the knowledge base and skills that persons seeking to teach in early childhood settings must demonstrate. Twenty-six states have defined ECEPC, although the content of the competencies and the programs/persons to which they are applicable differ from state to state. Some states have defined ECEPC as part of the preservice requirements for degrees and licensure, whereas others have implemented ECEPC as part of their in-service professional development and career ladder system, and still others have competencies in both areas (National Center for Research on Early Childhood Education [NCRECE], 2008).

Often the ECEPC specify broad areas of knowledge, each of which is further defined with specific statements of what an early childhood educator should know or be able to do (NCRECE, 2008). ELS have implications for the content of ECEPC in two ways. First, ECEPC typically define content teachers should know regarding child development. ELS speak to this area of teacher competencies directly, defining the areas of child growth, development, and learning deemed important for children. Second, ECEPC define what teachers should know and be able to do to be an effective teacher. Although ELS define what the state wants children to learn, the ECEPC standards should promote the knowledge and skills teachers need to facilitate the child outcomes described in the ELS.

There is evidence to suggest that states are defining and refining their ECEPC based on their ELS. In the survey of 47 states plus the District of Columbia, CCSSO (2009) reported that at least 33 states have developed or revised their ECEPC based on their state's ELS. For example, Virginia developed *Competencies for Early Childhood Professionals* based on their ELS (known as Milestones of Early Childhood Development) in 2007. Colleges and universities are required to incorporate the competencies into their coursework. Similarly, North Carolina has revised their core competencies for 2- and 4-year programs based on the content of their ELS, which are known as Foundations. Arizona, Georgia, and Massachusetts are developing or revising their teacher certification requirements and have used their respective state's ELS as they have defined what is expected of teachers. ELS have defined goals and expectations for children's development and learning, and states have taken them into consideration as they have defined expectations for what teachers must know and be able to do to be credentialed to work with young children.

Professional Development Initiatives to Improve Program Quality

To promote the child outcomes described in ELS, teachers must be competent and effective. Educators, researchers, and policy makers recognize that adults need assistance in developing the knowledge and skills necessary to work with children effectively, and therefore provide professional development to teach teachers how to teach. There are two basic types of professional development—preservice professional development, typically provided through institutions of higher education, and in-service professional development, typically provided by various agencies and institutions and often separate from a degree program offered through institutions of higher education. However, there has been a melding of the two types of professional development as more and more practicing professionals without degrees return to school for further education. States have launched a number of initiatives to infuse ELS into the professional development provided through institutions of higher education and through in-service professional development.

Preservice Professional Development Institutions of higher education play an increasingly important role in preparing teachers to use ELS. In 2002, only four states reported that institutions of higher education (IHE) were utilizing early learning standards in their curricula. In 2005, 24 states indicated IHEs were incorporating the early learning standards in coursework, and 7 additional states indicated that their state was in the process of engaging the higher education community (Scott-Little et al., 2007). In 2008, representatives from approximately 30 states indicated that their state's institutions of higher education were using their state's ELS in some way. Since the 2002 survey, the number of states reporting that their state's ELS were being used in IHEs has increased, and the ways in which the ELS documents were being infused into preservice professional development has changed as well. That is, in 2008 the ELS were being used to support and determine the content and delivery of courses. Furthermore, in 2002 many examples of how ELS were being used in institutions of higher education were examples of individual faculty members incorporating the ELS into their course content early in the ELS movement; more recent efforts have focused on incorporating ELS systematically into coursework at the institutional level. In Maine, for example, community colleges and 4-year-degree programs have embedded their state's ELS content in early childhood curriculum coursework. Professors or instructors are including their state's ELS in course content. An Early Childhood Higher Education Training Committee, comprising representatives from community colleges, 4-year institutions, and others, serves as a vehicle for providing information about teacher-preparation programs and discussing how the ELS are used in early childhood coursework. In Connecticut and Iowa, 2- and 4-year institutions have incorporated the ELS into their coursework, using specific activities to promote students' knowledge of the ELS and requiring that students use the ELS in planning activities for children as part of their practica experiences. In several states, ELS documents are required or recommended texts for various courses (CCSSO, 2009).

States have recognized that for faculty to use ELS effectively in their coursework, they must be knowledgeable of the document and how it is intended to be used. Therefore, several states have implemented professional development for faculty members who teach in institutions of higher education. For instance, faculty from 2- and 4-year institutions of higher education in South Carolina participated in ELS "train the trainer" institutes to learn how to implement the ELS within their coursework. At the institutes, participants received a copy of the South Carolina ELS, as well as nine video-based training modules for use in courses. Similarly, California's Faculty Initiative Project (FIP) provides professional development for faculty teaching in the state's 2- and 4-year institutions to help them integrate the content of their publications into coursework. States have recognized that institutions of higher education are important vehicles through which they can prepare teachers to use their ELS and have instituted various types of initiatives to promote the use of the ELS in higher education settings (CCSSO, 2009).

In-Service Professional Development States have also developed a variety of in-service professional development resources to support teachers as they use ELS. In 2008, respondents from almost 40 states indicated that their state has developed some type of in-service professional development related to their ELS. Arizona is developing a statewide comprehensive training system that will be available to child care, Head Start, school, and tribal community programs and will include both awareness-level training to familiarize teachers with their ELS and in-depth training on the ELS. Rhode Island has developed three levels of training: one to introduce participants to the ELS, another to provide in-depth credit-bearing sessions, and a third to provide sessions for administrators. Using a "train the trainer" model, Kentucky has provided training sessions to the Regional Training Center and Child Care Resource and Referral staff across the state. These staff, in turn, provide training to teachers to help them infuse the state's ELS into their teaching practices. Nevada has developed a statewide professional development system to provide training on the content of the ELS and to help teachers work more effectively with children from diverse backgrounds (i.e., children with diverse cultural backgrounds, dual language learners, and children with disabilities) as they implement the ELS. North Carolina requires that all professional development provided by the state's Office of School Readiness address the ELS in some way. Presenters must demonstrate how their training will include content of the ELS and help teachers implement them (CCSSO, 2009).

States have also developed a variety of resources to promote the use of ELS. For example, North Carolina and a number of other states have developed an online "toolbox" of materials to support the use of their state's ELS. In Rhode Island, a group of parents designed resource materials for parents that are disseminated through early childhood programs and available online (Scott-Little et al., 2007). Through both in-service training and targeted materials, states are seeking to support in-service teachers as they learn to use their state's ELS.

Curriculum and Child Assessment

In addition to helping teachers use the ELS, states have recognized that the curriculum and assessments used in the classroom can have a tremendous impact on what children learn and the extent to which they make progress on the knowledge and skills described in ELS. Therefore, states have begun to look at the extent to which early childhood curricula and child assessments are consistent or aligned with their state's ELS. In 2005, representatives from 26 states reported that their state had completed some type of activity to address alignment between ELS and curricula, and 7 were in the process. The activities ranged from conducting alignment analyses to requiring programs to choose curricula that are aligned with their ELS (Scott-Little et al., 2007). Minnesota and North Carolina recently convened committees to develop criteria for curricula, review curricula, and recommend curricula. For example, both states established criteria that required curricula to have a mechanism for using observations or results from instructional assessments to plan activities, to address how families are included in instructional planning, and to be developed based on a clearly articulated theoretical or research base or both. Programs involved in these two states' QRISs will receive recognition as part of their rating system for using approved curricula, and North Carolina's More at Four prekindergarten program will require local programs to use one of the approved curricula. In both states, alignment with the ELS was an important criterion, and curricula that did not align with their ELS were not recommended (Minnesota Parent Aware, n.d.-b; North Carolina Division of Child Development & Office of School Readiness, 2008).

To help children make progress on the knowledge and skills articulated in ELS, teachers also need to use instructional assessments that are aligned with the ELS. Aligned assessments can provide teachers with information on children's progress toward the ELS, whereas misaligned assessments may mean that teachers collect assessment data on areas of children's learning that are not included in the ELS or neglect to assess areas that are addressed in the standards. In 2005, 10 states reported having developed an assessment based on their state's ELS. Five states required programs to choose an assessment that is aligned with the ELS (Scott-Little et al., 2007). Connecticut is an example of a state that has developed an assessment based on ELS. The observational assessment, known as the Preschool Assessment Framework (PAF), was developed based on the skills and abilities outlined in their ELS, known as the Preschool Curriculum Framework (PCF) (Connecticut State Department of Education, 2008). In Minnesota, a committee was established to review assessments and make recommendations as to which should be used in the state's pilot QRIS, known as Parent Aware. Alignment with the Minnesota Indicators of Progress, their ELS, was an important criterion for an assessment to be approved (Minnesota Parent Aware, n.d.-a). By promoting curricula and assessments that are aligned with ELS, states hope to foster teachers' abilities to promote children's progress on ELS.

CHALLENGES

Although there are good intentions behind the development of ELS and their use in quality enhancement efforts, there are several challenges that must be considered when using the ELS within initiatives designed to improve the quality of programs. Many of these challenges relate to the content of the ELS themselves, as well as the capacities of teachers and programs to use the documents. We discuss some of these challenges next.

ELS Content

If ELS are going to be used within professional development and other initiatives designed to improve the quality of programs, they must articulate developmentally appropriate and developmentally significant content (National Association for the Education of Young Children [NAEYC], 2009a). Otherwise, the other components of the system are aligning to standards that are inappropriate or incomplete. Results from content analyses (Scott-Little et al., 2005, 2006, 2008) show that in some cases, the standards have overlooked particularly critical areas of development or articulated inappropriate expectations of infants, toddlers, or preschoolers. ELS must articulate balanced and developmentally appropriate expectations for children's learning and development to provide a firm foundation upon which program quality efforts can build. It is important, therefore, for state agencies that are writing or revising ELS to ensure that they include a diverse group of stakeholders in the development process, including persons with in-depth knowledge of child development and early education. Systematic analyses should be conducted on the content of draft ELS before they are finalized to determine that the ELS have addressed developmentally significant content and that the ELS are age appropriate.

Classroom- and Teacher-Level Issues

Often teachers lack adequate educational background to interpret the standards successfully. Without in-depth knowledge of children's development, it can be extremely difficult to understand ELS and, even more important, how they relate to daily classroom practices. In-service professional development on use of ELS can assist teachers in appropriate use, but it does not replace the broader understanding of child development that teachers can obtain through higher education programs. On-site consultation may provide the most effective professional development to promote the use of ELS, but it may also be cost prohibitive. It seems that a multifaceted approach that includes a variety of professional development delivery strategies and professional development providers is needed to promote effective use of ELS.

The appropriateness of most early learning standards for children with disabilities is also a practical issue that must be addressed. As the number of inclusive classrooms grows, ELS must overtly address children with disabilities within the document, and teachers working with children with disabilities must learn how to use the ELS to guide instructional practices with children with disabilities. Teachers must be knowledgeable of the ELS and must know how to make appropriate modifications and adaptations to be inclusive of all children. If teachers utilize different documents to guide their instruction, using ELS for typically developing children and individualized education programs (IEPs) for children with disabilities, a two-tiered system of education far beyond what is already an unequal system will develop. Ideally, IEP goals and goals based on ELS will be integrated and work together to support the progress of children with disabilities in areas that are specifically related to their disability and, at the same time, support the children's progress on the more general goals outlined in the ELS. The idea of using ELS and IEPs together is a relatively new concept within the field and requires a great deal of sophistication on the part of the teacher. Data from the recent CCSSO (2009) survey suggest that states are according significant attention to this issue as they develop and implement ELS.

Professional Development Providers

Finally, there are challenges related to incorporating the new ELS content into professional development that stem from the providers of professional development themselves. Professional development providers (e.g., higher education faculty, in-service trainers) may not be fully knowledgeable of the content of the ELS or how to promote intentional, standards-based education in a manner that is consistent with developmentally appropriate practices. The shift to using ELS may be particularly difficult in institutions of higher education, where faculty have to submit revised course syllabi and obtain administrative approval to make changes in their course content. The professional development teachers receive in institutions of higher education may lag slightly behind the momentum of the ELS. States may find it particularly beneficial to provide professional development on ELS to professional development providers in a "train the trainer" model or in other ways.

ELS AND QRIS—TOWARD A SYSTEMIC APPROACH TO QUALITY IMPROVEMENT EFFORTS

Despite challenges such as these, states are using various strategies to improve program quality as they implement their ELS. Using ELS as a guide toward the child outcomes their state is seeking to promote, various agencies are promoting intentional and effective teaching to support children's growth and development in the areas defined by the ELS. At the same time that ELS have gained momentum within states, QRISs have also become increasingly important quality improvement efforts.

The National Child Care Information Center (2009) defined a QRIS as "a systemic approach to assess, improve, and communicate the level of quality in early care and education programs." The state develops criteria to define requirements for varying levels of quality and establishes a process of evidence-based validation. For example, through a process of validation, programs are identified in their state's QRIS based on the level at which they meet basic or enhanced criteria of professional practice, professional development, curriculum, and licensing/program standards. Furthermore, programs are identified and often rewarded for meeting different levels of quality validated through the QRIS. Some states, such as North Carolina, have tiered subsidy reimbursement rates for early education programs. Programs that meet voluntary higher licensing standards receive higher subsidy rates. Quality enhancement initiatives are also tied to licensing/program standards. These incentives motivate early care and education programs to achieve and maintain quality.

QRISs have typically been developed out of states' departments of social services/human resources (sometimes in collaboration with states' departments of education) in an effort to improve the quality of early childhood programs and are being adopted by 18 states across the nation with another 27 in progress (NAEYC, 2009b). QRISs are structured differently across states and often are not implemented by a single program or agency. In fact, numerous agencies can be involved in the implementation of the QRIS. One agency may be responsible for setting the QRIS criteria for quality levels. The responsibility for monitoring the extent to which programs meet the requirements may be carried out by this agency, by a contractor, or by another agency. In some states, differential funding for programs that meet higher criteria may be provided by yet another agency. There is also great diversity in the way the systems have been developed and the weighting given to various aspects of the system. For example, in North Carolina, rating scale scores are included in the number of points awarded in the program requirement section of the system, whereas other states only require that the scales be completed but do not require a minimum score to achieve a certain point or star level. Because the nature and structure of QRISs differ from state to state, we are electing to refer generically to QRISs, knowing that within many states the QRIS is not one agency or entity but a collection of coordinated standards, monitoring mechanisms, and incentives that work together to recognize and reward higher quality programs.

Although many states have made a concerted effort to improve the quality of programs by infusing ELS into various systems, and a significant number of states are working on QRISs, we believe that thinking about the two quality improvement strategies together can yield a more systematic and synergetic means to improving the quality of early care and education. ELS define child outcomes the state is seeking to promote, and QRISs provide a framework for organizing various quality improvement efforts, articulating requirements, and deciding how programs will validate or be held accountable for meeting the requirements. With ELS at the center of quality improvement efforts and the QRIS as a framework for holding programs accountable for quality improvements, we believe states can develop a more cohesive and effective system to support effective programs.

Figure 4.1 provides a model for how the ELS and QRIS can be used together to promote quality. Located at the center of the model, ELS can be used to inform what is required of programs, teachers, and curricula and assessments that guide teachers' practices. This aspect of the model is represented by the inner circle that surrounds the ELS and represents the requirements that programs participating in the QRIS must meet. In addition to developing requirements that programs must meet, the QRIS also determines methods for collecting data to validate that programs are meeting the requirements. Depicted in the middle ring, these accountability requirements of the QRIS, when aligned with the ELS, can provide information on the extent to which children experience learning environments that promote the knowledge and skills articulated in the ELS. The requirements and accountability measures within the QRIS are, however, not sufficient to produce the type of program quality improvements that many in the field aspire toward. Agencies and organizations outside the QRIS must have policies and professional development that support the use of ELS. These outside supports are depicted in the outermost circle of the figure. A description of each of these components of the model is provided below, along with ideas on how ELS can inform QRIS requirements and can be considered in the measures or validation strategies used to document that programs are meeting the requirements of the QRIS.

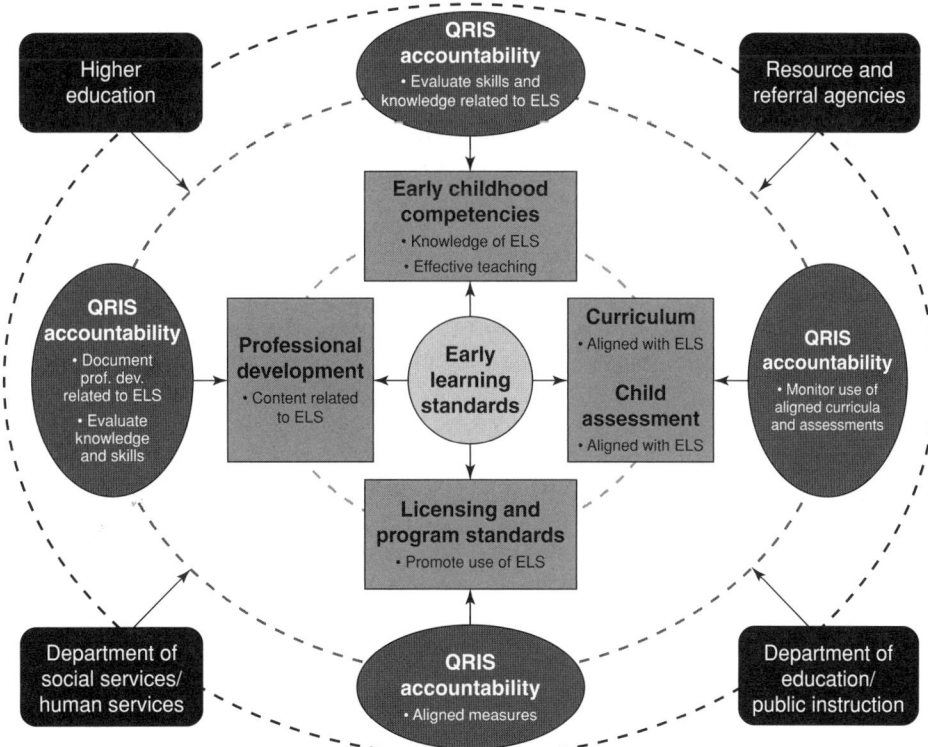

Figure 4.1. Early learning standards (ELS) and quality rating and improvement systems (QRISs) used to promote quality.

Licensing and Program Standards

Licensing regulations and program standards define the basic requirements that programs participating in the QRIS must meet. Figure 4.1 includes licensing and program standards at the bottom of the model. Licensing requirements typically focus on structural features of quality (e.g., adult–child ratios, group size) and requirements related to children's health and safety. Program standards may address aspects of quality included within licensing standards, but they often have requirements that promote quality above and beyond the basic licensing requirements. If ELS are used as a foundation for looking at licensing requirements and program standards, we believe that states can more effectively promote the child outcomes defined in ELS. For instance, if ELS stress the importance of children's ability to develop secure attachment relationships with their teachers, licensing requirements or program standards that promote low adult–child ratios and small group sizes would be in order. Likewise, if a state's ELS articulate the importance of children learning about science through experimentation with a variety of science-related materials, then program standards would call for classrooms to be stocked with a variety of science-related materials. in addition, if ELS include problem solving within its approaches to learning, then program standards may require teachers to have completed training on how to facilitate children's problem-solving skills. Program standards will also ensure that the classroom is stocked with manipulative materials that will require students to solve problems. States that develop their licensing requirements and programs standards with an eye toward the knowledge and skills described in their ELS can increase the likelihood that programs will be able to promote the child outcomes they have articulated in the ELS.

Similarly, states should keep their ELS in mind as they make decisions about the types of measures or processes that will be used to validate whether programs are meeting the licensing requirements or program standards. These accountability requirements are depicted in the middle circle within the model presented in Figure 4.1. Following the example from above, a state that emphasizes children's ability to form close attachment relationships with caregivers would need to measure adult:child ratios to ensure they are small enough to give children the opportunity to interact frequently with adults and would also want to incorporate a measure of teacher–child interactions that addresses the warmth and responsiveness of the caregiver to see if program staff are supporting children's ability to form close attachment relationships. When selecting measures to be used as part of a QRIS, it is important to look at alignment with the skills and knowledge outlined in the ELS and to select measures that promote the type of learning environment necessary for children to make progress on the ELS.

Drawing from an international example, we noted that there has been some effort to develop program measures that are consistent with the child outcomes articulated in ELS. England has national learning goals/standards (called Curriculum Guidance for the Foundation Stage) that include curriculum objectives and developmental expectations of children 3–5 years old. The Department for Children, Schools, and Families of England funded a nationally representative longitudinal study to examine preschool quality and children's outcomes through 16 years, including their educational, training, and employment choices following year 11 of public schooling (EPPSE 3–14 Project: Institute of Education, 2009).

In this study it was important to evaluate programs based on the learning goals the country had defined. To reflect the national learning goals, Sylva, Siraj-Blatchford, and Taggart (2006) developed the Early Childhood Environment Rating Scale–England (ECERS-E) to be used along with the Early Childhood Environment Rating Scale–Revised (ECERS-R) to evaluate program quality and for self-assessment. The ECERS-E contains four subscales reflective of the national early learning goals or standards including: literacy, numeracy, science, and diversity. According to Sylva, Siraj-Blatchford, Taggart, Sammons, et al., "The ECERS-E is specifically tailored to tap the dimensions of quality as defined by the new curriculum in England and by notions of emergent academic skills" (2006, p. 79). Although this international example is not associated with a QRIS, it illustrates how states might begin to think about selecting measures that address the teaching practices that facilitate the learning and development described in their ELS.

Curriculum and Child Assessments

Other important aspects of program quality are the curricula and assessments being used in programs. This component of program quality is depicted on the far right-hand side of the model. If ELS are being used as a foundational premise of a QRIS, it stands to reason that programs participating in the QRIS would be required to use curricula and child assessments that are consistent with the ELS. As we have seen in the previous section, North Carolina and Minnesota are two examples of states that have begun to designate aligned curricula and/or assessments and then to offer incentives for programs participating in the QRIS to use the aligned curricula and/or assessments. The idea behind this development is that programs are more likely to support children's development in the areas articulated in ELS if they are using curricula and/or assessments that are consistent with the ELS. We noted in both Minnesota and North Carolina that "consistency with the ELS" meant that not only did the curricula seek to teach the same skills articulated in the ELS but that the general approach toward educating young children was consistent with the approach the state envisioned when writing their ELS.

The middle circle of the model indicates that states must also think about how they will document or validate that programs are actually using aligned curricula and/or assessments. For instance, a state might require that programs submit a plan that describes what curricula and assessments they are using and how they use the aligned curricula and assessments. To hold programs accountable for documenting that the aligned curricula and child assessments are being used, programs might require documentation of the curricula and/or assessments on lesson plans and then check to see that the lesson plans used in a program actually do include features of the approved curricula and/or assessments. At a still more in-depth level of monitoring, states might choose to use an implementation evaluation guide or checklist that accompanies a curriculum as part of their monitoring process to document the extent to which the curriculum is being used or might train QRIS monitoring staff on features of various curricula that should be present in the classroom if a particular curriculum is being used. By including some type of monitoring of the use of aligned curricula and/or assessments in the QRIS monitoring system, states are taking yet another step toward ensuring that the learning environments children experience are environments that promote children's progress on the areas articulated in the ELS.

EARLY CHILDHOOD EDUCATION PROFESSIONAL COMPETENCIES

At the top of Figure 4.1, we see that the framework for using the QRIS and ELS together to promote quality includes efforts to ensure that the skills and knowledge teachers need to have (i.e., the ECEPC) are consistent with what is expected of children. Previously we described how the content of ECEPC should be consistent with the content of the ELS—teachers should be required to demonstrate knowledge and skills necessary to help children make progress on the ELS. This means that ELS must be considered when the content of the ECEPC is developed. It also means that the QRIS must, in some way, take the state's ECEPC into account within the requirements programs must meet. For this quality improvement strategy to be useful within the QRIS, the ECEPC must define competencies at a variety of levels of professional practice, not just at the 4-year-degree level, for teachers and for administrators. The ECEPC must include entry-level practitioners and articulate competences at higher levels of professional development and experience. Without this stairstep approach to ECEPC, the competencies will not fit the varying levels of education and experience teachers have within the programs participating in the QRIS.

States must also keep their ELS in mind when deciding how teachers will document that they have met the ECEPC. Within the system that is used to ensure that ECEPC are met, there must be some way for the QRIS to validate that the person's level of competency would be sufficient for him or her to help children make progress on ELS. For instance, if prospective teachers take a test to document that they have mastered the state's ECEPC, then the test should include content that is related to the state's ELS. If observations of prospective teachers are conducted to determine if they have met the competencies of the ECEPC, the observational measure should be consistent with the state's ELS. In this way it can be used to document that teachers understand the ELS and meet the ECEPC, which are aligned. In North Carolina, a new standardized evaluation instrument has been developed to assess teacher competencies at the preservice level and then continue on with the teacher as an in-service evaluation scale to be used by administrators. The new teacher evaluation, known as the Pre-Kindergarten and Kindergarten Teacher Performance Appraisal Instrument (PKKTPAI), includes standards and indicators of evidence upon which teachers' practices can be evaluated (North Carolina Department of Public Instruction, 2009). The standards and indicators of evidence are based on North Carolina's ECEPC, which are aligned with the state's ELS. The requirements for ECEPC, as well as the means for documenting that persons have met the competencies, should be viewed through the lens of ELS to ensure that the competencies are consistent with the knowledge and skills articulated within the ELS.

Professional Development

The left quadrant of the diagram addresses the relationship of ELS to QRIS and professional development requirements within the QRIS. The QRIS typically includes requirements for both preservice and in-service professional development. Similar to the professional competencies, professional development activities of the teachers and providers in the QRIS should include content related to the state's ELS and what teachers need to know to ensure the ELS are implemented effectively. Professional development of teachers working in programs that are participating in the QRIS should be approved by the QRIS with content tied to the ELS and with presenters who have been trained to conduct in-service training related to the ELS. Perhaps a certain percentage of the in-service training hours should be required to focus on ELS. Although currently states utilize child care resource and referral agencies and a variety of other systems to monitor the content of in-service training, the QRIS could systematically determine that the content of professional development is inclusive of ELS. It may be advantageous to develop online training modules including ELS content so that information could be provided more systematically to teachers and providers. In some states, including North Carolina, training provided by the QRIS (much of it through webinars) relates specifically to the classroom evaluation instrument required for the star rating. If the QRIS and ELS were more closely aligned, the scope of training provided by the QRIS could relate to all aspects of the diagram described as it relates to ELS, particularly, in this case, to the in-service professional development.

If the professional development is through the higher education system, then the coursework should define which aspects of ELS are the focus of the individual courses. Rather than simply articulating requirements that teachers complete certain degrees or a certain number of credits/hours, the QRIS should specify the types and number of courses related to ELS content that teachers must complete in their 2-year and 4-year-degree programs. Although the QRIS could not dictate what courses are offered in institutions of higher education, the system could be set up so that staff within programs participating in the QRIS must document how many of their courses address ELS content.

The QRIS could also provide a means of accountability to address the professional development completed by teachers working in participating programs (i.e., the middle ring in the model). At least two strategies for documenting that teachers meet professional development requirements come to mind. First, a QRIS could develop a system to monitor documentation teachers provide regarding the type of professional development they have completed. QRIS staff could examine documents such as college transcripts and in-service professional development logs to determine if teachers have completed courses and in-service training related to the state's ELS. Second, the QRIS might choose to monitor actual classroom performance of teachers to determine if they have had sufficient professional development experiences to prepare them to use the ELS effectively. A teacher performance instrument developed with an eye on the states' ELS could determine the extent to which teachers attend to ELS in their activities and interactions with the children. This system could provide a coherent connection between professional development and actual teacher performance as related to the early learning standards and could be used to document whether professional development experiences are effective in preparing teachers to use ELS. In an aligned system where both the ECEPC and professional development requirements are aligned with the state's ELS, the same measure might be useful to document both that teachers demonstrate the required ECEPC and that the professional development they have completed was sufficient to enable them to use the ELS.

Systems-Level Challenges to Utilizing ELS and QRIS Together to Improve Quality

Ideally, the ELS content would serve as a foundation or framework upon which requirements for the QRIS could be based, focusing on systemic quality improvement efforts on the skills and knowledge the state would like children to develop. There are, however, a number of systems-level or institutional challenges associated with this type of aligned approach. In addition to challenges related to the content of ELS documents, the capacity of teachers to implement ELS, and the ability of professional development providers to incorporate ELS into professional development described previously, states hoping to implement an aligned approach that brings together program improvement efforts based on ELS within the QRIS face several other challenges. These challenges relate to coordination and implementation of quality improvement efforts across agencies and programs involved in the QRIS.

Agency Responsibilities We noted that often ELS for preschoolers have been developed by one agency, and ELS for infants and toddlers sometimes have been developed by a different agency within the state's government. Frequently, ELS for preschoolers are developed by departments of education and infant-toddler standards are developed by departments of human services/human resources. Although the impetus for this separation by age is sometimes obvious—the department of education often does not administer programs that serve infants and toddlers—the potential implications for the development and implementation of ELS for different age groups are important considerations. The development of ELS within separate systems can create not only a lack of coordination between the two sets of standards but also inconsistency in dissemination, including inconsistent messages to teachers and providers about the purpose and use of the standards. Many states have addressed this issue by including persons who helped write the preschool ELS on committees that are writing the infant-toddler ELS, and vice versa. Carefully coordinated implementation is needed to avoid problems associated with separate agencies and programs implementing different ELS as children transition from one system to another. If ELS for different age groups (and their corresponding systems) are not clearly articulated and aligned, then the expectations for preschoolers will not proceed logically and developmentally from what was outlined for infants and toddlers.

A related issue is that often standards are endorsed or implemented by one agency serving preschoolers (or infants and toddlers) but not by other agencies serving the same age group. For example, although Head Start and prekindergarten children will be transitioning into the same public school kindergarten classrooms, their teachers may have used completely separate ELS to guide their practices because the Head Start programs implement requirements developed at the federal level and state prekindergarten programs implement state-level ELS. Furthermore, teachers in child care facilities may not have adhered to any particular set of ELS. Although we have no specific data indicating the impact of such disparities, it is highly likely that this contributes to inequity for the children as they enter kindergarten classrooms.

Finally, ELS may emanate from one agency, while quality improvement efforts such as the QRIS may be spearheaded by another agency within the state. In fact, the state department of education that developed the ELS may have its own program standards and professional development system developed specifically for prekindergarten programs and completely separate from the QRIS. As different quality improvement efforts emanate from different agencies, communication can be difficult and strategic plans misaligned. It may, however, be beneficial that the ELS and QRIS are overseen by different departments or agencies. Both departments share some common goals, most notably the goal to optimize early learning experiences and outcomes for children. In addition, a system of checks and balances is created. That is, the department of education serves as an informant for the field by developing ELS, and the QRIS creates a mechanism of accountability or validation through another agency. Subsequently, as the ELS and QRIS are developed and revised, they support each other through an iterative process. There is, however, potential for misalignment as one agency develops and implements ELS and a separate agency develops and administers the QRIS.

Monitoring   QRISs that are aligned with the ELS should present a more coherent set of requirements for programs and teachers. There are, however, numerous challenges related to monitoring the extent to which the aligned approach is being implemented within programs. The QRIS must develop some type of system to document that teachers are actually using the state's ELS. Although notations of how the ELS have been used to develop a lesson plan are one form of documentation, such documentation does not necessarily guarantee that teachers have actually implemented a lesson plan that is consistent with the ELS. New ways of documenting the use of ELS are needed for the ELS to be a meaningful component of the QRIS and other quality improvement initiatives. Research is needed to document how teachers use ELS, what effect the ELS have had on their practice, and how having ELS may, in turn, affect child outcomes for children enrolled in classrooms where ELS are used.

Multifaceted and Constantly Changing Systems for Quality Improvement   A final, and perhaps most daunting, challenge to the use of ELS in quality improvement efforts and the QRIS is the number of components that must be addressed and the fact that requirements and components of the systems are in a state of constant flux. It can be quite overwhelming to think about revisions to ECEPC, program standards, professional development systems, curricula and assessments, and other quality improvement efforts all at once. Yet, to achieve a cohesive system, each component must be developed and implemented with the requirements of the other components in mind. On top of the multifaceted planning that is necessary to infuse the ELS into the different components, there is the fact that many states have revised (or intend to) the content of their ELS every 3–5 years—just when the ELS have been infused into the QRIS, courses within institutions of higher education, and the professional development system, the content of the ELS may be revised. What results is a dynamic system that requires constant attention. Our advice is that as states begin to think in a way that infuses ELS across program quality efforts, they start by addressing the components of the system that make the most sense for their state's unique situation—look for the place where changes need to be made, or start with the component that will have the most impact across programs. Once that area is identified and addressed, move to another component. That way the systemic changes needed to truly infuse the ELS into program improvement efforts and the efforts to produce changes in programs and teaching practices that promote children's progress on ELS are not so overwhelming. Equally important is the "mind shift" that this type of systemic approach requires—recognition that a change in any one of the components should be viewed from how the change reflects the ELS, the impact it has on both program requirements and accountability requirements, and the implications for other components of the system.

ALIGNMENT AT THE SYSTEMS LEVEL—POLICIES AND PROFESSIONAL DEVELOPMENT TO SUPPORT AN ALIGNED QRIS

Up until this point, we have discussed various components of a QRIS, the importance of requirements that are consistent with ELS, and some of the systems-level challenges that may impede efforts to implement an aligned approach to quality improvements. We believe that this type of aligned approach could improve the quality and the effectiveness of programs. In short, QRIS requirements for programs, teachers, and curricula and assessments that take into account the state's goals for what children will learn and how they will develop the ELS can result in a more coherent approach to early childhood programs and provide better support for children's learning and development. We realize, however, that the ELS and the QRIS do not exist in a vacuum. There are several agencies/systems outside the QRIS that affect the degree to which this type of aligned program improvement approach can be implemented. These systems promulgate policies and provide professional development services that have a direct impact on the degree to which an aligned QRIS approach will be successful. ELS, therefore, must also be an important consideration in these other systems, which are depicted in the outer ring of the model in Figure 4.1. The organizations and systems that make policies and provide professional development in a state must also incorporate the state's ELS into their system for an aligned approach within a QRIS to work. Some of the considerations related to the policies and professional development that are not directly a part of the QRIS, but have important implications for the aligned approach to a QRIS, are discussed next.

Policies to Support an Aligned Approach to QRIS Organizations or systems that are outside the direct purview of the QRIS set policies and implement regulations that can have a direct impact on the QRIS and the programs participating in the QRIS. First, the ELS documents, not the QRIS, are typically written and implemented by the state's department of education or department of social services/human services. These agencies usually convene stakeholder groups to write the ELS and then implement professional development to support their use. It is important that representatives from the QRIS are included in the ELS development process. If representatives from the QRIS are involved in developing the ELS, they will be more knowledgeable of the ELS and likely will have a greater interest in investing resources to implement the ELS through QRIS requirements. Including representatives from the QRIS in the ELS development process can also increase the likelihood that the QRIS is taken into account as the ELS document is written. Departments of education and/or social services also are typically the developers of the ECEPC, and they dictate the knowledge and skills that teachers must demonstrate to be credentialed and specify the amount and type of professional development teachers must complete. Depending on the state, representatives from the QRIS may have limited input in developing these requirements, or, conversely, they may be intimately involved in crafting the requirements for teachers' professional development and their knowledge and skills. By setting the requirements for professional development and the ECEPCs, these outside systems have an impact on the QRIS. Therefore, it is important that the agencies developing the professional development requirements and the ECEPC seek to align the requirements with the ELS and involve the QRIS representatives in some way during the development process.

Professional Development to Support an Aligned Approach Even if policies that facilitate alignment between ELS and the requirements of a QRIS are developed, the success of an aligned approach is dependent on agencies and institutions that provide professional development. The professional development for teachers must address ELS and teach teachers how to implement their state's ELS in their classrooms. Teachers also need training on curricula and child assessments that are aligned with the ELS. It is therefore essential that institutions of higher education, resource and referral agencies, and other entities that provide professional development (shown in the outer ring of Figure 4.1) offer professional development that supports the use of ELS. Ideally, the professional development offered across these various organizations and agencies would be coordinated so that there is some consistency and coordination between what teachers learn in the professional development offered across the various organizations. For instance, the resource and referral agency might offer "awareness"-level training, and an institution of higher education might focus on the same elements of the ELS but offer a more in-depth study of the research and theory that support the ELS. A coordinated and consistent approach to the professional development offered across the various agencies could produce a workforce that is knowledgeable of the state's ELS and how to use them. Lack of consideration for ELS within the professional development offered by various organizations means that teachers working in programs participating in the QRIS will not be well prepared to meet the requirements that relate to the ELS.

We have presented a model for how ELS can be infused into various aspects of a QRIS and have postulated that the ELS must also be incorporated into policy making and professional development systems outside of the QRIS for the aligned approach to work. The ELS must be afforded significant attention within these other systems for teachers to receive training on the ELS and programs to meet the requirements of the QRIS.

CONCLUSION

Although the challenges are many, the potential rewards of a coherent, coordinated system of standards and accountability are great. In such an aligned approach to quality improvement efforts as described in this chapter, not only would all aspects of an ELS-based system be articulated and assessed, but the field would make progress toward a more intentionally coordinated system to serve families and children. ELS can be used as a framework to bring together the fragmented services and programs and facilitate movement toward shared goals for children and coordinated standards for quality. In addition, the movement of the early childhood field to a more professionally recognized one would undoubtedly be an outcome of such careful development and monitoring.

We are articulating a model that suggests that quality improvement efforts, particularly those included in a QRIS, use the state's ELS as a basis from which to consider what will be required of teachers and programs and how teachers and programs will document that they have met the requirements. We realize, however, that this type of aligned system requires an immense amount of thoughtful planning and time on the part of states, and we suggest that states will benefit from thinking through all the linkages necessary for an aligned system, as well as taking the time needed to develop each of the components. Every state is different. States differ in their political context, the culture of the state, the size and nature of early childhood programs that serve children, etc. It is important that each state take the time to develop and evaluate each of the components of their own system, their own ELS, and their own quality improvement efforts. The process of developing an aligned system is just as important as reaching the ever-moving target or goal. The opportunity to create an aligned system that integrally connects quality improvement efforts and ELS has great potential for improving the quality of services for families and children. The profession should move quickly to capitalize on the momentum of the ELS movement.

REFERENCES

Ackerman, D.J., & Barnett, W.S. (2006). *Increasing the effectiveness of preschool programs.* New Brunswick, NJ: National Institute for Early Education Research.

Bodrova, E., Leong, D., & Shore, R. (2004). *Child outcome standards in pre-K programs: What are the standards; what is needed to make them work?* New Brunswick, NJ: National Institute for Early Education Research.

Connecticut State Department of Education. (2008). *Connecticut preschool assessment framework.* Hartford: Author. Retrieved April 4, 2009, from http://www.sde.ct.gov/sde/lib/sde/PDF/DEPS/Early/Preschool_Assessment_Framework.pdf

Council of Chief State School Officers, Early Childhood Education Assessment Consortium. (2009). *State early childhood standards and assessments: A half-decade of development.* Washington, DC: Author.

EPPSE 3–14 Project: Institute of Education. (2009). *Effective Provision of Pre-School Education (EPPE) project.* Retrieved April 17, 2009, from http://eppe.ioe.ac.uk/index.htm.

Minnesota Parent Aware. (n.d.-a). *Child assessment review process summary.* St. Paul, MN: Author. Retrieved April 3, 2009, from http://www.parentawareratings.org/providers-educators/preparation.html

Minnesota Parent Aware. (n.d.-b). *Guide to curriculum review approval process.* St. Paul, MN: Author. Retrieved April 3, 2009, from http://www.parentawareratings.org/providers-educators/preparation.html

National Association for the Education of Young Children. (2009a). *Developmentally appropriate practice in early childhood programs serving children from birth through age 8* (3rd ed.). Washington, DC: Author.

National Association for the Education of Young Children. (2009b). *NAEYC quality rating and improvement systems toolkit.* Washington, DC: Author.

National Association for the Education of Young Children & National Association of Early Childhood Specialists in State Departments of Education. (2002). *Early learning standards: Creating the conditions for success* (Joint position statement). Retrieved April 2, 2009, from www.naeyc.org/dap

National Center for Research on Early Childhood Education. (2008). *Ensuring effective teaching in early childhood education through linked professional development systems, quality rating systems and state competencies: The role of research in an evidence-driven system.* Charlottesville, VA: Author.

National Child Care Information and Technical Assistance Center. (2009). *Quality rating systems: Definition and statewide systems.* Washington, DC: Author. Retrieved December 16, 2009, from http://nccic.acf.hhs.gov/pubs/qrs-defsystems.html

North Carolina Department of Public Instruction. (2009). *Public school employee evaluation. Pre-kindergarten–Kindergarten Teacher Performance Appraisal Instrument.* Retrieved July 13, 2009, from http://www.ncpublicschools.org/fbs/personnel/evaluation/

North Carolina Division of Child Development & Office of School Readiness. (2008, November). *North Carolina approved early childhood curricula.* Raleigh, NC: Author. Retrieved April 3, 2009, from http://ncchildcare.dhhs.state.nc.us/general/instructorsfor submittingcurriculum.asp

Scott-Little, C., Kagan, S.L., & Frelow, V.S. (2003a, Fall). Creating the conditions for success with early learning standards: Results from a national study of state-level standards for children's learning prior to kindergarten. *Early Childhood Research and Practice, 5*(2). Available at http://ecrp.uiuc.edu/v5n2/little.html

Scott-Little, C., Kagan, S.L., & Frelow, V.S. (2003b). *Standards for preschool children's learning and development: Who has standards, how were they developed, and how are they used?* Greensboro: SERVE Center at University of North Carolina at Greensboro.

Scott-Little, C., Kagan, S.L., & Frelow, V.S. (2005). *Inside the content: The breadth and depth of early learning standards.* Greensboro: SERVE Center at University of North Carolina at Greensboro.

Scott-Little, C., Kagan, S.L., & Frelow, V.S. (2006). Conceptualization of readiness and the econtent of early learning standards: The intersection of policy and research? *Early Childhood Research Quarterly, 21,* 153–173.

Scott-Little, C., Kagan, S.L., & Frelow, V.S. (2008). Infant-toddler early learning guidelines: The content that states have addressed and implications for programs serving children with disabilities. *Infants & Young Children, 22,* 87–99.

Scott-Little, C., Lesko, J., Martella, J., & Milburn, P. (2007). Early learning standards: Results from a national survey to document trends in state-level policies and practices. *Early Childhood Research and Practice, 9*(1). Retrieved from http://ecrp.uiuc.edu/v9n1/little.html

Sylva, K., Sirag-Blatchford, I., & Taggart, B. (2006). *Assessing quality in the early years: Early childhood environment rating scale (ECERS-E).* Staffordshire, England: Trentham Books.

Sylva, K., Siraj-Blatchford, I., Taggart, B., Sammons. P., Melhuish, E., Elliot, K., et al. (2006). Capturing quality in early childhood through environment rating scales. *Early Childhood Research Quarterly, 21,* 76–92.

CHAPTER 5

Quality Rating and Improvement Systems

Achieving the Promise for Programs, Parents, Children, and Early Childhood Systems

Kathryn Tout and Kelly L. Maxwell

Since Oklahoma initiated "Reaching for the Stars" in 1998, quality rating and improvement systems (QRIS) have been implemented, are being piloted, or are under development in over half of the states.[1] A QRIS is a systematic approach "to assess, improve, and communicate the level of quality in early care and education programs" (Mitchell, 2005, p. 4). With the potential to accomplish multiple goals and address vexing problems in the early childhood field, the expectations for QRISs are high. A QRIS can fill the gap between basic licensing requirements and national accreditation by delineating multiple levels of quality. Limited resources can be targeted to programs providing certain levels of quality. Subsidy reimbursement rates for child care can be linked to quality, thereby increasing the likelihood that poor children will receive high-quality care. Programs of all types (licensed child care centers, family child care homes, school-age programs) can be supported in quality improvement efforts and rewarded for achieving high quality. Parents can have tools to better understand the quality of care available and to more easily select high-quality care for their children, presumably driving the market toward production of higher quality care and increasing the likelihood that children receive services that promote positive child development. A notoriously fragmented set of services and resources can be brought together through the potential of a QRIS to build an aligned, comprehensive system of early care and education.

With 10 years of experience and some research on QRIS, the field is now at a critical point for examining progress toward meeting the promise of QRIS for programs, families and children, and early care and education systems. The purpose of this chapter is to contribute to this examination by describing key indicators of QRIS effectiveness, outlining measurement challenges, and highlighting areas for evaluation within and across the three themes highlighted previously: programs, parents and children, and early childhood systems. We begin with a brief overview of QRIS and introduce basic issues addressed in this chapter.

---

[1] A quality rating and improvement system may begin as a pilot program in a selected geographical region of a state or may be created specifically at a city or county level. Thus, there are a number of QRISs that are not implemented statewide. However, for the sake of simplicity, we refer to states as the agents charged with developing and implementing QRISs.

BASIC HISTORY, STRUCTURES, DEFINITIONS, AND GOALS OF QRIS

QRISs were developed over a decade ago in response to evidence showing that quality is linked to young children's development and that quality tends to be low (Mitchell, 2005). QRISs were developed initially as a strategy for promoting quality improvement by bridging the standards between licensing and accreditation and providing "manageable increments" and incentives for moving upward (Mitchell, 2005, p. 5). These increments, or steps, served as a structure for aligning funding to programs through increased child care subsidy payments (with rates increasing at higher quality levels) and through bonuses and other incentives for achieving higher quality levels. Although improvement in child outcomes was viewed by early QRIS developers as an expected consequence of higher quality early care and education, the goal of improved child outcomes has not always been explicitly stated in QRISs (see Zellman & Perlman, 2008, for a logic model with child outcomes as an explicit goal). Many early QRISs were focused on improving the quality of settings and improving access to quality among low-income children (Mitchell, 2005; Zellman & Perlman, 2008), while more recent QRISs have articulated the additional explicit goal of improving child outcomes (Child Trends, 2009a).

Another important contextual factor underlying the advent of QRIS was a confidence on the part of developers and supporters that the early childhood field had defined *quality* adequately and that the science and measurement of quality was advanced enough to support the development of a rating system. This intersection of basic science, practice, and public policy in early care and education has resulted in exciting innovations in QRISs, while at the same time it has generated an increased awareness of the difficulties and unanswered questions that emerge when translating knowledge from research and practice into a policy context. These difficulties are heightened by the fact that decisions about what to include in a QRIS and how to measure it are shaped by logistical constraints and costs as much as by guidance from research. Thus, what began as a reasonable extrapolation of research findings to generate a solution for the problem of low quality has in fact motivated new questions and new concerns about the evidence base and how it should be expanded to provide better support for quality improvement initiatives. It is our hope that this chapter contributes to the ongoing dialogue about QRISs, highlighting the need for more systematic inquiry while also recognizing states' urgent needs for practical knowledge that can be applied to their pressing questions.

Structure of Quality Rating and Improvement Systems

QRISs generally include five common elements: quality standards, a process for monitoring the quality standards, outreach and support to programs and practitioners, financial incentives, and dissemination of ratings and information to parents and consumers (Child Care Bureau, 2007; Mitchell, 2005; Tout, Zaslow, Halle, & Forry, 2009; Zellman & Perlman, 2008). These elements have emerged as common components of QRISs; they were not predefined by a federal agency or national organization, and a state QRIS may not have all of the elements in their particular system. States have developed QRISs in part through reviews and partial replication of existing QRISs but without much systematic, evidence-based guidance on best practices. This has led to much variation across state QRISs in details, priorities, and incentives.

The development or selection of quality standards is perhaps the most salient example of variation across QRISs. Some states, such as North Carolina, focus on a few quality dimensions (staff education and program standards), while other states, such as Colorado, focus on more dimension (learning environment, family partnerships, training and education, adult–child ratios, and accreditation). A 2007 summary of categories of quality standards indicated that most states included teacher qualifications/professional development, parent involvement, and the learning environment (Child Care Bureau, 2007). Few states included standards related to health and safety or provisions for children with disabilities in their QRIS (Buysse & Hollingsworth, 2008). Based on a review of QRISs in 2008, no state includes a quality component specifically related to cultural and linguistic competence (Bruner, Ray, Wright, & Copeman, 2009). Within each quality dimension, QRISs vary in the number of quality indicators included to tap that dimension and the process used to collect data on the indicator (i.e., observation, self-report, review of documents).

Definition of Quality Although many states develop their QRIS standards based in part on general evidence from early childhood research, there are also political and contextual influences that result in variation across state definitions of quality (Zellman & Perlman, 2008). Availability of funds is one important factor that determines the parameters included in the QRIS. A QRIS with more funds available may include an observational assessment and relatively generous incentives, whereas a QRIS with fewer funds may not include these components. Context also influences the development of a QRIS. A QRIS must differentiate programs (i.e., programs can't all be at one level of a QRIS) and be developed in a way that motivates providers to participate in it. Thus, there is often a tension between the ideal and reality of quality practices that can influence the definition of quality at various levels. If, for example, no programs met the highest quality level, state QRIS developers may adjust the QRIS so that at least a few programs could meet the highest quality rating. In a study of early QRIS adopters, Zellman and Perlman (2008) reported that the rapid time frame in which QRISs were launched and the lack of a pilot period in most sites resulted in numerous revisions to different components of the QRIS. They also described the challenges QRISs encounter in deciding what quality standards to include and exclude, given the lack of measures for some important constructs (an argument for exclusion of certain standards) but also the potential to devalue critical standards by leaving them out (an argument for inclusion of certain standards).

Resources such as accreditation standards and the Head Start Performance Standards exist to inform a definition of *quality,* but there is not a national consensus document with guidance or recommendations for indicators to include in a QRIS. Thus, statewide and pilot QRISs have continued to include a range of components. This has allowed for innovation in QRIS—for example, the inclusion of indicators related to family partnerships and family involvement—but has also highlighted the difficulty of translating research findings into specific rating structures. Likewise, identifying priorities and selecting and developing measures for QRISs demonstrate the challenges of translating the field's values and beliefs about families, culture, and inclusion into concrete indicators and measures.

To measure quality, states often use a combination of existing tools and self-developed tools in measuring components of the QRIS. In addition to requirements for documentation and self-report of different quality indicators, a significant proportion of statewide QRISs use the Environment Rating Scales by Harms, Cryer, and Clifford (2005) to observe classroom quality (ECERS-R Harms, Cryer, & Clifford, 2003; FCERS Harms, Cryer, & Clifford, 2007; ITERS Harms, Jacobs, & White, 1996). In addition, some QRISs have expanded the use of observational measures to include the Classroom Assessment Scoring System (CLASS; Pianta, La Paro, & Hamre, 2008) and the Early Childhood Environment Rating Scale-Extension (ECERS-E; Sylva, Siraj-Blatchford, & Taggart, 2006). Although these tools are among the most widely used to measure quality and have been used frequently in research, practitioners and researchers are discussing a range of issues in measuring program quality, including concerns about the content coverage of existing measures, the use of measures for multiple purposes (e.g., for rating and for quality improvement), and the challenges inherent in using the existing set of tools in high-stakes settings like QRIS in which the assessment results are tied to financial incentives for programs (Zaslow, Tout, Halle, & Forry, 2009; Zellman & Perlman, 2008).

For components other than observed classroom quality, many states develop their own measures. The RAND study of Colorado's Qualistar QRIS highlights the challenges in developing a measure of parent involvement that varies across programs (and therefore provides meaningful information about differences among programs) and is appropriate for both centers and family child care homes (Zellman, Perlman, Le, & Setodji, 2008). It also points to the complexity in measuring seemingly simple components such as adult–child ratios (Zellman et al., 2008) due to variability throughout the day. Additional discussion of measurement issues is provided in Chapter 3.

Goals for Quality Rating and Improvement Systems Central to the task of measuring quality and selecting quality indicators is the specification of goals for a QRIS. Goals influence what is measured and what is prioritized in a QRIS. As noted, improved child outcomes has emerged as an *explicit* goal of QRISs in recent years in addition to the already stated goals of quality improvement and increased access to quality. This reframed goal highlighting child outcomes may require that quality indicators be added or emphasized in QRISs that focus more specifically on the practices in early care and education settings that influence desired child outcomes articulated by state early learning guidelines (see Chapter 4). New work is underway to recommend changes to existing measures to improve alignment with child outcomees (Child Trends, 2009b). For example, a workgroup examining the connections between families and early care and education settings is exploring the development of a construct called "family-sensitive caregiving" to capture the practices in settings that are linked to positive family engagement and high-quality program–family relationships and ultimately improved outcomes for children (Bromer et al., in press). In addition, the National Association for the Education of Young Children (NAEYC, 2009) is working to develop measures of cultural competence that could be included in a QRIS to capture more precisely the practices that are supportive of young children. These are first steps in the revision or development of measurement strategies that can capture practices relevant for the prediction of child outcomes. New strategies must also acknowledge and address the different types of care, ages and abilities of children, and cultural and linguistic diversity present in early childhood settings (Child Trends, 2006).

Once each particular component is measured, the information must be combined in some way to create a single quality assessment for a program. States typically rely on either a building-blocks model or a point system in determining the overall program assessment (see Child Care Bureau, 2007, for more information). A building-blocks model requires programs to meet each and every criterion within a level (e.g., must meet all of the criteria in Level 1 plus all of the criteria in Level 2 to earn a rating of 2). This model ensures that each program at a higher rating has met the same standards. A point system assigns points to criteria and requires a program to earn a specified number of points to reach higher ratings, but programs can earn points by meeting different criteria. Thus, one program may earn a two-star rating by having well-qualified teachers but lower observed classroom quality, while another program may earn a two-star rating by having higher observed classroom quality but less qualified teachers.

With this basic overview of quality rating and improvement systems in the United States, we turn now to a more in-depth look at the promise of QRISs for programs, parents and children, and early care and education systems.

THE QRIS PROMISE TO PROGRAMS

The QRIS promise to programs has two parts. The first is the opportunity for programs to be recognized and rewarded for offering and maintaining a level of quality that goes above that required by licensing. The second is that programs have access to services, financial incentives, and resources that can help them improve their quality. This piece may not always be in place (i.e., some systems focus on ratings without providing improvement services), but the majority of systems include both rating and improvement efforts. To achieve these two promises of recognition and support, a QRIS must have a valid and reliable measurement strategy, provide effective improvement supports for programs to achieve the quality standards, and reward and incentivize the provision of high-quality care and education services. What evidence exists that these indicators of effective QRIS functioning for programs are being met and that they are having the desired impact? In this section, we describe the few findings in the literature that address this question and summarize the implications for next steps.

Are QRISs Founded on a Valid Measurement Strategy?

The measurement strategy used by a QRIS encompasses a variety of elements, including the quality indicators that are selected for inclusion in the QRIS, the measurement tools and data that will be used to examine the indicators, the staff and training infrastructure used to collect and verify the data, the oversight and control provisions put in place to ensure compliance with procedures, the method used for relaying scores and feedback to participants, and the process for dealing with appeals due to perceived errors in measurement. Developing and managing each of these aspects and coordinating across the staff and partner agencies responsible for these activities is a complex task that is typically undertaken with limited information (i.e., practical knowledge from the field) and financial resources (Zellman & Perlman, 2008). Yet, because of the consequences ratings have for programs, the level of precision expected in a QRIS is high. This section focuses primarily on the quality indicators and measurement tools that are used in a QRIS, but it is important to note that a valid, reliable measurement strategy requires attention to all of the elements outlined above.

The issue of validity of QRISs was raised early in the development of the systems. In the limited research literature on this topic to date, questions of validity have been addressed by examining how well the ratings generated by the QRIS relate to other measures of quality. Early studies in Oklahoma and North Carolina found that the ratings designated by the QRIS were differentially related in predictable ways to other quality measures (Bryant, 2001; Norris, Dunn, & Eckert, 2003). However, a more recent validation study in Colorado examining links between ratings and measures of process quality found no consistent patterns over the 3 years of the study (Zellman et al., 2008).

Studies underway in Indiana, Missouri, Minnesota, and Ohio will examine validity of a QRIS by including measures of child outcomes (Tout et al., 2009). These studies are not designed to assess the impact of the QRIS on children per se but rather to examine how QRIS ratings are linked to children's developmental gains from fall to spring in the year before kindergarten. The strategy used in these studies is to not only understand the relationship between inputs and program quality improvement but also to understand the effects on children's outcomes and to use the information to conduct a critical assessment of the components in existing QRISs. Do certain components of the rating product children's outcomes better than other? QRISs can then use this information to refine their current measurement strategies to align with practices that best support children. This forthcoming cohort of studies on QRISs reflects an emphasis on children's outcomes and the role that program quality can play in improving children's school readiness among a "new generation" of QRISs (selected programs launched in the late 2000s) on children's outcomes and the role that program quality can play in improving children's school readiness. The goals for children are explicit in this new generation of QRISs compared to early systems that emphasized the improvement of quality as the primary goal (Tout et al., 2009).

Composite Ratings Building on the general issue of validity, a number of specific issues can be raised that relate to how QRISs measure quality and create quality ratings. First is the issue of creating composite ratings using either a building-blocks or point-system approach. Little research is available to understand the strengths and challenges associated with each approach to creating a composite quality score. Findings from a pilot test of Rhode Island's QRIS demonstrate the complexity of using the building-blocks approach to develop levels that adequately differentiate programs (Maxwell, 2008). A pilot test of the draft Rhode Island QRIS framework using data from 25 randomly selected licensed child care centers and preschools suggested that programs would not earn more than a one-star rating with the original framework. Based on the pilot data, QRIS leaders adjusted the BrightStars Child Care and Preschool Framework before officially implementing the system statewide. Across all states, though, more research is needed to better understand questions like, "How much better is a five-star program than a four-star?" and "For how long is the composite rating of a program valid, especially since teacher turnover rates tend to be high?"

Weighting Components Within either the building-block or point-system models, a second measurement issue is the weighting of components, often implicitly, in assigning an overall rating to programs. For example, Kentucky's STARS for KIDS NOW for licensed child care centers measures five quality components: ratios, curriculum, training, regulatory compliance, and personnel (Kentucky Department of Education, 2008). Within the ratio component, programs must meet current licensing standards for ratios and post the ratios in each classroom. Within the curriculum component, each level assesses between three and six different aspects of curriculum. The Level 1 criteria for curriculum, for example, require programs to meet current licensing standards, complete the STARS for KIDS NOW overview, post a plan of program activities, post a daily schedule, host at least one family involvement activity, and agree to complete the Environment Rating Scales. Levels 2–4 for curriculum include fewer criteria, resulting in curriculum being weighted more at Level 1 compared to other levels. Across components, there is also variability in the number of criteria measured, which may result in certain quality components being weighted more than others. Similar examples in other systems highlight the various weighting strategies that are used and the need for research to identify those that are working effectively and those that are not (Zellman & Perlman, 2008).

QRIS Levels A third measurement issue requiring validation is the number of levels in a QRIS. From the perspective of programs, levels can represent manageable steps toward the goal of providing high-quality services for children and families. Indeed, QRISs have been characterized as building a path between licensing and accreditation, given that accreditation may not be attainable for certain programs due to cost or other barriers (Mitchell, 2005). A QRIS can thus recognize smaller steps toward quality and provide support and incentives toward meeting those steps. If, however, it is assumed that the steps or ratings levels must be related to improved child outcomes, then validating the system becomes more complicated. A critical issue for the field to address is the extent to which the indicators in a QRIS should be linked to child outcomes in general or whether each level of the system should distinguish meaningfully different outcomes for children. Does a "three-star" need to be different from a "two-star" program in the child outcomes that it produces? Or is it acceptable for the system to provide evidence that the dimensions of quality included in the QRIS are correlated with child outcomes in predictable ways—but not necessarily predictive of statistically significant differences in outcomes for children at each level? Perhaps there are thresholds in a QRIS whereby improved outcomes are expected only at the higher ratings. If this is the case, rating systems could be structured to recognize these thresholds rather than steps of quality for providers.

In sum, validation studies are needed to address the content of the QRIS as well as the mechanisms for combining, weighting, and assigning cut points and levels to the quality indicators. To date, QRISs have been constructed without specific guidance from research about where to set cut points of scales and how to combine a mixture of indicators from self-report, observational measures, and other sources (Zellman & Perlman, 2008). Current QRISs have been created with the best available current research, but the proliferation of these systems and the stakes attached to the ratings that programs are assigned provide a compelling reason for conducting systematic research on these issues.

Are QRISs Founded on a Reliable Measurement Strategy?

Underlying the issue of valid tools and strategies for creating a rating is the issue of reliability. In essence, reliability means that the QRIS processes are administered in the same way regardless of the particular staff person or group of staff assigned to the program. To date, reliability has been addressed primarily by establishing criteria for consistency in the use of observational quality measures (if the QRIS includes these). Other aspects of the rating process, however, also rely on subjective judgments that could undergo reliability checks as well. For example, review of documentation and written materials could be conducted with adherence to written guidelines and regular reliability checks to show that assignment to a particular staff for review of materials has no bearing on the rating received. Clear protocols and training procedures for establishing reliability in QRISs are necessary for ensuring integrity of the rating process, but little is known currently about the reliability procedures in use across existing QRISs.

Do QRISs Provide Effective Quality Improvement Supports?

Although it is a central feature of a QRIS from the perspective of programs, little systematic information exists about the type and intensity of quality improvement supports being provided in QRISs and how these supports are linked to professional development systems. Even less information exists about the effectiveness of these supports. In this section, we provide a brief overview of the types of strategies states are using and make recommendations for research and evaluation needed to document how well quality improvement supports are working.

Most QRISs use a cyclical process to establish ratings and to provide quality improvement services. Typically, programs complete an application for the QRIS that they submit to begin the rating process. In some QRISs, programs are expected to complete a quality self-assessment at the time of application that provides initial information about the QRIS quality indicators and how well the program might score on each dimension. These tools might be used by programs to begin their own informal quality improvement process so that their quality level can be improved before they enter the QRIS. Some QRISs, like that in Pennsylvania, may offer financial support in the form of grants to help with quality improvements prior to enrollment. These early experiences with the QRIS are a critical time for programs that need to consider both the potential for further quality improvement supports if they enroll in the QRIS as well as the possibility of negative consequences associated with receiving a low rating upon entering. A QRIS may target these programs in particular to ensure that they aren't attracting only programs at higher quality levels. To date, little systematic information exists across states about the degree to which QRIS programs reflect the characteristics of programs that have not enrolled in a QRIS and the degree to which QRISs target programs at lower quality levels for improvement supports.

After a program has applied to the QRIS, their experience will depend on whether the application contains all of the information necessary to issue a rating. In a number of QRISs, the program will receive an on-site visit so that assessors can collect observational data using standardized tools. When an observational visit is included in the QRIS, states may provide orientation or training sessions to programs so that they are informed about the content of these visits. In addition, information that is collected from the observers may be shared with a technical assistance provider (sometimes referred to as consultants, coaches, or mentors) who is working with the program. A systematic review of the roles and responsibilities of quality improvement staff is underway as part of the QRS Assessment Project funded by the Office of Planning, Research, and Evaluation in the U.S. Department of Health and Human Services. Without current data, it is difficult to provide a full description of how QRISs have implemented technical assistance to support quality. We do know that across QRISs, strategies vary widely for identifying the programs' needs, creating a quality improvement plan, and determining the level and type of assistance that will be offered. QRISs report that they use individualized approaches to working on quality improvement. This may mean, however, that even within one state QRIS, there is not a specific set of services available or formal plan established for working with programs.

Another element of quality improvement strategies that is not well understood is the degree to which QRISs are linked and aligned systematically with state professional development systems. Although this may seem to be a logical point of connection, evidence of integration has not yet been documented (Howes et al., 2008). It is clear that infrastructure elements such as Professional Development Registries and Career Lattices are incorporated in QRISs and that many of the agencies in charge of implementing components of the QRIS are the same agencies contracted to provide professional development services. However, it is not clear that these connections promote integration or that QRIS quality standards are linked to what is supported and promoted in the professional development system (Howes et al., 2008). Because the majority of QRISs are voluntary, it may be the case that states separate the set of quality improvement services in the QRIS from the broader professional development system so that providers and programs not participating in the QRIS perceive open access to the professional development system. Working with limited resources, it will be critical for QRISs and professional development systems to develop more formal and meaningful integration. Howes and colleagues (2008) described these linkages as offering mechanisms for both accountability and feedback. QRIS data can document the effectiveness of professional development in improving the competencies of practitioners and can also be used to link practitioners to the professional development needed to foster a competency that they are lacking. As such, systematic data collection and evaluation of the professional development experiences and quality improvement strategies used in QRISs will be critical for building new knowledge.

To date, research from a handful of state QRISs indicates that quality improvement does occur over time, though changes in quality are not always statistically significant (Barnard, Smith, Feine, & Swanson, 2006; Cheatam, Pope, & Myers, 2005; Norris et al., 2003; Pope, Denny, Magda, Homer, & Cunningham, 2007; Zellman et al., 2008). Because of the designs of the studies, it is not possible to make causal attributions about the QRIS and its role in supporting quality improvements, and very few studies provide information about the *process* of quality improvement (see Ackerman, 2008, for an exception). New research on quality improvement will be beneficial if it can link changes in quality to particular quality improvement provisions, such as different modes or intensities of technical assistance. To make this research most useful for generating practical knowledge, researchers and practitioners should identify common definitions and data elements that can be used to characterize quality improvement supports. Although individual terms may vary that reference the type of supports provided (e.g., coaches, consultants), presentation of common data elements such as average frequency and duration of quality improvement sessions and mode of support(s) used (role-modeling, discussion, reflective practice) will be important for building a shared knowledge base about effective practices.

Do QRISs Provide Adequate Rewards and Incentives for Programs?

Similar to the provision of quality improvement supports, little systematic information exists documenting the types of rewards and incentives used to encourage enrollment in the QRIS, support quality improvement, and assist programs with maintenance of quality over time. It is clear that the range of available financial support (in the form of grants, awards, bonuses, scholarships, and tiered reimbursement) is wide, with some QRISs offering substantial awards for achieving quality levels and others offering amounts that are quite small. Much more information is needed about the effectiveness of financial incentives. An analysis of Ohio's QRIS highlights the importance of analyzing the increased costs to providers in meeting higher quality standards and the extent to which those increased costs are supplemented by state incentives or financial supports to parents (Brandon & Stutman, 2009). One cannot assume that the resources offered to parents and programs through a QRIS are enough to improve and sustain high levels of quality. Planned-variation studies about incentives (i.e., amount, type, and frequency) would provide critical information to QRIS leaders across states that are working to implement a range of technical assistance and financial incentives to improve quality.

Summary of Progress Toward Effective QRISs for Programs

There is mixed evidence suggesting that QRIS quality measures are related to other measures of process quality and no evidence to date that shows clear linkages between quality levels of programs and child outcomes. Further evidence is needed to sort out the degree to which the mechanics of QRIS—such as the weighting strategies and number of levels in the system—are related to meaningful differences in outcomes. Research evidence regarding the effectiveness of different quality improvement strategies for programs and options for providing financial incentives is not yet available.

THE QRIS PROMISE TO PARENTS AND CHILDREN

The QRIS promise to parents has both short-term and long-term components. In the short term, as a QRIS is being established in a state or community, parents can use information and ratings to select care and education settings for their children. Similar to restaurant or movie ratings, the hope is that a simple rating system (often a star system) will make it easier for parents to select high-quality programs that can enhance their children's development. In the long term, it is expected that this selection process (or demand) by parents, in which parents select care of the highest quality, will eventually cause lower-quality settings to leave the market (Zellman & Perlman, 2008). Thus, a QRIS is assumed not only to increase the number of higher quality sites available to parents but also encourage improvement among sites so that they can meet parent demand for quality.

To what extent is this promise for parents, children, and the child care market in general being achieved through QRISs? Although some research has documented the factors that parents care about when choosing care and education settings, little research exists that examines the assumptions underlying the demand model described above (Zaslow & Forry, 2009). Even the most basic premise—that parents will use ratings to make child care decisions—has not yet been established empirically. Nevertheless, emerging research can help us better understand four critical questions about parents, children, and quality information: 1) do parents want *comparative* information about quality, 2) can parents access quality information, 3) do parents use quality ratings to make their child care decisions, and 4) do children benefit from the decisions parents make based on quality ratings? Each of these issues could be considered indicators of an effective QRIS if/when it is established that they are in place.

Parents' Interest in Quality Information

From the perspective of generating parent demand for quality through QRIS, several key assumptions are made. One is that parents lack information about the quality of care and education settings available in their community. Although information about basic features of programs such as type, location, and hours can be accessed through child care resource and referral (CCR&R) services available in most communities in the United States (National Association of Child Care Resource and Referral Agencies [NACCRRA], 2008), information about quality from the perspective of "experts" isn't typically available in CCR&R referrals or through other sources (Mitchell, 2005; Zellman et al., 2008). In addition, research indicates that parents make judgments about quality that differ from experts (Cryer & Burchinal, 1997). Thus, information about quality is a gap for parents, partly because objective information doesn't exist and partly because parents may need external help discerning the quality of settings.

A second assumption is that parents want information that will help them compare the quality among settings. The implications of this assumption go beyond those of a more simple information gap to suggest that parents want quality information that is ranked and that, in theory, could help them determine if one setting is better than another setting. Research conducted by state QRISs supports this premise to some extent. For example, 88% of parental respondents in a Missouri survey said they would use information from a quality rating system to help them look for child care (Thornburg et al., in press). Similarly, 88% of parents in a Minnesota survey reported that a quality rating system would be "very" or "somewhat" helpful (Chase et al., 2005). Parents in Minnesota who had low incomes or who spoke languages other than English were more likely than other parents to indicate that a quality rating system would be helpful. This emerging state research is beginning to build an understanding of the information parents may desire, although more detailed findings would be useful for the design and refinement of QRISs.

Parents' Ability to Access Quality Information

A second set of issues to consider concerns the ability of parents to access quality information in sources that they trust and in the languages that they speak. To date, very little evidence exists to document the success of QRISs on the issue of access. Most existing QRISs offer information on the Internet or provide toll-free phone numbers that parents can call for assistance or to request written information. The extent to which parents can or will access information from these sources likely depends on their resources and characteristics. A telephone survey of parents in Washington state, for example, revealed that only 20% of parents trust the Internet "a lot" as a source for information about early learning (including information to help parents make decisions about services and child care; Golan et al., 2008). Similar percentages trusted materials in the mail (16%) or a toll-free parent advice line (19%) "a lot." Resources such as health care providers and child care providers were much more likely to be trusted "a lot" as a source of information about early learning (71% and 53%, respectively). Significant differences among subpopulations (primary language and income level) were noted for a number of the information sources examined in the needs assessment.

Likewise, in Minnesota, focus groups conducted with low-income parents revealed that parents don't trust unfamiliar institutions for information about child care. Recommendations from the marketing firm that conducted the focus groups emphasized the importance of using peer-to-peer marketing strategies and engaging health care professionals and other credible social service agencies to distribute information about the QRIS being piloted in Minnesota. In contrast to the findings from Washington State (Golan et al., 2008), data from a separate set of focus groups with parents in Minnesota showed that the Internet was the top response when parents were asked where they would like to access information about quality child care (Minnesota Department of Education and Minnesota Department of Human Services, 2007). Yet, findings from a survey of low-income families indicated that approximately 40% of low-income families in the urban area where the QRIS is being piloted do not use the Internet in their homes (although 20% reported using the Internet someplace else; Chase & Moore, 2008).

Marketing strategies are also important to take into account when examining issues of access. QRISs vary in the resources available for marketing or in the degree to which they are ready to launch a marketing campaign. Promoting the program too early in implementation (before a sufficient number of programs have enrolled) could spread dissatisfaction among parents who look for rated programs and find very few from which to select. Although not conducting a study of a QRIS, Witte and Queralt (2004) noted a large jump in "hits" to a web site (an increase of over 16,000 hits in 1 month) after a marketing campaign was used to make parents aware of data available online about child care licensing inspections and complaint reports. Thus, parents may respond swiftly to effective marketing strategies about QRIS. Tracking hits to web sites is one potential source of data for QRIS, although additional data-collection strategies are recommended to track more in-depth characteristics of parents using the QRIS information.

Looking across the emerging data, it is clear that there is no perfect formula for determining whether parents can or will access information about child care quality from a QRIS. It appears that a variety of factors including parents' own characteristics and the source of the information will play a role as well as the degree to which effective marketing and outreach strategies are used by the agency or organization implementing the QRIS.

Parents' Use of QRIS Information to Make Decisions

A third broad issue related to parent demand is the extent to which parents will *use* quality information to make decisions about care and education for their children. Data from a variety of studies indicate that parents do value dimensions of quality such as the learning environment and activities, the training of the caregiver, and safety and cleanliness (e.g., NACCRRA, 2009). However, parents report that they also must weigh factors such as cost and convenience when making care and education decisions (NACCRRA, 2009). Quality is thus an important factor in decision making but not the *only* factor that parents use.

The extent to which parents understand the terms used in QRIS is also of concern. Recent research by NACCRRA (Smith & Sarkar, 2008) revealed that parents (especially military parents who move frequently between states) are confused by the distinctions between key terms used in QRIS and early learning systems, such as *licensing, certification,* and *accreditation.* They also have misperceptions about the requirements for licensing and the regularity of inspections in child care settings (NACCRRA, 2009). It will be important for future research to address questions about the terms used in QRIS as well as other issues affecting how parents may use the ratings, such as the format (e.g., the availability of summary ratings and individual component ratings) and the number of levels (e.g., do parents prefer multiple levels, or is a two-level system sufficient?). Zaslow and Forry (2009) recommended that future research on the use of QRIS information focus on three additional dimensions: timing (at what point in the decision-making process is QRIS information most useful?), characteristics (do characteristics such as income and language restrict the way that parents use the ratings?), and efficiency (do ratings simplify or complicate the process of finding high-quality care and education?). Understanding each of these dimensions would help in the design and refinement of QRISs so that they can be more effective for parents.

Children's Outcomes and QRISs

A critical indicator of QRIS effectiveness for families is the extent to which the provision of information to parents results in child care placements for children that are linked to improved developmental outcomes. This means that the QRIS not only has provided parents with information that they can access, understand, and use but also that the designations of quality—the ratings—in the QRIS are valid reflections of quality that can enhance children's development (as described earlier in this chapter). This is at the core of the QRIS framework. There are numerous design issues that surface when considering how QRIS research could examine child outcomes, and to date no summative evaluation has been conducted to study how child outcomes are affected by a QRIS. It is our assertion that the essential steps in the QRIS logic model leading to child outcomes should be established empirically first before turning to the more difficult research challenge of studying child outcomes. As noted earlier, this work would involve research findings documenting the validity of the process used to identify quality in a QRIS as well as findings showing that parents are using quality ratings in the process of their decision making about child care. Research on child care decision making is particularly challenging given the complex array of factors that parents weigh when choosing a child care arrangement. However, it will be important to demonstrate how a QRIS influences this process if we want to fully understand whether and how a QRIS has affected child outcomes.

Summary of Progress Toward Effective QRISs for Parents and Children

A growing body of evidence provides insights into the information parents value and the way that parents wish to access information about early care and education.

There is, to date, a dearth of information about whether parents access information from QRISs and, if so, whether and how they use information to make early care and education decisions to promote more positive outcomes for their children. This research is necessary to create QRISs that work effectively for parents and to examine the extent to which parent demand can play a driving role in improving the quality of early care and education settings.

THE QRIS PROMISE TO BUILD A SYSTEM

The third major promise for a QRIS is that it will help build an integrated early childhood service system. Merriam Webster's Collegiate Dictionary 11th Edition defines a system as "a regularly interacting or independent group of items forming a unified whole"[2] (2010). What is the "whole" of interest—an early care and education system for children birth to 5, an early care and education system for children birth through age 8, or a broad service system for all aspects of young children's well-being that goes beyond early care and education? And what is the "set" of things needed to make that "whole"? Various definitions of *early childhood systems* and their components have been described in the literature (Bruner, 2004; Gallagher, Clifford, & Maxwell, 2004; Johnson & Knitzer, 2006; Kagan & Cohen, 1997), with varying scopes—from those focused only on licensed or regulated preschool education (Gallagher et al., 2004) to the broadest array of components for health, family support, early intervention, and early care and education (Bruner, 2004). To date, no state has one integrated service system for young children; states have multiple agencies serving young children birth through age 5 that vary in the extent to which they coordinate their efforts. Projects like the BUILD Initiative and the Maternal and Child Health's Early Childhood Comprehensive Systems support states as they move toward developing and integrating systems (see Coffman, Wright, & Bruner, 2006, for examples of state efforts to build a system). Although an in-depth discussion of systems in the broadest sense is beyond the scope of this chapter, we will highlight possible roles of a QRIS in the particular effort of developing an integrated *early care and education system* for young children.

Indicators of Success in Using a QRIS to Build a System

QRIS is often purported to serve as the center spoke that links together various aspects of the early childhood care and education "system": licensing, state prekindergarten (pre-K), Head Start, early learning standards, and other components (Mitchell, 2005). With a QRIS as an umbrella describing aspects of quality, policy makers and administrators can use it as a framework for organizing and aligning key components of an early childhood care and education system. What would it mean for the QRIS to fulfill its promise to build a system of early care and education? The section below highlights three indicators that would suggest that the QRIS has fulfilled this promise.

Indicator 1: The QRIS Administrative Partners Coordinate   A QRIS is often housed or affiliated with state agencies like the department of health and human services and the department of education. Other groups, like Early Intervention or Mental Health, may be less tied to the QRIS but are important partners in building an early care and education system. QRIS-related legislation may serve as a lever for change in its requirements for particular agencies or organizations to work together. In this role, the QRIS could provide the necessary funding and

---

[2] Reprinted by permission. From Merriam-Webster's Collegiate® Dictionary, 11th Edition ©2010 by Merriam-Webster, Incopated (www.Merriam-Webster.com).

support for states to develop a more integrated early care and education system. QRIS leaders, for example, could articulate professional competencies and then measure those competencies as part of the quality rating system (see Howes et al., 2008, for more discussion of the links between professional development and QRIS). Guidelines for North Carolina's More at Four, the state-funded pre-K program for at-risk 4-year-olds, require participating programs to be either a four- or five-star–rated program (North Carolina Office of School Readiness, 2008). Requirements such as this could help strengthen ties between state agencies responsible for licensing child care programs and state agencies that oversee K–12 education.

States also can move toward a coordinated early care and education system by blending some of the supports provided by the multiple agencies that serve young children (Gallagher, Clifford, & Maxwell, 2004). For example, a QRIS could offer the structure under which multiple agencies conduct cross-agency planning. A QRIS could also help build a coordinated data system if QRIS staff gathered and stored data related to program quality for multiple types of care (licensed centers, homes, state pre-K, Head Start).

Indicator 2: The QRIS Includes Evidence of Alignment Across System Components

Alignment is important for multiple aspects of an early childhood system: program standards, professional standards, and desired child outcomes. One could argue that child outcomes are the force that drives the broad early care and education system: We strive for a high-quality system to ensure that all children in America receive the best foundation possible for lifelong health and success. As one piece of the broader system, the QRIS could delineate child-level results as its ultimate goal and include components that would likely promote those desired child outcomes in early childhood settings (Kagan, 2008). This would help ensure that early childhood programs strive toward similar long-term child-related goals. The program standards needed to support those desired outcomes could also be delineated within the QRIS rating system in such a way that they build on or coordinate, rather than compete, with existing program standards (e.g., Head Start, Title I, state pre-K).

Finally, the professional standards for teachers articulated in the QRIS should be aligned with both state professional development systems and competencies for early childhood educators (Howes et al., 2008) to form an integrated professional development system that focuses on who receives professional development, what is covered, and how the professional development is delivered (Buysse, Winton, & Rous, 2009; Winton, McCollum, & Catlett, 2008). To help move toward an aligned system of early care and education, QRIS leaders could, for instance, work with higher education and in-service professional development providers to ensure that the teacher competencies and skills delineated as important in the QRIS are adequately addressed in preservice and in-service professional development efforts. In these ways, the QRIS could become an important mechanism for aligning a state's program standards and professional development efforts with its early learning standards.

Indicator 3: Multiple Types of Programs Participate in the QRIS

To effectively build a system, all kinds of programs must participate in a QRIS: for-profit and not-for-profit centers, Head Start/Early Head Start, state pre-K programs, family child care homes, and programs and providers that serve dual language learners. In states with voluntary QRISs, a recent case study of five QRIS pioneer states suggests that participation rates vary widely across states (10%–68% in the Zellman & Perlman, 2008, report). Participation rates are also likely to vary by program type (e.g., family child care homes may be less likely to participate).

Without high participation rates among most providers and programs, it will be difficult for the QRIS to fulfill its promise of building an integrated early care and education system. If many providers continue to operate outside the QRIS, then it may have limited influence over the larger system of early care and education. Agencies may not want to invest in creating a shared data system, for example, if they serve only a small number of the same clients. Under these circumstances, the QRIS may be beneficial in articulating child, professional development, and program standards but may be less effective in other ways, such as blending supports across agencies and programs.

This section has focused on the need for involving as many licensed or regulated providers as possible if the QRIS is to be successful in moving states toward a system of early care and education. We want to acknowledge a broader system issue, though, of *all* types of care for young children. If states are interested in developing a broad system of early care and education, then they must also consider family, friends, and neighbors who care for children. More than 1 million individuals are estimated to care for young children in licensed or registered programs, and at least another 800,000 are estimated to care for children outside the licensing or regulation system (Burton et al., 2002). So far, state QRISs have focused on licensed and regulated care. Inclusion of informal providers may occur by extending certain components of the QRIS to family, friend, and neighbor caregivers. For example, Illinois provides higher reimbursement rates to family, friend, and neighbor caregivers who complete different levels of training. In contrast, other models may be created for family, friend, and neighbor caregivers in the tradition of family support and parent education rather than framing it as quality improvement support (Porter, 2007). These supports may be peripheral to the QRIS but provide a critical resource for family, friend, and neighbor caregivers in the early care and education system.

Summary of Progress Toward Effective QRISs for System Building

The field of early care and education is newly recognizing the potential for QRISs to play a role in system building. Little is known, though, regarding the role of QRISs, in moving toward an integrated, high-quality early care and education system. State evaluations focus primarily on determining the validity of the quality rating and the change in quality of participating programs over time. A challenge to the field is to agree upon the scope and components for a system and to gather data documenting the impact of QRISs on the system. As states work toward building a system, they will continue to face these and other challenges.

Finally, we offer a caution about the role of QRIS in system building. The QRIS promise of helping to build an early care and education system implies that the system is high quality and accessible to children and families who want or need care. Although a QRIS can help leaders move toward a system, it is likely not the "silver bullet" to ensure a high-quality system. We must acknowledge the high cost of making high-quality care accessible to families in America and the limited ability of families, programs, providers, and private foundations to support this cost. Estimates of the cost of universal, high-quality care range from $45 to $100 billion (Barnett & Masse, 2003; Helburn & Bergmann, 2002). Without significant investments in early care and education, we should expect limited—albeit possibly important—improvements in the overall system of early care and education.

ACHIEVING THE QRIS PROMISE ACROSS PROGRAMS, PARENTS, AND SYSTEMS

As QRISs continue to be developed in states and localities, tracking the effectiveness of existing strategies and evaluating planned variation in QRIS are necessary. Researchers, policymakers, and practitioners recognize the exciting potential of QRIS to achieve multiple goals but are also calling for an approach to new growth that incorporates emerging information about effective practices (Child Trends, 2009a). Many decisions will still be "best guesses" as innovations are built into QRIS to meet the needs of target populations and key stakeholders. Yet there is also an increasing call for making evidence-based decisions in QRIS. In particular, as pilot and existing programs are reshaped by fiscal constraints, policy makers need information about which elements of their QRIS are working as intended and which are not contributing to desired outcomes. Implementing this information should be part of a predictable cycle in which participants in the QRIS—programs and parents—know when changes are going to be made and are informed about the purpose of revisions to existing practices and policies.

Structures are being developed to support the field with information about best practices in design and implementation and to build direct connections with researchers who can assist with evaluation efforts and synthesis of findings. For example, the National Child Care Information and Technical Assistance Center has produced a number of resources on QRIS. In addition, the National QRIS Learning Network founded by the Build Initiative and the Smart Start's National Technical Assistance Center is a new initiative that will create opportunities for sharing information about best practices, learning from new research, and providing targeted technical assistance. At the federal level, the Office of Planning, Research, and Evaluation has supported a series of meetings convening researchers, policy makers, and practitioners to identify and discuss pressing issues in the measurement of quality and in the evaluation of quality initiatives and QRIS (Child Trends, 2006, 2009a, 2009b). These meetings have led to the funding of new research on QRIS (the Child Care Quality Rating System Assessment project) and initial support of a Quality Initiatives Research and Evaluation Consortium (INQUIRE) that will make research findings more available to stakeholders and provide opportunities for planning and discussing new approaches and new questions for research on QRIS. These and other efforts will provide a forum for sharing new evidence on QRIS, asking questions about the effectiveness of QRIS practices, and for acknowledging successes and challenges in the quest to better support early childhood programs, parents, and children.

With increased federal attention and funds through efforts like the proposed Early Learning Challenge grants, we expect states to continue developing and refining quality rating and improvement systems. This chapter has highlighted some of the promises made with the QRIS framework, many of which are yet to be fulfilled. As researchers, we have underscored in this chapter the need for more systematic evaluation to define indicators of an effective quality rating and improvement system in improving program quality, helping parents make informed child care choices, and moving toward an integrated system of early care and education. We and other researchers are also working to help support state leaders as they aim to design, implement, and evaluate their QRIS based on the best possible evidence and methodology.

As observers and participants in many conversations about QRIS, we believe that the development of QRISs in the United States is at a critical juncture. The current path involves continued development of individual QRISs that are created within the confines of available resources and political and economic contexts, and, to some degree, building on and learning from other QRIS examples. The resulting QRISs vary in the definition of *quality* that is used, the effectiveness of the services, and the degree to which innovations in measurement or service delivery can be implemented. An alternative path is also possible. This path may involve, for example, the collective development of a "core" set of recommended QRIS components that could be implemented in QRIS, with flexibility to add other components that suit stakeholders' particular interests and needs. This path would also articulate expected outcomes for systems, programs, families, and children and highlight the importance of managing expectations to match inputs and resources. We believe that investment of federal, state, and private resources in research and evaluation of planned variations would greatly improve the evidence base needed to inform the development of these support structures. We hope that this chapter can serve, in part, to spark discussions about the creation of a roadmap for the future of QRISs.

REFERENCES

Ackerman, D.J. (2008). Coaching as part of a pilot quality rating scale initiative: Challenges to—and support for—the change-making process. *Early Childhood Research and Practice, 10*(2). Retrieved on September 29, 2009, from http://ecrp.uiuc.edu/v10n2/ackerman.html

Barnard, W., Smith, W.E., Fiene, R., & Swanson, K. (2006). *Evaluation of Pennsylvania's Keystone STARS quality rating system in child care settings*. Pittsburgh: University of Pittsburgh School of Education, Office of Child Development. Retrieved on September 29, 2009, from http://www.pakeys.org/docs/Keystone%20STARS%20Evaluation.pdf

Barnett, W.S., & Masse, L.N. (2003). Funding issues for early childhood education and care programs. In D. Cryer & R.M. Clifford (Eds.), *Early childhood education and care in the USA* (pp. 137–166). Baltimore: Paul H. Brookes Publishing Co.

Brandon, R.N., & Stutman, T.J. (2009). Potential improvements to Ohio's Step Up to Quality program: Quality-based costs to providers, families, and funding agencies. University of Washington: Human Services Policy Center. Retrieved August 30, 2009, from http://hspc.org/publications/financeECEpubs.aspx

Bromer, J., Paulsell, D., Porter, T., Henly, J.R., Ramsburg, D., Weber, R. & Families and Quality Workgroup Members. (in press). Family-sensitive caregiving: A key component of quality in early care and education arrangements. In M. Zaslow, I. Martinez-Beck, K. Tout, & T. Halle (Eds.), *Measuring quality in early childhood settings*. Baltimore: Paul H. Brookes Publishing Co.

Bruner, C., Ray, A., Wright, M.S., & Copeman, A. (2009). Quality rating improvement systems for a multi-ethnic society. Retrieved July 15, 2009, from http://www.buildinitiative.org/content/diversity-and-equity

Bruner, C. (2004). Building an early learning system: The ABCs of planning and governance structures. Retrieved July 15, 2009, from http://www.buildinitiative.org/content/governance

Bryant, D.M. (2001). *Validating North Carolina's 5-Star child care licensing system.* Chapel Hill, NC: Frank Porter Graham Child Development Center.

Burton, A. Whitebook, M., Young, M., Bellm, D., Wayne, C., Brandon, R., & Maher, E. (2002). *Estimating the size and components of the U.S. child care workforce and caregiving population: Key findings from the child care workforce estimate.* Washington, DC, and Seattle, WA: Center for the Child Care Workforce and Human Services Policy Center. Retrieved August 7, 2009, from http://www.ccw.org/storage/ccworkforce/documents/publications/ccw_exec_final.pdf

Buysse, V. (2009). Program quality and early childhood inclusion: Recommendations for professional development. *Topics in Early Childhood Special Education, 20*(5), 1–10.

Buysse, V., Winton, P.J., & Rous, B. (2009). Reaching consensus on a definition of professional development for the early childhood field. *Topics in Early Childhood Special Education, 28*(4), 235–243.

Chase, R., Arnold, J., Schauben, L., & Shardlow, B. (2005, December). *Child care use in Minnesota: 2004 statewide household child care survey.* St. Paul, MN: Wilder Research.

Chase, R., & Moore, C. (2008, February). *Early learning conditions among low-income families in Minneapolis, Saint Paul, Blue Earth and Nicollet Counties. Baseline report prepared for the Minnesota Early Learning Foundation.* St. Paul, MN: Wilder Research.

Cheatam, J., Pope, B., & Myers, G. (2005). *Evaluating quality in state child care licensing: The Tennessee Report Card and Star-Quality Child Care program.* Retrieved September 29, 2009, from https://www.sworps.utk.edu/ann_rep_2005/docs/germanypaper.pdf

Child Care Bureau. (2007, Winter/Spring). *Child care bulletin.* Retrieved September 29, 2009, from http://www.nccic.acf.hhs.gov/ccb/issue32.pdf

Child Trends. (2006). *Roundtable on measuring quality in early childhood and school-age settings: At the junction of research, policy, and practice.* Washington, DC: Meeting notes prepared for the U.S. Department of Health and Human Services, Administration for Children and Families, Office of Planning, Research, and Evaluation. Retrieved March 6, 2009, from http://www.researchconnections.org/location/ccrca12621

Child Trends. (2009a). *Meeting on evaluation of state quality rating systems.* Washington, DC: Meeting notes prepared for the U.S. Department of Health and Human Services, Administration for Children and Families, Office of Planning, Research, and Evaluation. Retrieved from the Early Care and Education Research Connections Web site at http://www.researchconnections.org.

Child Trends. (2009b). *Roundtable on developing the next wave of quality measures for early childhood and school-age programs.* Washington, DC: Meeting notes prepared for the U.S. Department of Health and Human Services, Administration for Children and Families, Office of Planning, Research, and Evaluation.

Coffman, J., Stover Wright, M., & Bruner, C. (2006). Beyond parallel play: Emerging state and community planning roles in building early learning systems. Retrieved July 15, 2009, from http://www.buildinitiative.org/content/build-issued-research-and-policy-briefs.

Cryer, D., & Burchinal, M. (1997). Parents as child care consumers. *Early Childhood Research Quarterly, 12*(1), 35–58.

Gallagher, J., Clifford, R.M., & Maxwell, K.L. (2004). Getting from here to there: To an ideal early preschool system. *Early Childhood Research and Practice, 6*(1). Retrieved September 29, 2009, from http://ecrp.uiuc.edu/v6n1

Golan, S., Spiker, D., Peterson, D., Mercier, B., Snow, M., & Williamson, C. (2008, June). *Parent voices: A statewide look. Washington State Department of Early Learning parent needs assessment: Phone survey.* Menlo Park, CA: SRI International.

Harms, T., Clifford, R.M., & Cryer, D. (2005). *Early childhood environment rating scale–revised.* New York: Teachers College Press.

Harms, T., Cryer, D., & Clifford, R.M. (2007). *Family child care environment rating scale–revised.* New York: Teachers College Press.

Harms, T., Cryer, D., & Clifford, R.M. (2003). *Infant/toddler environment rating scale–revised.* New York: Teachers College Press.

Harms, T., Jacobs, E.V., & White, D.R. (1996). *School-age care environment rating scale*. New York: Teachers College Press.

Helburn, S.W., & Bergmann, B.R. (2002). *America's childcare problem: The way out*. New York: Palgrave.

Howes, C., Pianta, R., Bryant, D., Hamre, B., Downer, J., & Soliday-Hong, S. (2008). *Ensuring effective teaching in early childhood education through linked professional development systems, quality rating systems and state competencies: The role of research in an evidence-driven system*. National Center for Research in Early Childhood Education. Retrieved July 10, 2009, from http://www.ncrece.org/wordpress/products/publications/

Johnson, K., & Knitzer, J. (2006). *Early childhood comprehensive systems that spend smarter: Maximizing resources to serve vulnerable children* (Issue Brief 1). National Center for Children in Poverty. Retrieved July 10, 2009, from http://www.nccp.org/projects/thrive_pubs.html

Kagan, S.L. (2008). *On buckets, banks, and hearts: Aligning early childhood standards and systems*. Presentation at the Build Conference on Quality Rating and Improvement Systems, Minneapolis, MN.

Kagan, S.L., & Cohen, N.E. (1997). *Not by chance: Creating an early care and education system for America's children*. New Haven, CT: Bush Center in Child Development and Social Policy, Yale University.

Kentucky Department of Education. (2008). *STARS for KIDS NOW Child Care Quality Rating System Standards: Licensed Type I Centers*. Retrieved May 30, 2009, from http://www.kde.state.ky.us/KDE/Instructional+Resources/Early+Childhood+Development/STARS++for+KIDS+NOW+(Quality+Rating+System).htm

Maxwell, K.L. (2008). Pilot test of the draft Rhode Island BrightStars child care center and preschool framework. Chapel Hill: University of North Carolina at Chapel Hill. Retrieved August 27, 2009, from http://www.rikidscount.org/matriarch/MultiPiecePage.asp_Q_PageID_E_665_A_PageName_E_RIQRS

Merriam Webster's Collegiate® Dictionary, 11th Edition ©2010 by Merriam-Webster, Incorporated (www.Merriam-Webster.com).

Minnesota Department of Education and Minnesota Department of Human Services. (2007, January). *Child care information and rating system-Parent focus group results*. DHS-4965-ENG 1-07. St. Paul, MN: Authors.

Mitchell, A.W. (2005). *Stair steps to quality: A guide for states and communities developing quality rating systems for early care and education*. Alexandria, VA: United Way of America, Success by 6.

National Association for the Education of Young Children. (2009). *Quality benchmark for cultural competence*. Retrieved September 29, 2009, http://www.naeyc.org/files/naeyc/file/policy/state/QBCC_Tool.pdf

National Association of Child Care Resource and Referral Agencies. (2009, January). *Parent perceptions of child care in the United States: NACCRRA's national poll, November 2008*. Washington, DC.

Norris, D.J., Dunn, L., & Eckert, L. (2003). *"Reaching for the stars": Center validation study final report*. Norman, OK: Early Childhood Collaborative of Oklahoma.

North Carolina Office of School Readiness. (2008). More at Four pre-kindergarten program guidelines and requirements. Retrieved July 10, 2009, from http://www.osr.nc.gov/MoreFour/ProgramGuidelines.asp

Pianta, R.C., La Paro, K.M., & Hamre, B.K. (2008). *Classroom assessment scoring system*. Baltimore: Paul H. Brookes Publishing Co.

Pope, B., Denny, J.H., Magda, J., Homer, K., & Cunningham, M. (2007). *Tennessee Report Card & Star-Quality program—Year 5 annual report*. Knoxville: University of Tennessee College of Social Work, Office of Research and Public Service.

Porter, T. (2007). Assessing initiatives for family, friend and neighbor care: An overview of models and evaluations. *Research to Policy Connections, No. 5*. New York: Child Care and Early Education Research Connections.

Smith, L., & Sarkar, M. (2008). *Making quality child care possible: Lessons from NACCRRA's military partnerships*. Washington, DC: National Association of Child Care Resource and Referral Agencies.

Sylva, K., Siraj-Blatchford, I., & Taggart, B. (2006). *Assessing quality in the early years: Early Childhood Environment Rating Scale Extension (ECERS-E)*. London: Trentham.

Thornburg, K.R., Mauzy, D., Mayfield, W.A., Hawks, J.S., Sparks, A., Mumford, J., et al. (in press). Data-driven decision making in preparation for large scale quality rating system implementation. In M. Zaslow, I. Martinez-Beck, K. Tout, & T. Halle (Eds.), *Measuring quality in early childhood settings*. Baltimore: Paul H. Brookes Publishing Co.

Tout, K., Zaslow, M., Halle, T., & Forry, N. (2009). *Issues for the next decade of quality rating and improvement systems* (OPRE Issue Brief #3). Washington, DC: Child Trends.

Winton, P.J., McCollum, J.A., & Catlett, C. (2008). A framework and recommendations for a cross-agency professional development system. In P.J. Winton, J.A. McCollum, & C. Catlett (Eds.), *Practical approaches to early childhood professional development:* Evidence, strategies, and resources (pp. 263–272). Washington, DC: ZERO TO THREE: National Center for Infants, Todders, and Families.

Witte, A.D., & Queralt, M. (2004, January). *What happens when child care inspections and complaints are made available on the Internet?* (Working Paper #10227). Cambridge, MA: National Bureau of Economic Research.

Zaslow, M., & Forry, N. (2009, March). *Understanding parent use of child care quality information*. Paper presented at the National Association of Child Care Resource and Referral Agencies 2009 National Policy Symposium, Washington, DC.

Zaslow, M., Tout, K., Halle, T., & Forry, N. (2009). *Multiple purposes for measuring quality in early childhood settings: Implications for collecting and communicating information on quality* (OPRE Issue Brief #2). Washington, DC: Child Trends.

Zellman, G.L., & Perlman, M. (2008). *Child-care quality rating and improvement systems in five pioneer states*. Santa Monica, CA: RAND Corporation.

Zellman, G.L., Perlman, M., Le, V.-N., & Setodji, C.M. (2008). *Assessing the validity of the Qualistar Early Learning Quality Rating and Improvement System as a tool for improving childcare quality*. Santa Monica, CA: RAND Corporation.

CHAPTER 6

Professional Development and Quality Initiatives

Two Essential Components of an Early Childhood System

Pamela J. Winton

Quality in early childhood programs clearly must be built upon a foundation of a highly competent workforce equipped with the knowledge, skills, and decision-making abilities to positively influence young children's learning. Such a high-quality workforce results from an efficient and effective professional development (PD) system. For this reason, any initiative for monitoring quality in early childhood programs and rewarding excellence aligns with a solid PD system. Only with an integrated system of quality monitoring for building continuous improvements through professional development for the workforce can we ensure positive outcomes for all children and families.

Ideally, a human service system develops, is implemented, and is managed in a cohesive fashion, whereby the ultimate outcomes for the individuals being served drive the other components of the system (e.g., determine the practices that achieve those outcomes, the competencies needed to implement those practices, the professional development needed to build those competencies, and the quality monitoring approaches that must guarantee that those skills and practices are implemented). The system must operate in a dynamic fashion with efficient feedback loops between the components. Child and family outcome data from intervention effectiveness studies inform what constitutes effective practices. Quality assurance processes evolve to mirror and support the newly defined practices and the PD needed for practitioners to implement those practices.

Creating these dynamic, data-driven systems is a challenge for all human service agencies. In the early childhood field, the challenges in creating such a system are enormous. First of all, there is no early childhood system. The fragmentation and misalignment of these key components of an early childhood system have been described in recent literature (Howes & Pianta, in press; Winton & West, in press) and some of the root causes identified (Winton & West). These causes include the historical lack of political will and public investment in early childhood. As a result, the demand for early childhood services has led to a conglomeration of programs (e.g., public prekindergarten [pre-K]; Head Start, private for-profit child care, private nonprofit child care, early intervention) with a range of funding sources, motives, and missions. This has meant that parallel early childhood systems have been developed at national and state levels with duplication across personnel standards and competencies, certification and licensure requirements, program standards, outcome measures, monitoring and quality assurance initiatives, and PD networks (Winton & West). This duplication is important in understanding the complexity of the fragmentation challenges. Each sector (e.g., Head Start, pre-K, child care, early intervention) struggles with efforts to integrate PD with teacher competence and practices, child and family outcomes, and quality assurances. Solving these same struggles across multiple sectors and then integrating the results into one dynamic, data-driven early childhood professional development system is particularly daunting.

The purpose of this chapter is to first examine the systems-level challenges from the perspective of one component—professional development—and to identify ways that the interface between quality assurance initiatives and PD could be strengthened to ensure a high-quality workforce. Quality assurance refers to planned and systematic processes (e.g., monitoring, accreditation, licensing, credentialing) that provide confidence in a product's suitability for its intended purpose. The product in this case is high-quality early care and education. The first section of the chapter examines and defines PD and what we know about it from research, followed by an examination of the interface between PD and two quality assurance initiatives. The chapter includes a focus on gaps and challenges and concludes with a set of recommendations for improving PD. The recommendations focus on systematic changes to existing structures, with one exception. The final recommendation proposes a paradigm shift in how professional development curricula are conceptualized and developed. As such, it qualifies as a disruptive innovation, described in Chapter 9 of this book, a dramatic but positive change to the status quo.

DEFINING EARLY CHILDHOOD PROFESSIONAL DEVELOPMENT

Being a professional is generally defined as being competent in a particular field or discipline demonstrated by having met certain academic qualifications or other criteria established by a licensing body. In the field of early childhood, there are no agreed-upon criteria or measures for demonstrating competence or academic qualifications that must be obtained to teach young children. In addition, there is no uniform, agreed-upon definition or terminology related to professional development to prepare or support individuals entering or practicing in the field. Sometimes the term *workforce development* rather than *professional development* is used to reflect the fact that there are no academic qualifications for entering the field. A variety of other terms—*teacher education, preservice, personnel preparation*—have been used to describe professional development provided for those seeking academic credit or degrees under the auspices of institutions of higher education (IHEs), as distinguished from the terms *training, inservice training,* or *continuing education,* which often refer to learning experiences primarily provided outside of IHEs.

The definitional challenges persist when describing approaches to PD. A host of different "relationship-based" approaches to PD—such as mentoring, coaching, consultation, and Communities of Practice—are sometimes referred to in interchangeable ways and have no agreed-upon operational definitions or clearly defined sets of procedures that set them apart from one another.

The absence of academic criteria or demonstrated competence for entering the field, the lack of agreement on terms for describing professional development, the absence of operational definitions for approaches to PD, and the bifurcation of PD into two separate systems of *preservice* and *inservice* are all factors that have negatively affected efforts to study and make improvements to PD.

For the purposes of this chapter, a broad, all-encompassing definition of PD, inclusive of all the examples of PD provided above, is used. PD is defined as "facilitated teaching and learning experiences that are transactional and designed to support the acquisition of professional knowledge, skills and dispositions as well as the application of this knowledge in practice" (Buysse, Winton, & Rous, 2009; National Professional Development Center on Inclusion [NPDCI], 2008, p. 3). The key components of the PD definition include 1) characteristics and contexts of the learners and the children they serve and the PD providers (the *who*); 2) the content focus of professional development (*what* professionals should know and be able to do); and 3) the organization and facilitation of learning experiences (the *how*, or the methods and approaches used to implement PD).

The consumers of PD in the early childhood field (the *who*) represent a myriad of disciplines, organizations and backgrounds, and education levels. They serve a changing population of children and families with increasing numbers of children who are nonwhite and dual language learners (U.S. Census Bureau, 2008). That change and the growing number of children with disabilities being served in regular early childhood settings (Data Accountability Center, n.d.) are

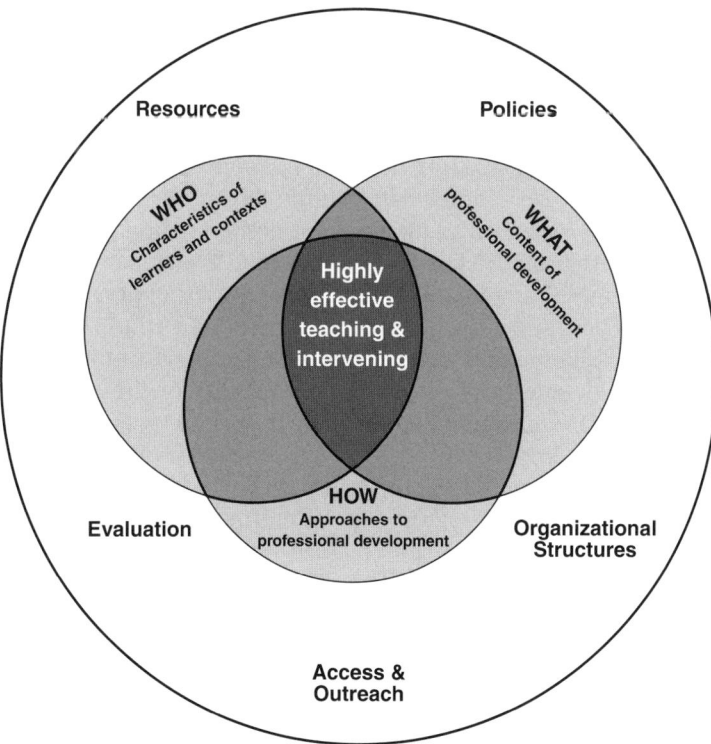

Figure 6.1. NPDCI conceptual framework for professional development in early childhood. (From National Professional Development Center on Inclusion (2008), Reprinted with permission.)

contextual changes that must be considered when thinking about the needs of the consumers of professional development. The characteristics and backgrounds of those who provide PD (e.g., faculty, trainers, consultants, mentors, coaches) are another aspect of the *who*. PD providers serve a critical role as "knowledge mediators" and as such are generally expected to have early childhood content knowledge and competence in providing PD effectively. Because the competencies and qualifications for being a PD provider have not been defined in early childhood, this is an additional aspect of the *who* that is varied and ill defined in terms of backgrounds, experiences, and PD needs.

The guidance to PD providers about the *what* of PD comes from multiple sources. One source for foundational content are the personnel standards and recommended practice guidelines developed by national professional organizations, such as the National Association for the Education of Young Children (NAEYC), the Division for Early Childhood (DEC) of the Council for Exceptional Children (CEC), the Council for Professional Recognition, and the National Board for Professional Teaching Standards. Winton and West (in press) provide more information about each of these sets of national standards. In addition to national personnel standards, a number of states (80%) have developed personnel competencies for early educators (National Child Care Information and Technical Assistance Center [NCCIC], 2007).

The *what* is also shaped by current and emerging research on effective practices. The evidence-based practice movement, which emphasizes both a decision-making process (Buysse & Wesley, 2006) and a set of research-based practices that have been validated through a rigorous review process (Odom et al., 2005), has become a focus in early childhood. It has brought needed attention to skills for implementing specific research-based practices and the ability to take into account multiple factors (e.g., relevance of research to specific situation, related policies, family perspectives, and unique context) in deciding on and implementing a practice approach. A challenge for PD providers and planners is how to find, organize, and distill the various sources of information into relevant, useful PD curricula.

The *how* of PD (approaches and methods for designing and facilitating learning) is guided by research on effective approaches to PD coupled with the needs of the *who* in terms of the knowledge, skills, dispositions, and practices they must master (the *what*). The importance of this alignment is a central theme of the NPDCI PD definition. Challenges to achieving that alignment, outlined by Winton and West (in press), include the following: 1) variability of the *who* in terms of levels of education and competency expectations; 2) lack of agreement on the *what* because of different sets of standards and competencies from national organizations and states that are neither consistent with each other nor organized and updated to reflect changing demographics, emerging research-based practices, and the evidence-based practice movement; and 3) inadequate attention paid to the quality of the *how*.

DEFINING PROFESSIONAL DEVELOPMENT SYSTEMS

A multitude of contextual factors contribute to the effectiveness of PD and constitute what is often called a PD system. Several early childhood PD systems frameworks and accompanying resources (Lemoine, 2008; NCCIC, 2007; NPDCI, 2008) have been proposed. Each has included the importance of planning and situating PD within a broad context that includes factors such as supportive and dynamic organizational structures, policies, outreach and access, data systems, standards and evaluation, and quality assurance, such as credentialing and certification. Feedback loops among these components of the PD system are important for ensuring the effectiveness and continuous improvements of PD so that it functions effectively within the broader early childhood system described in the introduction.

RESEARCH ON PROFESSIONAL DEVELOPMENT

Volumes have been written about PD, and lots of money has been spent studying it, which makes the next sentence unexpected. Very little rigorous research is available to address the question often posed by policy makers: What is the best PD investment to ensure quality teaching and positive child and family outcomes? That question is hard to answer because there are few rigorous studies that make the complete causal connection from PD to teaching practices to child and family outcomes. That is true in general K–12 education (Whitehurst, 2002) and special education (Goe, 2006) and is the case for studies focused specifically on preservice education (Cochran-Smith & Zeichner, 2005) or on inservice education (Wei, Darling-Hammond, Andree, Richardson, & Orphanos, 2009). Studies of child care conducted in the 1990s provided correlational evidence that higher quality early childhood programs and positive outcomes for children were associated with early childhood teachers having degrees (Cost, Quality, and Child Outcomes Study Team, 1995). However, the strength of that relationship has been called into question by recent re-analyses of datasets from several large-scale studies (Early et al., 2006; Early et al., 2007). The reanalyses elevated the need to focus more intentionally on the quality of early childhood PD and identify effective approaches for implementing it. Ensuring that teachers have access and support to enroll in degree-granting early childhood programs is important but must be considered as one of many interrelated strategies for achieving a high-quality workforce.

The most definitive statement about PD approaches from reviews on the topic is that episodic, one-shot workshops are not effective in building skills (Whitehurst, 2002). This may come as no surprise. What makes it disturbing is that research indicates that workshops are the most likely approach to training and technical assistance (TA) taken by state agencies (Center to Inform Personnel Preparation Policy and Practice in Early Intervention and Preschool Education, 2007a, 2007b). State policy makers need access to the best available research to make decisions about PD approaches to fund. That guidance is available from research summaries of studies representing a broad array of methodologies that do not necessarily meet the gold standard for research (i.e., random assignment to treatment and control groups, valid, reliable observation of practices and outcomes) but nevertheless provide some direction.

A recent review by Wei and colleagues (2009) identified key principles in the design of learning experiences that affect teacher knowledge and practices. The review included studies representing a range of methodologies. From this review, some broad themes were identified about the content, context, and approaches for delivering PD. The conclusions were similar to those made in a PD analysis report by Snow-Renner and Lauer (2005) and a research synthesis conducted by Trivette (2005) on the guided design approach to PD. That is, PD is more likely to positively affect learner outcomes if it is focused on specific content and/or instructional strategies rather than general content, is of considerable duration, is infused with active learning opportunities, is characterized by collective participation (e.g., team based), and incorporates or is aligned with standards, curriculum, and assessments. The key principles identified in the literature review extend the broad assumptions of adult learning as described by Knowles, Holten, and Swanson (1998) a decade ago. That is, the process of learning is optimized when methods ensure that learners are ready to learn, self-directed, and actively involved in content. The recent reviews extend the assumptions about adult learning by demonstrating the importance of focusing PD on practice-centered knowledge.

These basic design principles provide guidance to faculty and PD providers at a broad level, and are an important source of evidence for designing effective PD. In addition, PD approaches must match the context and characteristics of the learners with the content and the level of learner outcome desired as a result of the PD. In some situations learners may need basic content information. To address this need a PD approach such as a workshop designed to impact knowledge at an awareness level might be appropriate. In most situations the desired outcomes of PD are at the level of skills and/or implementation. This would require a different approach to PD (e.g., active learning, of considerable duration, situated in practice context) in order to impact learner outcomes at skill and implementation levels. Given the extent to which workshops are used as a PD approach, being clear that the expected impact of a workshop is awareness level should cause PD planners to rethink their PD methods. Figure 6.2 is an illustration of how a PD provider might think about aligning the PD approach with the level of learner impact desired.

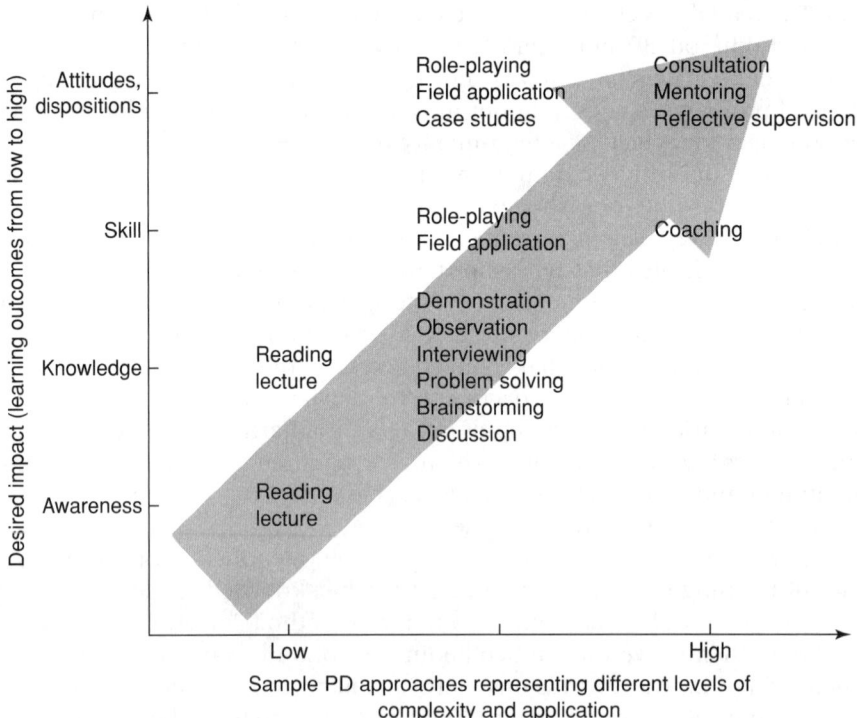

Figure 6.2. Matching PD approaches to desired PD outcomes. (From Harris, B.M. (1980), Improving staff performance through in-service education, Needham, MA: Allyn & Bacon, Adapted with permission.)

In summarizing what is known about PD in early childhood, the following are some of the identified challenges:

- There are no agreed-upon competencies or educational criteria for being admitted to the field of early childhood.

- Definitional issues abound. There are no agreed-upon terms for professional development as an overarching concept, nor are there agreed-upon methods for reaching consensus on proposed definitions of PD, such as the one recently put forth by NPDCI (see p. 115). In addition, there are no operational definitions of different PD approaches.

- Research on effective PD approaches is limited, although some important principles can be identified from the literature to guide PD planning and decision making.

- The research that does exist suggests that most PD is provided at basic levels. There is little evidence that PD affects teacher practices in ways that improve child outcomes.

PROFESSIONAL DEVELOPMENT AND QUALITY ASSURANCE INITIATIVES

PD systems, in their current state, are not adequate to the task of preparing and supporting a competent and high-quality early childhood workforce. From a systems vantage point, it is fitting to examine how quality assurance initiatives—such as accreditation, certification, and monitoring—might bring improvements to the PD system or offer avenues for improvement. These initiatives should serve as the linchpin of a PD system. They motivate learners to participate in PD, they shape the focus of the PD content, and they undergird the quality of the PD experiences available to practitioners. A number of national and state-based quality assurance initiatives with links to professional development are in place in early childhood, some more recently as part of the overall accountability movement in education. These initiatives include the following: national accreditation of early childhood teacher education programs in IHEs, state teacher licensure and certification, NAEYC early childhood program accreditation, early learning guidelines as specified by the Good Start, Grow Smart initiative, state child care program licensing, state quality rating and improvement systems (QRISs), and the State Performance Plan Annual Performance Report (SPP APR) required of state Part C and Section 619 agencies by the U.S. Department of Education, Office of Special Education Programs. This next section of the chapter describes two of them briefly (accreditation of IHE programs and QRIS). Then, using the NPDCI PD Conceptual Framework (see Figure 6.1), this section examines the PD associated with each, including the targeted learners, the content focus, and the method of delivering the PD. This analysis provides a means for exploring the interrelationships of quality initiatives and PD and the extent to which the initiatives could bring improvements to PD.

Accreditation of IHEs

A quality initiative focused directly on PD is the accreditation of early childhood teacher preparation programs in IHEs. There are two separate programs that administer this voluntary initiative: one for early childhood 4-year (bachelor of arts [B.A.] and graduate degree) programs housed in schools of education, through the National Council for Accreditation of Teacher Preparation (NCATE), and the other for 2-year early childhood programs, launched in 2006 and administered by NAEYC (http://www.naeyc.org/accreditation). The NCATE program relies on the national early childhood personnel standards of NAEYC for reviewing teacher education programs with an early childhood specialization. NCATE-approved teacher education programs that also receive NAEYC recognition demonstrate that their graduates have been assessed on the NAEYC standards and that they use student performance data to improve the program. The early childhood special education standards of CEC/DEC guide the review process for early childhood special education programs. The NAEYC accreditation program of associate degree programs relies on NAEYC personnel standards in its review. These accreditation programs play an important role in assuring consumers that they are investing in PD that meets a certain basic level of quality in terms of broad content coverage (i.e., link with national standards) and in terms of some of the important characteristics of PD approaches (i.e., dispersed over time and usually includes a field experience, practica, or student teaching, thus situating PD within a practice content). Examining some of the gaps in the accreditation programs is helpful in identifying how they can more be more effective in building a high-quality workforce through PD.

One gap relates to the incomplete coverage of the target audience (the learners or the *who*) involved in this quality initiative. Although NAEYC's 2-year IHE accreditation is an important but emerging program and a small but growing number of programs are participating, the majority of accredited early childhood programs are those accredited by NCATE at the B.A. and graduate level. Not all early childhood B.A. and graduate programs participate in NCATE. Programs that participate are those providing licensure and housed in schools of education. A recent national survey indicated that 27% of early childhood B.A. and graduate level programs have their administrative homes in a variety of other university departments other than education (Maxwell, Lim, & Early, 2006). In addition, even those early childhood programs that are part of NCATE-approved teacher education programs may not be NAEYC recognized. The voluntary nature of the accreditation program and the many early childhood teacher preparation programs not under any accreditation system at this point means that not all consumers of PD provided in degree-granting programs (the *who*) have an assurance of basic quality.

One contributor to the content gap (the *what*) in the accreditation process relates to the lack of agreed-upon national standards. As mentioned earlier, the two major national early childhood professional organizations (NAEYC and CEC/DEC) have separate sets of standards, a tradition dating to the era when young children with disabilities were educated in separate specialized settings. Early childhood teacher education (ECE) programs seeking NCATE and NAEYC accreditation must demonstrate how NAEYC standards are addressed in coursework and practica, and early childhood special education (ECSE) programs must do the same but with CEC/DEC standards. There are some early childhood teacher education programs with a blended program, usually located in the small number of states with blended state licensure. Stayton and colleagues (2009) identified seven states whose departments of education have dispensed with separate ECSE and ECE licensures. These states have created a single licensure that serves both groups. The early childhood teacher preparation programs whose graduates are awarded blended licensure must demonstrate how they address both NAEYC and CEC/DEC standards in their coursework and practica in order to receive NCATE accreditation. This is not an easy task given the large number of standards and competencies in each set of national standards that must be integrated. NCATE provides no guidance in how to do that. A bigger gap in adequate coverage of content related to children with disabilities exists in the NAEYC accreditation program of 2-year programs. Accreditation is based solely on NAEYC personnel standards. Although efforts have been made to ensure alignment between NAEYC and CEC/DEC standards, the absence of inclusion of CEC/DEC standards as a rubric for ensuring the quality of 2-year early childhood programs is a shortcoming. It is inconsistent with survey research indicating that the majority of early childhood teacher preparation programs (approximately 60%) state that preparing early childhood special educators and early interventionists is part of their primary mission (Early & Winton, 2001). The implication is that IHEs have embraced the early childhood inclusion mandate (at least at the level of stated mission), and the national organizations and accreditation process have not fully supported that direction.

It is important to look beyond mission statements in examining another aspect of the content gap—the extent to which course and practica content reflects emerging research findings and the changes in demographics of children being served. Survey data indicate that early childhood teacher preparation programs do not provide adequate coverage of certain key areas (i.e., disabilities, ethnic and linguistic diversity, and infants and toddlers) (Chang, Early, & Winton, 2005; Early & Winton, 2001; Lim & Maxwell, 2009; Ray, Bowman, & Robbins, 2006). A specific case in point is that of the 60% of early childhood teacher preparation programs that include preparing early childhood special education/early intervention (ECSE/EI) practitioners as part of their primary mission, only 40% required at least one course focused on young children with disabilities (Early & Winton, 2001). In terms of how NCATE accreditation affects key content, findings are disappointing. A national survey by Ray and colleagues (2006) indicated no differences in coverage of diversity content in NCATE- and non-NCATE-accredited early childhood teacher education programs.

In summarizing content issues related to IHE early childhood program accreditation, three are critical: the lack of national standards; inadequate attention to ethnic, linguistic, and ability diversity; and absence of attention to how faculty are kept abreast of emerging research so that content can be incorporated into PD. Too often faculty and instructors depend on textbooks that become outdated almost the moment they are released. PD for PD providers is not a high priority at national, state, or local levels and is done in a scattered fashion when done at all.

An additional gap in the accreditation programs is that little is known about *how* the PD is delivered in accredited programs. For instance, the extent to which active learning and collaborative approaches are infused in the PD is not directly addressed by the accreditation programs. Research indicating that graduate students in early childhood teacher preparation programs, the group most likely to be faculty, do not have exposure to adult learning principles. Research indicates that graduate students in early childhood teacher preparation programs, the group next likely to be faulty, do not have exposure to adult learning principles. (Maxwell, Lim, & Early, 2006) suggests that future faculty are not being adequately prepared to implement effective PD practices.

In summary, accreditation of IHEs is a quality assurance initiative that directly addresses the quality of PD. It ensures that learners are exposed to nationally endorsed content in ways that honor some of the key principles of PD. The shortcomings of this quality assurance system outlined above suggest that a more consistent and integrated approach to accreditation of early childhood teacher preparation is warranted. Having a single set of national standards to guide accreditation is an important aspect of solving the challenges of the national accreditation programs. Providing a focus in the accreditation process on how PD is provided and how PD providers are kept abreast of emerging research and PD approaches is a missing aspect of this quality initiative. It is also important to recognize the inherent limitations of an accreditation system. Agreed-upon measures for assessing learner performance through direct observation are not in place.

QRISs

An emerging and promising quality assurance initiative with a PD component focus is state-implemented QRISs focused on early childhood programs. Approximately 14 states have developed QRISs with more in process (NPDCI, 2008). QRIS is based heavily on a consumer education model. The reasoning is that if consumers have a method for easily identifying high-quality early childhood programs, they will choose these programs over others, thereby putting pressure on all programs to pay attention to program quality. Being a licensed child care program is often a required first step for programs desiring to participate in a QRIS.

There is tremendous variability in these state-developed systems, although generally they have five components that are used to assess and promote program quality (NCCIC, 2007). Two of the five components—practitioner support and quality standards—have a specific focus on PD. The practitioner support component includes certain PD requirements for staff, some linked to licensure, credentials, and degrees. The other link with PD is through the technical assistance (TA) efforts being made by states to promote the quality standards that are part of the QRIS. As described in Chapter 7, the TA varies from state to state in terms of philosophical orientation, practice guidelines, implementation rubrics, and TA provider characteristics. The extent to which the TA needs of early childhood practitioners are aligned with personal standards and research-boxed practices and how that information guides the TA provided, is unknown. A review of QRIS by Howes and colleagues (2008) found few apparent requirements that indicated states were linking the content of PD to competencies. There is also a lack of consistent attention to how QRIS can ensure that each child, including those with disabilities, can be adequately served (NCCIC, 2007; NPDCI, 2008).

The promise of QRIS is strong because it could become a quality assurance system that is used to assess and improve quality across an array of early childhood programs (e.g., Head Start, child care, pre-K, Part C and Section 619) (LeMoine, Lutton, McDonald, & Daniel, in press). Because it is a system still in development, the chances to involve all sectors is strong. The TA approach to PD being used by many states is also promising, in that the approach in its broad definition reflects what is known about effective PD. That is, TA can be intensive and of some duration and situated in practice with active involvement of participants. The absence of agreed-upon credentials or competencies for TA providers and the absence of TA practice guidelines are unmet challenges to this quality initiative.

GAPS AND CHALLENGES

The major gaps and challenges in linking professional development and quality assurance initiatives relate to the weakness of some of the basic building blocks of an early childhood system. These basic gaps include the following:

- The lack of agreement on definitions of key terms related to early childhood systems, such as *competencies, standards,* and *professional development*
- The lack of one set of national standards and competencies tied to a uniform and distinctive early childhood certification
- The lack of attention to the quality of PD and to the needs, characteristics, and quality of those who provide it (i.e., faculty, consultants, TA providers, mentors)
- The voluntary nature of most quality initiatives, meaning that quality is uneven and contingent upon factors, such as consumer pressure, that are not powerful enough to affect broad-scale improvements in quality or incentives to change by participating in PD.

These gaps are further exacerbated by the fragmentation across the weak building blocks comprising standards, competencies, monitoring, and PD. The fragmentation is both within and across sectors. It is common for state efforts to focus on one aspect of the early childhood PD system, such as early childhood competencies, without ensuring that the competencies are being used to guide the professional development materials or activities being implemented within that sector (Winton & West, in press). Trying to collaborate across all PD sectors in terms of competencies, quality assurances, and PD to reduce fragmentation is extraordinarily difficult.

RECOMMENDATIONS: TRADITIONAL AND DISRUPTIVE

The recommendations grow out of the challenges and focus on how to systematically and intentionally strengthen, align, and evaluate the basic structures of the early childhood professional development and quality assurance systems. These recommendations are considered traditional within the concept of disruptive innovations described in Chapter 9. They require intentional and systematic focus on slow and incremental improvements to existing structures. The traditional recommendations are followed by the suggestion of a disruptive innovation, which proposes a different way of conceptualizing PD and PD curricula.

Traditional Recommendations

- Develop national early childhood standards and competencies that are inclusive of all sectors (i.e., higher education, child care, pre-K, Head Start, Part C and 619) and that are updated in a dynamic fashion based on emerging research findings on effective practices and changing demographics.

- Develop a uniform certification program that is linked with the national standards and provides a clear pathway for practitioners to make progress through levels of recognition.

- Develop an agreed-upon set of competencies for PD providers and a system for supporting their professional development on effective intervention practices and effective PD approaches.

- Examine quality assurance and PD systems for points of intersection to unify the disparate systems that exist now. Ensure that the systems are linked to the standards and certification.

- Develop data and evaluation systems that allow for continuous improvements to all key components of the early childhood system (e.g., the standards, certification processes, PD approaches).

- Invest in PD research that takes into the account the complexities of studying the phenomenon. Longitudinal studies are needed that follow learners into work settings and observe the impact of PD on actual practices and child outcomes. Validated, reliable, and agreed-upon measures of early childhood teacher knowledge, skills, and practices are needed so that studies of PD approaches across multiple sites can be aggregated. Operational definitions and fidelity measures of promising PD approaches, such as consultation and coaching, are needed.

Disruptive Innovation: An Evidence-Based Practice Approach to PD

Several years ago, Tom Guskey (2003) made the observation that most PD planners start with the method for delivering the PD (e.g., "Let's plan a workshop, a seminar, a series of trainings") and then map backward to the content and the needs of the learners. Rarely do planners consider the ultimate beneficiaries of the PD—that is, the children and families being served and the outcomes for them that are desired. He suggested that PD planners turn this approach on its head and start with the desired outcomes for children and families. Although this suggestion was made years ago and has been described in subsequent literature as important to follow (Winton & McCollum, 2008), it has not appeared to make an impact on PD planners. The disruptive innovation being recommended extends Guskey's recommendation and reflects the emphasis on practices that has emerged as part of the evidence-based practice (EBP) movement. It suggests that the starting point for PD should be those practices that have been proven through the best available research to be effective in achieving desired outcomes for children and families. It is based on the emerging expectation that early childhood teachers should know about and use EBP to meet the individual learning and socialization needs of each child. It is in keeping with the admonition by the Office of Special Education Programs (OSEP) of the U.S. Department of Education that the early childhood personnel preparation programs they fund should incorporate EBP into their coursework and practica. It is an approach in which two disruptive innovations identified in Chapter 9 (EBP movement and the importance of PD) are integrated to equal a third disruptive innovation (EBP approach to PD). It is an approach to PD being developed by the leadership team of the National Center to Mobilize Early Childhood Knowledge (CONNECT) and is reflected in the online instructional modules they are developing on key content areas identified by the field (http://community.fpg.unc.edu/connect-modules).

A challenge in embedding EBP into PD is the lack of clarity around the meaning of the term *evidence-based practice*. Two meanings have been discussed in the literature. One focuses on identifying certain practices that have been found to be effective through research (Odom et al., 2005). The other focuses on a process by which practitioners reach a practice decision by appraising and integrating various sources of evidence (research, policies, values, and context) (Buysse & Wesley, 2006). This challenge has been addressed by including both approaches to EBP in the design of the CONNECT EBP approach to PD and in the organization of PD curricula that reflects this approach.

The following section provides a description of the EBP approach to PD and the sequence of procedures used by CONNECT in developing online instructional modules for faculty and PD providers based on the approach. The development of the online modules reflects the contributions of the CONNECT leadership team and core staff. Some examples from the CONNECT module on early childhood inclusion are provided next as illustrations of the approach.

The first task in the design sequence is identifying the discrete practice focus for the PD within a broad key content area such as inclusion. For instance, early childhood inclusion has recently been defined through the DEC/NAEYC *Position Statement on Inclusion* (Division for Early Childhood, 2009) as having three key components: access, participation, and support. A discrete set of research-based practices (embedded interventions) that support the participation of young children with disabilities in inclusive settings has been defined and validated through a rigorous review process and research synthesis developed by Snyder (2009). The position statement and the research synthesis were important assets in helping CONNECT with the definition of a practice focus related to inclusion for the development of the CONNECT module on embedded intervention.

The second task in the design sequence relates to organizing content and sources of evidence into a five-step learning cycle modified from Buysse and Wesley's (2006) adaptation of the five-step decision-making process developed in evidence-based medicine. In Step 1, the learner considers a realistic dilemma to be solved. The dilemma is presented from the perspectives of family members and the practitioners in the dilemma. This grounds the PD in a realistic practice context that runs as a thread through the entire module. In Step 2, the learner identifies a practice-focused question within the dilemma that can be answered through various sources of evidence, including the best available research. This step helps the learner move from the dilemma, which raises all kinds of possible foci and questions, to a specific practice focus and establishes the problem-solving context for the learner. The learner is guided in using the Patient Intervention Comparison Outcome, a tool developed in evidence-based medicine, to identify characteristics and intervention needs of the child, family, and program and an intervention practice to investigate in Step 3 that could be effective in addressing those needs. In Step 3, the learner identifies and appraises key sources of evidence related to the practice focus. This process includes further defining the practice focus and learning to recognize examples of it by observing video clips of the practice, followed by observations in real practice settings. The sources of evidence that learners are exposed to include the following: 1) a distillation of laws, policies, and consensus statements from the field related to the practice; 2) a summary of the best available research evidence on the practice; and 3) a resource called Parents Speak Out, which reflect experience-based knowledge about the implementation of the practice from family perspectives. In Step 4, the learner integrates that information and then appraises its relevance to the unique context of the dilemma (e.g., the practice settings, characteristics of child, values of family, their own values and experiences) to make an informed decision and develop a plan for implementation. In Step 5, the learner describes how to evaluate the impact of the practice decision to assess and refine practice.

Each online module has a similar structure. Content is organized into the five-step learning cycle and includes learner activities, audio clips of interviews, video clips of practice, and self-assessment strategies. An instructor's guide for each module includes the following: NAEYC and DEC personnel standards related to the practice focus; U.S. Department of Education, OSEP, SPP APR indicators related to the practice; facilitation tips for implementing the learner activities; and learner assessment strategies. In addition, an online "faculty lounge" is available for sharing ideas, challenges, and approaches for using the modules.

Within that structure, modules are designed to be flexible to address individual learner needs and the variety of PD contexts in which modules might be used. These contexts include coursework, practica, seminars, workshops, consultation, coaching, supervision, and Communities of Practice. Within these contexts, instructors can implement the modules in a variety of formats, including online, face to face, or a combination of online and face to face.

The innovative aspect of the CONNECT modules is the focus on a discrete set of research-based practices and the organization into the five-step learning cycle designed to build evidence-based practice decision-making skills. This is why it is strongly recommended that the learning cycle be followed, regardless of the context or format used, if the desire is to incorporate EBP into PD. The approach acknowledges that all practitioners need certain foundational knowledge, which can be obtained through any number of PD approaches, but beyond that practitioners must be problem solvers who can draw upon funds of knowledge and evidence to address the daily practice challenges of working with young children and their families. They need practice-focused decision-making skills to do that. This approach to PD provides teachers with what they need on Monday morning to do their jobs.

The EBP approach to PD has implications for how PD curricula are organized. The concept of focusing curricula on key practices and organizing and distilling the huge glut of potentially relevant evidence (e.g., research, laws, policies) into digestible chunks for learners provides a focus for those who design professional development modules and textbooks (e.g., faculty, PD providers, agencies, organizations, publishers). The five-step learning cycle provides a framework for organizing the chunks of evidence into a meaningful learning sequence that reflects the literature on how adults learn (e.g., realistic cases to solve, active engagement in content, alignment with standards) and builds on a proven model from medicine for helping practitioners make practice decisions. The approach and related curricula have positive implications for PD providers, making it easier for them to stay abreast of the latest research. They have access to consolidated and focused evidence and practice demonstrations that are often hard to find and distill in relevant and useful ways.

The chapter began with a description of what an ideal early childhood system might look like. It would be managed in a cohesive fashion, whereby the ultimate outcomes of the children and families being served would be the driving force in determining the other components of the systems (e.g., the effective practices, the competencies needed to achieve those practices, the professional development to build those competencies, quality monitoring that guaranteed that the practices were implemented). Based on the content of this chapter, it is clear that a system of that sort is far from reality, hence the need for a disruptive innovation. The fact that an EBP approach to PD could be implemented in a variety of PD contexts with a focus on any key content area that has a set of discrete practices means that it fits one of the characteristics of a disruptive innovation identified by Buysse and Wesley (see Chapter 9); that is, it could be used or modified by anyone who has access to the specifications of the component parts. The fact that the innovation can be implemented even if the other systems-level recommendations related to PD and quality initiatives in this chapter were ignored represents another way the approach qualifies as a disruptive innovation. It can occur outside of the existing organizational structures.

Some aspects of the existing PD system may be further along than others and may provide fertile ground for a disruptive innovation. For instance, it appears that early childhood programs in IHEs are closer to embracing inclusion of children with disabilities as manifest in their stated missions than are professional organizations and accrediting bodies. However, this is an example where desire is ahead of practice, given the lack of attention to inclusion content in their coursework. Taking advantage of the apparent desire to address inclusion in their coursework, the disruptive innovation described above could first be provided to faculty in IHEs, around the topic of inclusion that they espouse to champion in their missions. It could focus on a specific practice, such as embedded interventions, that has been shown to be effective for supporting the participation of young children with disabilities in inclusive settings. An EBP approach to PD curricula on the practice of embedded interventions could be developed and widely disseminated to 2- and 4-year IHE early childhood faculty, accompanied by PD to the faculty so they are supported in their use of the curricula. The curricula could be evaluated to determine if the approach is effective in improving teachers' abilities to implement the practice. If effective, this could lead to further adoption of the EBP approach to PD. This is the strategy being used by the CONNECT project to introduce the EBP approach to PD. Whether this will tip the balance to a new conceptualization for PD is yet to be determined. Meanwhile, the small incremental changes to the PD and quality assurance systems related to PD are needed to supplement efforts to make rapid improvements. There is too much at stake; simultaneous traditional and nontraditional approaches to the PD challenges are necessary to meet the needs for a high-quality workforce capable of meeting the needs of each and every child.

REFERENCES

Buysse, V., & Wesley, P.W. (Eds.). (2006). *Evidence-based practice in the early childhood field*. Washington, DC: ZERO TO THREE.

Buysse, V., Winton, P.J., & Rous, B. (2009). Reaching consensus on a definition of professional development for the early childhood field. *Topics in Early Childhood Special Education, 28*(4), 235–243.

Center to Inform Personnel Preparation Policy and Practice in Early Intervention and Preschool Education. (2007a). *Study VI: State training systems for Section 619 personnel* (Vol. 6, No. 2). Farmington: University of Connecticut Health Center, Author.

Center to Inform Personnel Preparation Policy and Practice in Early Intervention and Preschool Education. (2007b). *Study VI: State technical assistance systems for Section 619 personnel* (Vol. 6, No. 4). Farmington: University of Connecticut Health Center, Author.

Chang, F., Early, D., & Winton, P. (2005). Early childhood teacher preparation in special education at 2- and 4-year institutions of higher education. *Journal of Early Intervention, 27*, 110–124.

Cochran-Smith, M., & Zeichner, K. (2005). Executive summary. In M. Cochran-Smith & K.M. Zeichner (Eds.), *Studying teacher education: The report of the AERA panel on research and teacher education* (pp. 1–36). Mahwah, NJ: Lawrence Erlbaum Associates.

Cost, Quality, and Child Outcomes Study Team. (1995). *Cost, quality, and child outcomes in child care centers public report.* Denver: University of Colorado–Denver, Economics Department.

Data Accountability Center. (n.d.). *Part B national trend data. Table B4D: Number and percentage of children (ages 3–5) receiving special education services in each environment, by race/ethnicity: 2006–2007.* Retrieved August 18, 2009, from https://www.ideadata.org/PartBTrendDataFiles.asp

Division for Early Childhood. (2009). *Early childhood inclusion: A joint position of the Division for Early Childhood (DEC) and the National Association for the Education of Young Children (NAEYC).* Retrieved December 4, 2009, from http://www.dec sped.org/uploads/docs/about_dec/position_concept_papers/PositionStatement_Inclusion_Joint_updated_May 2009.pdf

Early, D.M., Bryant, D.M., Pianta, R.C., Clifford, R.M., Burchinal, M.R., Ritchie, S., et al. (2006). Are teachers' education, major, and credentials related to classroom quality and children's academic gains in pre-kindergarten? *Early Childhood Research Quarterly, 21*(2), 174–195.

Early, D.M., Maxwell, K.L., Burchinal, M., Alva, S., Bender, R.H., Bryant, D., et al. (2007). Teachers' education, classroom quality, and young children's academic skills: Results from seven studies of preschool programs. *Child Development, 78*(2), 558–580.

Early, D., & Winton, P. (2001). Preparing the workforce: Early childhood teacher preparation at 2- and 4-year institutes of higher education. *Early Childhood Research Quarterly, 16*, 285–306.

Goe, L. (2006, November). *The teacher preparation–teacher practices–student outcomes relationship in special education: Missing links and new connections* (Research & Policy Brief). Washington, DC: National Comprehensive Center for Teacher Quality.

Guskey, T.R. (2003). Scooping up meaningful evidence. *Journal of Staff Development, 24*(4), 27–30.

Howes, C., & Pianta, R.C. (Eds.). (in press). *Foundations for teaching excellence: connecting early childhood quality rating, profession development, and competency systems in states.* Baltimore: Paul H. Brookes Publishing Co.

Howes, C., Pianta, R.C., Bryant, D., Hamre, B., Downer, J., & Soliday-Hong, S. (2008). *Ensuring effective teaching in early childhood education through linked professional development systems, quality rating systems and state competencies: The role of research in an evidence-driven system.* Charlottesville: University of Virginia, National Center for Research in Early Childhood Education.

Knowles, M.S., Holton, E.F., III, & Swanson, R.A. (1998). *The adult learner: The definitive classic in adult education and human resource development* (5th ed.). Houston, TX: Gulf.

LeMoine, S. (2008). *Workforce designs: A policy blueprint for state early childhood professional development systems.* Retrieved August 14, 2009, from National Association for the Education of Young Children web site: http://208.118.177.216/policy/ecwsi/pdf/Workforce_Designs.pdf

LeMoine, S., Lutton, A., McDonald, D., & Daniel, J. (in press). Putting the pieces together: Integrated professional standards for the early childhood workforce. In C. Howes & R. Pianta (Eds.), *Foundations for teaching excellence: connecting early childhood quality rating, profession development, and competency systems in states.* Baltimore: Paul H. Brookes Publishing Co.

Lim C.I., Maxwell, K.L., Able-Boone, H., & Zimmer, C.R. (2009). Cultural and linguistic diversity in early childhood teacher preparation: The impact of contextual characteristics on coursework and practica. *Early Childhood Research Quarterly, 24*, 64–76.

Maxwell, K.L., Lim, C.-I., & Early, D.M. (2006). *Early childhood teacher preparation programs in the United States: National report.* Chapel Hill: University of North Carolina, FPG Child Development Institute.

National Child Care Information and Technical Assistance Center. (2007). *Early childhood professional development systems toolkit.* Retrieved April 6, 2009, from http://nccic.acf.hhs.gov/pubs/goodstart/index.html

National Professional Development Center on Inclusion. (2008). *What do we mean by professional development in the early childhood field?* Chapel Hill: University of North Carolina, FPG Child Development Institute, Author.

Odom, S.L., Brantlinger, E., Gersten, R., Horner, R.H., Thompson, B., & Harris, K.R. (2005). Research in special education: Scientific methods and evidence-based practices. *Exceptional Children, 71,* 137–148.

Rakap, S., Snyder, P., McLaughlin, T., & Ryndak, D. (2009, July). *Embedded instruction: Reaching consensus on definition and application.* Presentation given in Barcelona, Spain.

Ray, A., Bowman, B., & Robbins, J. (2006). *Preparing early childhood teachers to successfully educate all children: The contribution of 4-year undergraduate teacher preparation programs.* New York: Foundation for Child Development.

Snow-Renner, R., & Lauer, P. (2005). *Professional development analysis.* Denver, CO: Mid-Continent Research for Education and Learning.

Stayton, V.D., Deitrich, S.L., Smith, B.J., Bruder, M.B., Mogro-Wilson, C., & Swigart, A. (2009). State certification requirements for early childhood special educators. *Infants & Young Children, 23*(1), 4–12.

Trivette, C.M. (2005). Effectiveness of guided design learning strategy on the acquisition of adult problem-solving skills. *Bridges, 3*(1), 1–18. Asheville, NC: Research and Training Center on Early Childhood Development, Orelena Hawks Puckett Institute.

U.S. Census Bureau. (2008). *U.S. Census Bureau news.* Retrieved August 11, 2009, from http://www.census.gov/Press-Release/www/releases/archives/american_community_survey_acs/012634.html

Wei, R.C., Darling-Hammond, L., Andree, A., Richardson, N., & Orphanos, S. (2009). *Professional learning in the learning profession: A status report on teacher development in the United States and abroad.* Dallas, TX: National Staff Development Council.

Whitehurst, G.J. (2002, March 5). *Research on teacher preparation and professional development.* Address to White House Conference on Preparing Tomorrow's Teachers. Retrieved April 26, 2005, from http://www.ed.gov/admins/tchrqual/learn/preparingteachersconference/whitehurst.html

Winton, P., & McCollum, J.A. (2008). Preparing and supporting high-quality early childhood practitioners: Issues and evidence. In P.J. Winton, J.A. McCollum, & C. Catlett (Eds.), *Practical approaches to early childhood professional development: Evidence, strategies, and resources* (pp. 1–12). Washington, DC: ZERO TO THREE: National Center for Infants, Toddlers, and Families.

Winton, P.J., & West, T. (in press). Early childhood competencies: Sitting on the shelf or guiding professional development? In C. Howes & R.C. Pianta (Eds.), *Foundations for teaching excellence: connecting early childhood quality rating, profession development, and competency systems in states.* Baltimore: Paul H. Brookes Publishing Co.

CHAPTER 7

Rethinking Technical Assistance to Support Quality Improvement

Patricia W. Wesley and Virginia Buysse

Across the country, states are implementing a variety of initiatives to improve child care quality. These efforts largely are based on the growing body of knowledge linking child care quality to children's language, math, social, and emotional outcomes (Bryant, Burchinal, Lau, & Sparling, 1994; Howes, Phillips, & Whitebook, 1992; Lamb, 1998; National Institute for Child Health and Human Development [NICHD], 2001, 2005; Peisner-Feinberg et al., 2001; Vandell, 2004), and research showing that many children were enrolled in early child care environments of poor to moderate quality (Cost, Quality, & Child Outcomes Study Team, 1995). For example, public–private partnerships have been established to develop comprehensive systems of early care and education. The goal of these systems is to coordinate and align multiple services and resources to address all aspects of children's early experiences, including their physical and mental health, development and education, and family involvement (Child Care and Early Education Research Connections, 2007). Some states and localities also implement quality rating improvement systems (QRISs) to monitor and increase quality of child care centers and homes and focus considerable resources on professional development activities to increase the knowledge, skills, and stability of the early childhood workforce. As a part of these efforts, technical assistance (TA) has emerged as a key approach to promote the changes necessary to improve program quality.

The early childhood field uses the term *technical assistance* in numerous contexts at the federal, state, regional, and local levels. TA may be provided by federal agencies to state agencies (e.g., to support state administrators' oversight of policy), by state agencies to community agencies (e.g., to support the implementation of state-approved curricula), and by community agencies to early childhood programs (e.g., to enhance global program quality). At the community level, programs including child care, Head Start, prekindergarten, and early childhood special education programs receive TA through multiple vehicles, including child care resource and referral agencies, Head Start, the local school system, and other

---

The authors wish to thank Ivelisse Martinez-Beck, Ph.D., Child Care Research Coordinator, Office of Planning, Research and Evaluation, Administration for Children and Families, U.S. Department of Health and Human Services, for her substantive contributions as a reviewer of this chapter.

organizations funded for this purpose. Policy makers, regulators, professional development providers, administrators, and early childhood educators rely on TA as a preferred mechanism for addressing a host of challenges, such as extending knowledge acquired through courses and workshops to classroom application, preparing programs for national accreditation, supporting compliance with regulatory requirements, and individualizing interventions to meet children's special needs. TA may include various on-site activities such as consultation, coaching, or mentoring or involve the provision of information or resources from a distance.

Overall, TA activities represent a major investment of federal and state dollars. For example, states participating in the Child Care Development Fund (CCDF) program, which provides block grants to states for child care, are mandated to spend a minimum of 4% of their CCDF budget to improve the quality of child care programs. The 2008 appropriation of funds included targeted money to expand activities to improve infant and toddler care, school-age care, and child care resource and referral services. Federal economic stimulus funds available through the American Recovery and Reinvestment Act of 2009 increased discretionary funding of the CCDF program for a 2-year period and targeted funds for quality improvements and for TA activities.

In the most recent reauthorization of Head Start, the Improving Head Start for School Readiness Act of 2007, Congress authorized the provision of TA and training for Head Start programs for the purpose of improving program quality and preparing children to succeed in school. The Office of Head Start is currently redesigning their TA activities to comply with the foci and purposes of TA as stated in the 2007 Head Start Act.

Currently there are at least 18 federally funded early childhood TA projects (including several national centers) working across the country to address such topics as language, literacy, social-emotional development, autism, mental health, inclusion, families, professional development, and the implementation of the Individuals with Disabilities Education Improvement Act. These projects share information about their work through a web site (http://www.ectaconsortium.org; click on "Consortium Participants") and occasional face-to-face meetings that are held to promote coordination and collaboration among them, as they work in many of the same states.

In spite of the funding and good intentions backing TA, the early childhood field faces many obstacles to providing a coordinated and consistent network of supports to programs. Many TA projects are funded to meet the needs of programs as required by different laws authorizing early childhood programs supported by public funds, as well as the specific needs of constituents in states and localities. Efforts to coordinate services are hampered by differences in purpose and requirements.

Another issue that has played a role in preventing more coordination of TA delivery is that the early childhood field has not reached consensus on the meaning of TA and its relationship to professional development. Nor is there agreement about the definition of professional development. Professionals use many words interchangeably to describe methods of working with adults, including *TA, consultation, coaching, mentoring,* and *on-site training.* For example, one guide to providing center-based TA, Opening the Door to Quality: Centers (National Association of Child Care Resource and Referral Agencies [NACCRRA], 2005), defined *TA* as consultation and *monitoring* as one of three types of TA visits, which suggests that one purpose of TA is monitoring. In our experience, conversations at the national and state levels to explore the possibility of shared definitions have sometimes been impeded by the recognition that some state and/or local agencies have operationalized their own definitions and prefer to keep them. The lack of a shared definition of various professional development approaches has contributed to confusion in the early childhood community, making it difficult to share lessons learned and to plan evaluation efforts.

Not only are terms defined differently, but most early childhood professionals providing TA lack a conceptual framework and consistent procedures for implementing activities such as consultation and coaching (Wesley, Buysse, & Skinner, 2001). They are not always able to differentiate among these models or make informed decisions about when to use one versus another model for a specific purpose. Viewed through the lens of program quality, little can be gained when TA providers interpret the meaning of TA differently and are not intentional in their approach and procedures (i.e., the TA services they provide are disconnected from broader quality improvement goals and initiatives). Numerous other aspects of TA delivery also present challenges. Concerns include the lack of consistent preparation and ongoing professional development of TA providers, high rates of attrition among them, the challenge of evaluating the effectiveness of TA services, and the absence of scientific research on TA methods (and the methodological challenges of evaluating TA).

Although agencies providing early childhood TA may have different missions and funding sources, they often deliver TA to the same states, communities, and programs. A lack of systematic planning and communication among TA providers results in inconsistent approaches to TA, duplication of effort, and a mottled landscape of quality enhancement services (and therefore quality) within counties and states and across the country. Although the availability of TA probably never has been so high in the early childhood field, much work remains to be done to maximize its efficiency and effectiveness for early childhood professionals.

The purpose of this chapter is to take a close look at TA and the challenges of creating an effective TA system to support program quality. We explore the development of TA across several fields during the past 50 years, propose a definition for the early childhood field, and consider principles of effective TA delivery. The chapter closes with the introduction of a new framework for conceptualizing state and local implementation of TA in the quality improvement movement and with a discussion of TA provider competencies.

WHAT IS TA?

Spending only a couple of hours on the Internet searching for current information about TA reveals numerous examples of its current application in multiple professional fields. There are web sites describing TA services provided through departments of the federal government (e.g., Human Services, Education, Transportation, Homeland Security, Commerce, Justice, Energy); international trade and development organizations; and diverse entities representing a host of interests including information technology, health, housing, mining, agriculture, finance, forestry, and textiles, to name only a few. What is striking, in contrast to the abundance of TA sites and topics on the Internet, is the absence of clear, current descriptions of the meaning and purpose of TA. TA seems to constitute everything from a resource pipeline to skills training in the field to complex, long-range organizational planning. Although much is assumed about the meaning of the term in its present-day uses, several decades ago many different professions were actively engaged in defining and evaluating TA and in developing guiding principles for the delivery of TA.

TA Definitions

Early influences on TA include at least four theoretical contributions, beginning with the principles of *planned change* and the related concept of *innovation diffusion*, which involve deliberate interventions to bring about change in individuals and their organizations. Key features of each include mutual needs assessment and goal setting by the change agent and members of the organization, shared power, and joint decision making and evaluation (Bennis, Benne, & Chinn, 1969; Havelock, 1973; Rogers & Shoemaker, 1971). The third influence was the literature on *adult learning* with its emphasis on the importance of the learners' active participation in the learning process, individualized needs assessment, and conducive learning environments (Knowles, 1978; Knox, 1980). *Consultation* provided a fourth source, especially the process concerns related to entry, using different consultant styles and roles as necessary to respond to the client, and follow-up (Lippett & Lippett, 1986).

Definitions of TA vary across professions, but a common feature is the provision of "information, methods, tools and support" (Sullivan, 1991, p. 290) or "specialized knowledge, skills, information, and technologies" (Richman & Clifford, 1980, p. 13) from one system to another that identifies a need for change. Early descriptions of TA in education emphasized as a defining feature the process of communication between two systems or entities, the TA provider and the TA receiver, and the development of a continuous relationship between them that promotes appreciation in each for what the other is and either needs or has to offer (Clifford & Trohanis, 1980; Sturgeon, Tracy, Ziegler, Neufeld, & Wiegerink, 1977). By describing TA as more than the simple transfer of knowledge from point A to point B, early thinking about TA valued the importance of collaboration between TA provider and receiver. Trohanis (1982) explained that TA is not a fragmented or reactive strategy to address one need at a time but rather a comprehensive approach using both content and process expertise to identify and address multiple goals. TA addresses current concerns of a client program while at the same time building internal support to sustain the changes and address similar concerns in the future. The success of TA depends on the capacity of both TA provider and recipient to solve problems. The TA delivery system must have the competence and resources to help various types of clients, and the TA receiver must have the willingness and resources to engage in self-improvement (Havelock, 1977).

In early childhood, TA providers use a variety of methods to plan and implement change, such as providing tools to assess needs, making site visits, sharing materials and resources, and linking professional networks through strategies such as conference calls, listservs, topical web sites, and webinars. What seems missing, however, is a well-grounded, intentional rationale for the use of these options, a shared understanding among TA agencies and providers of a logical process for drawing on these options to maximize outcomes, and, given the emphasis on increasing knowledge and skills, an understanding of how TA links to broader issues related to professional development.

A BRIEF HISTORY OF TA

A brief look at the history of consulting and the emergence of the term *technical assistance* in other fields provides an interesting backdrop for consideration of the development of TA in early childhood. TA in the areas of business and politics, for example, evolved from a technical and expert-oriented approach in which information, knowledge, and skills were expected to be transferred from the TA provider to the TA recipient, to a reciprocal and co-equal collaboration in which both parties experienced change.

TA in Business and Politics

During the late 1800s, a newly organized scientific management movement began applying the scientific method to solving production problems in factories. Industrial engineers (pioneers of management consulting) analyzed limited, technical problems with a focus on how to make factories more efficient and productive while improving the quality of the goods (Kubr, 2002). They conducted time and motion studies, waste-elimination studies, measured the impact of new machinery and processes on production, and used what they learned from this research to make changes. Although factory owners and managers were pleased with the profit resulting from increased efficiency, innovations were often objectionable to the workers, who were not a part of the decisions but were the people most affected by them (Kubr, 2002).

With the emergence of unions and changes in social and labor relations, industry consultants in the 1920s began taking a less prescriptive, more collaborative approach and adopted a wider perspective beyond the shop floor. They sought to improve overall strategy, structure, and performance and addressed personnel management, sales, and business expansion (Kubr, 2002). At the same time, they stayed abreast of new developments in power-driven, industrial machinery and linked factory managers with experts on their optimal use (McKenna, 1995).

During World War II, military leaders viewed the conflict as a management challenge and recognized the value of research, analytical techniques, and expert advice to solve problems, from weaponry to strategy, on and off the battlefield (Domergue, 1968). Building on the success of consultation in industry, the government hired consultants to address military concerns such as strategic planning and efficiency. Postwar reconstruction and the rapid expansion of businesses and technologies ensured the continued demand for management consulting and stimulated development of services that were either specialized for particular business sectors or bundled as comprehensive packages to meet broad needs (Kubr, 2002). The term *technical assistance* came to be used during 1947 and 1948 when it was recognized that this type of consulting could be exported as a means through which developed countries could extend their expertise internationally to aid less developed countries (Wilson, 2006).

Under President Truman's influence, a special agency of the United Nations (itself a fledgling organization) was created to deliver TA, which was at first conceptualized as a linear transmission of learning, knowledge, and techniques from a knowledge-rich, developed world to a knowledge-poor, underdeveloped world (Wilson, 2006). Subsequent debate in the TA literature acknowledged the challenges of transferring knowledge across cultural and societal boundaries and the need for the receiving countries to develop capacity to both articulate their needs and assimilate the TA. Participatory approaches in TA began to be recognized in the 1970s as a means for TA providers to find out about local context to maximize the effectiveness of the knowledge transfer. In the 1980s, however, participatory engagement was valued in international development as a mechanism through which aid-receiving countries learned about themselves in order to take ownership of their own priorities (Wilson, 2006). Increasingly, the TA literature referred to cooperation and partnership with TA recipients and the extension of that partnership to the clients' ownership of the change process. TA to build capacity was contrasted against TA that only fills content gaps, and descriptions of TA recipients being "in the driver's seat" became common. This shift in focus from transferring expertise to promoting the capacity of countries to identify and achieve their own developmental objectives produced a change in nomenclature, from technical *assistance* to technical *cooperation,* denoting the emphasis on collaboration and the intention to support the TA recipients' long-term self-management.

TA in Early Childhood Education

As illustrated in the description of TA in business and politics, the years between 1960 and 1980 were a critical developmental period. During this era there was great interest in theories of adult learning, models of information dissemination, and in effective planning for organizational development and innovation. Concern grew that traditional one-shot training approaches did not provide professionals with the continual exposure to the latest knowledge, skills, and products necessary for them to stay current in their jobs. As practices such as individualized needs assessment and action planning became popular approaches in professional development, TA evolved as a promising combination of instruction, consultation, and resources to build the capacity of people and programs to make and sustain changes. In early childhood, this evolution has taken place in the form of parallel activities across various sectors, including special education, child care, and early education.

Although never a part of the TA definition and not always the case, the term *technical assistance* was usually applied when federal or state agencies contracted with or awarded a grant to an organization of professionals who were competent to provide support to a group of service agencies that also received funds from the agency sponsoring the TA (Budde & Summers, 1991). For example, the emergence of TA in early childhood special education can be traced to 1971 when the U.S. Department of Education, Bureau of Education for the Handicapped, funded the Technical Assistance Development System (a forerunner of the National Early Childhood Technical Assistance Center) to support 20 demonstration centers implemented as a part of the newly passed Handicapped Children's Early Education Assistance Act (PL 90-538). In 1975, when the Education for All Handicapped Children Act (PL 94-142) was passed, this same TA network provided TA to recipients of state improvement grants to support implementation. Helping state education agencies respond to the numerous critical provisions mandating compliance (e.g., the development of individualized education programs, procedural safeguards, child evaluation) was an enormous undertaking, for which one-shot workshops or mini-courses were not likely to be effective. Although the TA system targeted specific areas to focus on (e.g., program development, public awareness, interagency collaboration), services were designed to allow significant variability in the types of supports provided, based on the input of schools about the kinds of assistance they felt they needed (Gallagher, Danaher, & Clifford, 2009).

The Cooperative Extension System provides another example from this era of how training and outreach activities were developed and modified to meet client needs and is important historically for its focus on early childhood. Drawing on the resources of the land-grant universities and with a presence in every county in all 50 states and 6 territories, the Cooperative Extension System had long been established as the direct educational link to rural America. Agency services included establishing farm demonstration projects and disseminating their research findings, as well as providing information and training in the areas of home economics and rural energy. Extension agents provided an array of TA, including training, on-site consultation, materials development, and resource lending as methods of communicating new technologies and empowering farms and communities to solve problems. In response to changing local needs, the focus of extension agencies expanded during the 1970s from increasing farm production to also working in nonagricultural realms (Scheuring, 1988). This expansion included providing education about child development, educating families about quality child care, offering training for child care providers, and facilitating community collaboration to create and administer child care programs—all services that continue to be provided through Cooperative Extension agencies today.

It was also during this time that child care resource and referral (CCR&R) agencies emerged as a grassroots response to the absence of federal funding for early childhood services and a national strategy to provide affordable, accessible, quality child care. CCR&Rs were established in the late 1960s in five pioneer states for the purpose of addressing the needs of parents and care providers. Since their beginnings, CCR&R agencies have emerged as a vital TA resource for communities and have grown steadily in response to many factors: the needs of individual families for vital child care and parenting information, the needs of communities to build the supply and improve the quality of care, employers' recognition of the importance of CCR&R to the corporate strategies for a family-friendly workplace, and new federal emphasis on parental choice and increased understanding of the key role of CCR&R in making such choice a reality.

In the mid 1990s, as part of welfare reform, the Personal Responsibility and Work Opportunity Reconciliation Act (PRWORA) of 1996 (PL 104-193) and the Balanced Budget Act of 1997 (PL 105-33) created the Child Care and Development Fund (CCDF), combining four major federal child care programs into a single block grant to states. It authorized much larger amounts of direct spending for child care and allowed states to transfer Temporary Assistance for Needy Families funds to the federal child care program, the Child Care and Development Block Grant (CCDBG). CCDF is administered by the Child Care Bureau in the Administration for Children and Families, U.S. Department of Health and Human Services. PRWORA authorized discretionary funds that are subject to annual appropriations, including targeting of specific amounts for child care quality improvement activities, infant and toddler quality improvement, child care resource and referral and school-age child care activities, and child care research, demonstration, and evaluation activities. In addition, federal regulations (45 C.F.R.

§ 98.60[b][1]) set aside one-quarter of 1% (0.25%) of the federal CCDF for TA. In each of FY 2004 and FY 2005, just over $12 million was targeted to the needs of state, territorial, and tribal grantees.

The Child Care Bureau delivers TA through links with the bureau's research team and its partners to help CCDF administrators build capacity to support working parents and promote learning and healthy development for children in child care. In partnership with a network of contracted TA providers and ACF regional offices, the bureau identifies exemplary research and promising practices and brings CCDF grantees together to learn from one another. The main role of the bureau's TA providers, many of whom have worked as state child care administrators, is to help lead agencies develop services and TA delivery systems and to disseminate evidence-based information related to key topics in early and school-age child care.

TA ROLES

The literature on both consulting and TA includes much discussion about the need for content experts and process facilitators. Content includes theory, experience, skills, values, and competencies, and process refers to the approaches, capabilities, and methods that are required for effective application of knowledge. In many fields this discussion is framed as a debate on the need for specialists as well as generalists. A specialist possesses a deep knowledge and skill in a particular area (or areas), while a generalist has broad knowledge and general skills across several areas. A specialist's collaboration with the TA recipient may be limited to providing information or advice on request; he or she may not be involved in addressing the social or behavioral aspects of the change process in the client program (Kubr, 2002). A TA specialist might be called in to give up-to-date information to improve a program's technical capability—for example, to answer specific questions about how to comply with regulatory requirements or performance-based standards. On the other hand, a generalist helps the client solve its own program problems by making the client aware of organizational processes and their consequences and of interventions or techniques to stimulate change. A generalist would focus on the interaction, coordination, and integration of several program areas or explore management processes, structures, and resource allocation to address a more complex problem—for example, staff turnover. Instead of passing on technical knowledge and telling the client *what* to change, the consultant shares his or her approach as a way of helping a program know *how* to change (Kubr, 2002).

A related issue about TA roles is the distinction between directive and nondirective approaches. In a directive approach, the TA provider assumes a leadership position. He or she initiates activities or tells the client what to do. In a nondirective approach, the TA provider expects the client to take initiative, including accepting or rejecting the TA provider's advice. In early childhood, TA providers and their clients report a natural tendency toward technical fixes that provide direct, simple solutions to problems (Wesley, Buysse, & Skinner, 2001), and yet quick fixes do not provide opportunities for collaboration and empowerment and may produce dependence on the TA system.

Considerable disagreement also exists in the early childhood field about whether TA providers should also be program monitors. This is worth noting, given that other professions make clear distinctions between the two functions and warn against combining collaborative and regulatory approaches (see, for example, Kubr, 2002, and the literature on management consulting). Whereas state regulatory agencies are expected to hire licensing monitors or inspectors, enforcement should not be the role of TA providers. Yet, whether because of philosophy or limited resources, some early childhood agencies (e.g., some agencies implementing a QRIS) combine the roles of regulator/enforcer (monitor) with collaborator/resource provider (technical assistant) in positions sometimes called quality enhancement specialist or consultant (Bryant, Wesley, & the QUINCE Study Team, 2009; RAND Corporation, 2008). TA providers playing such dual roles in implementing a QRIS look for compliance with performance-based standards and prescribe "improvement plans" where needed (Bryant et al., 2009). The expectation is that program staff will execute these plans using the technical advice or other resources provided by the monitor/technical assistant, who may then visit the early childhood program unannounced to check on progress. Lack of follow-through may result in the program's termination in the quality enhancement program and the withdrawal of TA. Understandably, TA providers report frustration in their dual roles of monitor and collaborator/helper and question their effectiveness to regulate the quality of early childhood programs while also building lasting relationships with clients based on mutual trust (Bryant et al., 2009). Such frustrations are not likely to resolve without professional development in collaborative consultation and a clear conceptual framework for the delivery of TA that clarifies functions and roles.

The limited literature on early childhood TA and consultation provides little guidance on how to combine roles and approaches. TA providers may believe they must choose to be either specialists or generalists, content experts or process facilitators. They may not understand that these and other roles fall along a continuum of directive and nondirective approaches, and they may not realize the potential of combining and changing roles to accomplish different functions as the TA relationship evolves. When TA providers lack opportunities to plan and discuss their practices with colleagues, it is likely that they drift through many other roles (e.g., fact finder, resource provider, trainer and educator, advocate, coach) without awareness or intention (Wesley et al., 2001). In the following section we continue to explore role confusion and other TA challenges in the early childhood field.

THE CONFUSING WORLD OF EARLY CHILDHOOD TA

Recent years have seen little scholarly attention paid to the topic of TA in human services. In education this presents a particular concern because, as in the period of rapid expansion 40 years ago, early childhood agencies across the country now are adopting TA with brush-fire speed as a means of enhancing program quality. The following scenario brings to life the typical TA experience for many communities and illustrates problems related to the revolving door of on-site quality improvement services.

Knock, Knock, Who's There?

Rainbow Child Care is a licensed early childhood center that has been open for 5 years. Through the years center staff have attended regional workshops on early childhood issues, and this year its director decided to participate in her county's quality rating improvement system. As a result, the program receives on-site TA from the local CCR&R. Every few weeks a person called a quality enhancement consultant visits the center to work with the director and staff to make program improvements. Rainbow Child Care also receives services from a behavior specialist who visits the toddler classroom to help the teacher address the challenging behaviors of a particular child and from an early childhood literacy coach who is focusing on the classrooms for 3- and 4-year-olds.

Both the quality enhancement consultant and behavior specialist are employed by the CCR&R that serves the community where Rainbow Child Care is located. The literacy coach is funded through the school system by a special statewide initiative to promote kindergarten readiness. Although it is required only for the literacy coach position, all three professionals have B.A. degrees in early childhood or a related field. Only the behavior specialist has previous early childhood classroom experience. None worked in a TA position prior to their current jobs, and none were oriented to TA by their employers. All three are aware of the research that links early childhood program quality to positive child outcomes and are committed to their work, but none have received training about how to motivate, teach, or support other adults to achieve this quality. Nor have they participated in any courses on general methods of working collaboratively with others or building capacity at the program level. Like other itinerant early childhood professionals who report lacking a collaborative and empowering framework for consultation practice (Wesley et al., 2001), two of these TA providers use a directive approach in which they observe the situation and then tell the child care staff what aspects of the environment or their teaching practices to change.

The CCR&R requires its technical assistants to use the Family Child Care Environment Rating Scale–Revised (FCCERS; Harms, Cryer, & Clifford, 2007), the Infant/Toddler Environment Rating Scale–Revised (ITERS-R; Harms, Cryer, Clifford, 2003), and the Early Childhood Environment Rating Scale–Revised (ECERS-R; Harms, Clifford, & Cryer, 1998) to assess program quality, but, other than caseload, it has not defined the parameters of the on-site work. On her first visit, the quality enhancement consultant administers the ECERS-R in two of the classrooms at Rainbow Child Care. She uses her scores to identify weak areas needing improvement but does not share the scores with the program staff. On her second visit, she discusses the goals she has written for quality improvement with the director and classroom teachers and leaves several copies of the improvement plan with them. The quality enhancement specialist returns every few weeks to see if the goals have been accomplished. The quality enhancement consultant sees her main role as making recommendations for room arrangement and instructional materials. She takes responsibility for creating purchase orders for any furnishings and supplies that Rainbow Child Care staff need to buy with the incentive money they were offered when they signed up to participate in the quality enhancement program.

The behavior specialist receives programmatic direction from a coordinator outside the CCR&R, who oversees the work of a total of 40 behavior specialists across the state. Although the specialist's paychecks come from the local CCR&R agency and his supervisor is the CCR&R director, his position is actually funded by a special initiative developed by the state using CCDF from the federal government. His intervention strategies include observing children who are referred to his caseload and administering the Devereaux Early Childhood Assessment (LeBuffe & Naglieri, 1999), developing behavior plans for them based on their assessment results and explaining the plans to classroom teachers for them to follow. He also provides periodic workshops on positive behavioral supports that are attended by early childhood professionals who are served by the local CCR&R for which he works. Although the statewide project states that its mission is to promote positive social and emotional development in young children, it measures the effectiveness of its services by a decrease in the number of children expelled from early childhood programs across the state and publicizes this as a desired outcome. As a result, behavior specialists are typically called in to address urgent concerns related to young children who are about to be "disenrolled" and feel they cannot take the time to thoroughly assess the needs of the program or focus on prevention.

Monthly staff meetings at the CCR&R agency attended by the quality enhancement consultant and behavior specialist are largely administrative, with much time focused on the new online reporting system that documents the number, type, location, and duration of their contacts. Although the two professionals try to touch base with each other periodically when they find they are working in the same early childhood program, their caseloads require much travel and time away from the office. When they do have time together, they often use it to vent their frustrations about the lack of follow-through by teachers and directors. They are not aware that a literacy coach is visiting Rainbow Child Care.

The literacy coach is using the Early Language and Literacy Classroom Observation (ELLCO) Tool (Smith, Brady, & Anastasopoulos, 2008) to assess the quality of classrooms and teaching practices and a checklist designed by the state project to familiarize teachers with developmental expectations for children headed to kindergarten. She sees her primary role as collaborating with teachers to assess their needs and making recommendations for activities that will increase children's use of language and awareness of print, and she shows teachers how to use storybook time to increase children's recognition of letters and their sounds. She attends periodic statewide meetings conducted by her project's director, where she learns about new early childhood literacy products and approaches. Although she is aware that other professionals are working with the staff at Rainbow, she has not thought much about it, as she believes their focus is not literacy.

Aside from brief, initial training on the instruments they use, there are no requirements for ongoing professional development for these itinerant positions. Minimum job qualifications do not include previous experience working in an early childhood classroom or previous experience providing TA. Although all three professionals visiting Rainbow Child Care hope to make a difference in the quality of young children's experiences, they have divergent ideas about what an early childhood classroom should look like, and, in fact, sometimes their recommendations about room arrangements and materials conflict. Similarly, because their experiences and knowledge of effective curriculum, interactions, and instruction vary widely, the advice that one consultant gives about these topics is sometimes inconsistent with that offered by the others. If these challenges alone are not enough to create confusion among the center staff, then there is the fact that only one of the visitors schedules appointments in advance, while the others prefer to "pop in."

Rainbow Child Care is a fictitious center and the description of TA is hypothetical, but there are real situations like this one all across the country. In some states, other TA providers would be visiting the early childhood program as well—people who focus on health and safety, outdoor play areas, infant-toddler classrooms, or teachers' professional development plans to meet QRIS requirements. In North Carolina, for example, approximately 568 TA providers visit child care programs throughout the state. They represent at least 142 different job titles and are employed by 242 different early childhood agencies (Ryan & Wesley, 2006). In most states, a child care licensing consultant also would be visiting Rainbow Child Care at least once a year, and it is possible that some of his or her views about policy and practice in the program would conflict with those of the TA providers.

In spite of the increasing availability of on-site TA to early childhood programs, the goal of raising and sustaining child care quality may be compromised by the lack of consensus about the meaning of TA and the absence of a coordinated approach within and across agencies providing TA. TA providers' complaints that early childhood program staff are not invested in change and fail to follow through with implementation (Wesley et al., 2001) are not surprising, given the TA providers' limited preparation for their roles as effective change agents and the lack of coordination of TA approaches. In short, the early childhood field has dispatched an army of helpers and troubleshooters across the nation without the necessary education and supports to ensure their success.

CURRENT TA CHALLENGES IN THE EARLY CHILDHOOD FIELD

In addition to the lack of a commonly accepted definition of TA, there is limited scientific research to guide the development of TA services. The field also lacks an effective infrastructure to support early childhood TA providers. Problems range from inadequate preparation of professionals for TA roles to inappropriate methods for evaluating the success of on-site services. Limited systematic planning and communication among TA providers result in inconsistent approaches to TA and a mottled landscape of quality enhancement services (and therefore quality) within counties and states and across the country.

Limited Research

In general, the literature on TA is long on theory and short on science. There is little rigorous research, for example, to guide the design of TA systems or decisions about the types, intensity, and duration of services. We do not know under what conditions the provision of TA is likely to improve program quality. Yet, as described previously, every year states spend millions of dollars on initiatives implemented by various agencies providing TA to enhance early childhood program quality (U.S. General Accounting Office, 2002). Unfortunately, evaluations of these quality initiatives cannot link program improvements to particular quality enhancement activities. Consider the example of North Carolina, where TA strategies, including on-site consultation and mentoring, have been popular for years among agencies funded by Smart Start, the comprehensive early childhood initiative. Four statewide assessments of early childhood classroom quality from 1994 to 2001 showed significantly improved quality over time (Bryant, Bernier, Maxwell, & Peisner-Feinberg, 2002; Bryant, Maxwell, & Burchinal, 1999), and numerous states continue to look to Smart Start as a beacon when designing their own early childhood system components. Although the Smart Start evaluation showed that programs participating in more of the quality enhancement opportunities made greater gains on quality measures, particular interventions that made the most difference in quality could not be identified, largely because TA activities were categorized under broad headings such as "resource and referral."

Although there is increased interest among researchers in studying TA in early childhood settings, such research is difficult and expensive to conduct because of the multiple points of contact in the TA process. There are TA providers, early childhood program administrators, classroom teachers and other program staff, and the children served in the classrooms where TA is provided. This "links in the chain" problem (Fuchs, Fuchs, Dulan, Roberts, & Fernstrom, 1992, p. 162) is illustrated in the following steps. First, a researcher must train the TA providers who will participate in the intervention study. The TA providers then must interact with TA recipients from diverse backgrounds in a variety of settings. The TA recipients, in turn, interact with the children they teach and other adults involved in their programs. Their work environment—an early childhood classroom, for example—is a functional system with many parts, all of which have the potential to be affected by the introduction of simple changes. These multiple transactions and contextual variables increase the difficulty of implementing TA interventions with the intended strength and integrity in terms of both the TA providers' adherence to the components of the TA process and the TA recipients' follow-through to address TA goals. Without clearly defining the TA intervention being studied and implementing it in a consistent and accurate way (and controlling for a wide range of variables that could influence the results), the research findings will not be useful to practitioners.

For the most part, we cannot say which TA approach is most effective with what professionals in what programs, and when. Yet, promising findings are emerging that identify significant quality improvements in family child care homes that receive systematic, intensive, and collaborative on-site consultation as opposed to less frequent and less collaborative quality enhancement services (Bryant et al., 2009). More research is needed to explore a range of TA outcomes, such as the recipient's ability to address similar problems in the future and to sustain quality changes and factors that contribute to the effectiveness of quality enhancement services.

Inadequate Professional Development of TA Providers

Many TA providers graduate from universities without preparation in consultation or other methods of working with adults (Bryant et al., 2009; Dinnebeil & McInerney, 2000), and most have not received professional development related to TA on the job. Although at the state level discussions are emerging about job qualifications and professional competencies for early childhood TA positions, within states, and certainly nationwide, we are a long way from reaching consensus about TA competencies, professional development, or even the need to reach consensus on these issues. As a result, there are huge variations in quality enhancement services offered to child care centers and homes within and across states. While some TA providers complete a brief checklist on-site, others visit programs for a set number of visits, while still others visit several times over many months for the purpose of developing and implementing an improvement plan (Bryant et al., 2000). TA providers are not always sure how to organize their services and often find themselves responding in an ad hoc or crisis-oriented fashion (Wesley et al., 2001). As mentioned earlier, sometimes they view themselves as monitors and resource providers more than change agents, and they describe their goals in terms of performance improvement rather than empowerment. This is not surprising, given the limited opportunities for professional development on topics such as effective communication strategies, consultation stages and tasks, interpersonal skills, and other aspects of how to be an effective catalyst for change.

The National Association of Child Care Resource and Referral Agencies (NACCRRA; 2007b) has adopted a 12-point plan for improving training and TA that calls for the development of "best practices" for TA delivery, a community-based tracking database to document TA services, training and TA evaluation models, and a national trainer credential, among other innovations. Advancement in these and other areas may be limited, however, by the lack of state and local agency leadership. Although NACCRRA describes the CCR&R network as poised to support a national system of training and TA, no single agency is responsible for TA across all sectors of the early childhood field (e.g., Head Start, child care, public prekindergarten), nor is it clear how funds could be combined to create an integrated system of TA services.

Attrition

The problem with teacher turnover is a familiar concern in the early childhood field, but two recent studies show that turnover among TA providers is equal or higher. A study of child care resource and referral agencies nationwide reported 26% turnover among TA providers (NACCRRA, 2007a), and a five-state study of on-site consultation to enhance quality reported a 37% loss of TA providers over 18 months (Bryant et al., 2009). Causes of attrition include TA providers leaving their jobs for personal and medical reasons, including finding better jobs outside their agencies, but also their reassignment to administrative and other positions within the same agency, the termination of funding for TA positions, and the closure of entire agencies. That agencies reassign TA providers to other positions and sometimes shuffle their TA caseload assignments (Bryant et al., 2009) may reflect an underestimation of the relationship-based nature of TA and a lack of long-term planning for the TA program.

Just as qualifications vary within counties and across states, so do salaries (Bryant et al., 2009), and the lack of a clear career path for TA providers only confounds the situation. Although one of the remedies to the attrition problem well may lie in the development of a statewide TA credential, without funding to provide a corresponding raise in salary, the promise seems hollow. For many agencies, however, the idea of providing salary increments tied to TA certification can barely be discussed at all because stabilizing the funding to retain the existing TA staff from year to year is a higher priority. In fact, the year-to-year funding uncertainties under which many of these agencies operate may be a primary impediment to building systems and a challenge for staff stability and morale.

Measurement Limitations

The effectiveness of TA to address program quality depends, in part, on the comprehensive assessment of the programs' needs. Certainly one of the most important accomplishments of the early childhood field has been the identification and measurement of many quality indicators in early childhood centers and homes. The use of the FCCERS, ITERS-R, and ECERS-R is common in TA initiatives to enhance quality, but attention across the nation also increasingly is turning to additional aspects of quality in centers and home-based care. For example, criticisms of the ECERS-R are that items do not sufficiently address the levels of learning in language, early literacy, mathematics, and science that increasingly are expected of young children (Espinosa, 2002; Sylva et al., 2006) or the specific instructional practices that lead to children's progress in learning. There is increased interest in the Classroom Assessment Scoring System (Pianta, LaParo, & Hamre, 2008; CLASS) which assesses interactions between students and teachers, but this instrument assesses instruction only at a very general level (National Research Council, 2008). The identification of and response to children's early learning challenges and the active engagement and participation by children with special needs are other dimensions that should be addressed in efforts to measure and enhance program quality. Others have pointed to the need to include in quality assessments indicators of sensitivity and supports for parents and families. The assumption here is that providers' sensitivity to the needs of parents, and activities to support them in multiple ways, increases the likelihood of children's stable participation in programs and of congruence among practices at home and in the care environment (Bromer & Henly, 2004). Collaboration among professional organizations such as the NAEYC, the Division of Early Childhood (DEC) of the Council for Exceptional Children, Head Start, ZERO TO THREE, and NACCRRA is essential as the field continues to refine the way we conceptualize and measure quality and to provide a unified set of standards for program quality.

Challenges in Evaluating TA

The evaluation of TA should answer specific questions and serve a stated purpose. A key evaluation question is whether the TA goals were accomplished, but other questions must be answered if a purpose of evaluation is to use the findings to guide future TA services. For example, what TA strategies were most effective to accomplish the goals, and were they the right goals to begin with? Do TA activities reflect the best available research on supporting the implementation of evidence-based practices (Fixsen, Naoom, Blasé, Friedman, & Wallace, 2005)? What were the effects of TA, anticipated and unanticipated, positive and negative? Was the TA recipient satisfied with the TA provider and process? Did specific skills of the TA recipient increase, and if so, how were they related to program quality improvement? Because of limited funds and other agency constraints, few early childhood TA initiatives approach evaluation in such a comprehensive way.

Driven by the culture of accountability, state and local agencies that provide TA are likely to design evaluation plans that produce numbers, as opposed to selecting more open-ended and discursive evaluation methods. Few agencies ask early childhood programs to evaluate the services they receive or the knowledge and skills of the TA providers (Bryant et al., 2009). Typically, TA agencies document the types and numbers of programs receiving TA and types and numbers of the quality enhancement contacts (e.g., phone calls, workshops, on-site visits). Most states track changes in child care registration or licensure, and those participating in a QRIS may document changes in scores on assessment instruments. Unfortunately, without clearly articulating a TA process, and without assessing what is actually happening during visits between TA providers and early childhood program staff, it is impossible to identify fully what may be causing changes in quality and how these changes may be affecting other distal outcomes. Concerns also exist that the measures being used to track improvements may not be sensitive enough to capture certain kinds of changes (e.g., changes in interactions or in a teacher's ability to scaffold instruction) and about how measurement results are being used to inform the change process.

State and local agencies that provide TA may operate with the expectation that TA will not only promote program compliance with performance-based standards but also that it can be linked to measurable child outcomes (Bryant & Ponder, 2004). It seems reasonable to anticipate that establishing a link between TA and positive outcomes for children will be a long-range proposition, and not the sort of activity that can be evaluated and reported within a fiscal year. Yet, in a high-stakes political environment, many state and local early childhood agencies providing TA are asked to justify their funding each year by demonstrating that funded TA activities produce measurable, positive results for children. It is easy to understand how, in an attempt to demonstrate more immediate effects of TA, agencies may select narrowly focused TA strategies over more comprehensive and intensive approaches to enhance quality. For initiatives that propose comprehensive TA programs, it may be challenging to implement and evaluate the full scope of activities within the fiscal year.

REFRAMING TA IN THE EARLY CHILDHOOD QUALITY MOVEMENT

Currently in early childhood, TA typically involves a cafeteria approach of discontinuous experiences and ad hoc responses offered by various community agencies and other organizations that may or may not discuss their TA services with each other. As we have described, such agencies include CCR&R, Head Start, early intervention, public schools (prekindergarten and early childhood special education programs), public health, Cooperative Extension, and any other TA initiatives that may be funded through a statewide early childhood partnership. TA also is provided by an increasing number of independent, private consultants who market their abilities to respond to program quality concerns. This group includes people who have established credibility (e.g., university employees, state agency retirees) and others who simply have hung a shingle outside their door to announce their new consulting business.

Although initial efforts to create a more integrated system of early childhood TA are underway in some states and communities, these efforts typically are not grounded in a shared definition of TA. Nor do they specify a conceptual framework for TA delivery and evaluation, although some discussion is beginning to distinguish between basic, content-focused TA and the more complex and intensive TA required for systemic change (Blase, 2009). In this section we explore the features and purpose of a systemic TA network that is part of a broader professional development system in early childhood and propose a definition of TA for the early childhood quality improvement movement.

Establishing a TA Network: Part of a Broader Professional Development System

Drawing from the TA literature and our own experience and research, we believe that the effectiveness of TA in early childhood would be enhanced if it were organized at the macro level as a continuous and coordinated network of services and activities in every state and part of the state's broader professional development system. To create such a continuous and coordinated network, the various state agencies and organizations providing TA would form a TA collaborative. The goal is to organize and coordinate the TA services within their own agencies and across sectors efficiently and effectively to support the professional development of the early childhood workforce. This is not an easy task, as state agencies have different TA priorities, with some developing their statewide TA plans based on priorities identified at the federal level (e.g., Head Start).

First steps in developing a cross-sector, integrated TA plan are to identify who currently provides TA and who receives it and to consider commonalities in TA focus and methods across sectors. Then it is important to examine how TA services relate to and support the state's comprehensive professional development plan. Where is there duplication of services? Where are there gaps? Are TA services accessible and relevant to diverse program needs along a variety of dimensions (e.g., the needs of low-quality and high-quality programs, the need for content and process expertise, the need for intensive and multiple visits or brief informational contacts). For example, do TA strategies support early childhood professionals who need basic information and skills to raise program quality and those who know how and why to raise quality but who seek new resources? Are there multiple types of TA that vary in duration and intensity? These and related questions can guide the members of the collaborative as they begin to think about TA as a coherent network of services. It is also critical to consider the qualifications of TA providers and their competence to do the job. Table 7.1 summarizes these and other goals of a TA collaborative.

Improving quality is a complex undertaking in which innovation is needed across and within multiple components of the early childhood system. How can we expect the quality of the early childhood system to increase without communication and careful planning within and among those agencies involved in supporting quality changes? By articulating a shared vision and outcomes, and collaborating to define, plan, deliver, and evaluate their services, agencies and organizations providing TA would enhance their understanding of both the landscape of early childhood programs and the landscape of individuals and agencies delivering TA. TA providers would help recipient programs know how to access

Table 7.1. Goals of a TA collaborative

- Assist in assessing the professional development needs of anticipated TA recipients and ensure that TA services support those needs.
- Reduce duplication in TA services.
- Address challenges and gaps in TA delivery.
- Identify effective TA strategies, develop shared terminology, and increase consistency in TA approaches across sectors.
- Expand TA services to reflect and address early learning standards, components of high-quality inclusion, and other guidelines and standards associated with quality.
- Promote universal competencies for TA providers that are tied to certification and compensation.
- Create cross-sector opportunities for TA providers to engage in shared reflection and professional development.
- Identify and enhance additional resources to support TA providers.
- Collaborate to evaluate TA, share data, and use those data in future.
- Identify and leverage funding to support TA, and share ideas and data to justify and expand funding resources.
- Overall, increase access to and the quality of TA across sectors.
- Build public will toward early childhood services and broad understanding about the importance of quality.

and use TA services in an efficient, effective, and empowering way to develop and implement their own goals to improve and sustain quality.

Several states have begun collaborative planning efforts to tackle innovations such as these, including South Carolina, Wisconsin, Missouri, and Colorado, to name a few. Their purpose is to coordinate elements of existing TA infrastructures to enhance efficiency, increase the quality of TA, and ultimately improve services for children and families. Ideally, this collaborative approach also would be implemented at the community level through similar efforts by professionals providing TA to local programs. The section at the end of this chapter entitled "A Promising New Direction" describes one approach that such a community collaborative of TA providers could use to organize their TA services.

Purpose of TA

The ultimate purpose of a continuous and coordinated early childhood TA network is to help early childhood programs and organizations acquire the knowledge, skills, and other resources necessary to identify and accomplish goals related to a particular content area, such as program quality. Stating the purpose of TA in terms of supporting what recipient programs hope to accomplish is different from describing the TA provider's purpose as raising early childhood program quality, which is the way some TA initiatives currently describe their work. When TA providers believe the purpose of their job is to raise quality, it is easy to understand their temptation to assume prescriptive and directive roles and to underestimate or ignore the value of the program's initiative and active participation, beginning with needs assessment. How can we expect the quality of early childhood programs to continue and strengthen without the program staff themselves developing the knowledge and skills to address it? For maximum effectiveness, TA does not simply diagnose and fix problems, but rather it is a resource that clients can draw on to build strength, fill gaps, and learn how to solve problems effectively in the future. TA should seek to empower rather than simply serve, and it should promote in TA recipients more steering and less mindless rowing (to borrow a phrase from Osborne & Gaebler, 1993).

Defining TA to Support Program Quality

In the movement to improve quality, TA can be defined as the provision of content and process expertise to help early childhood professionals 1) develop their capability to identify and implement high-quality practices for children and families and 2) sustain the operation and management of that capability in their programs. In other words, the TA provider helps TA recipients to acquire the resources (e.g., information, knowledge, skills, techniques, tools, dispositions) needed to identify and accomplish current goals and to develop their capacity to address related concerns in the future. The key components of TA to support program quality are 1) communication between TA provider and recipient to identify needs (e.g., what type, how urgent), clarify the purpose of TA, and select goals related to quality enhancement; 2) the intentional selection and implementation of TA strategies that reflect the realistic capabilities of the TA recipient to accomplish those goals; and 3) joint and ongoing evaluation of how and when goals are accomplished, coupled with discussion of how each goal contributes to early childhood program quality and what next steps are needed.

TA refers to many different services and activities, including consultation and coaching, which in a state or community TA network would be delivered by many different TA providers. There should be an active, long-term relationship between the TA "system" and the "system" of early childhood programs receiving TA. This enables the TA network to equip itself with responsive TA services and problem-solving approaches. It means staying abreast and evaluating the potential of current research findings, products, and techniques that are likely to address current problems in client programs and to be assimilated by client programs as part of their approach to future self-assessment and problem solving.

Early childhood TA providers promote their clients' understanding of what to do to improve and sustain quality, how to do it, and why it must be done. Ideally, early childhood TA providers and TA networks would develop multiple approaches to promote the TA recipient's capacity at three levels: 1) the individual level (i.e., equipping a person to do a job), 2) the program or organizational level (i.e., supporting individual capabilities to achieve program goals by effecting institutional procedures and frameworks), and 3) the system level (i.e., promoting the program's capability to effect mandates, standards, guidelines, policies, and modes of operation and engagement that influence interaction among programs or organizations) (United Nations Development Programme Practice Note, 2008). An example of building capacity at these three levels would be providing TA to 1) promote the understanding and skills of a teacher in an early childhood center to assess the quality in her classroom using reliable and valid instruments (individual level); 2) facilitate a planning process involving the director, teachers, and other program staff at the early childhood center to use the assessment results from all classrooms in developing long-range goals (program or organizational level); and 3) coordinate needs assessment and communication across early childhood centers in the community to inform a collaborative professional development plan (system level).

There are a range of TA activities, including providing general information, resources, and referral; consultation; coaching; training and education; and giving expert opinion and advice, to name a few (Wesley & Buysse, 1996; Blase, 2009). These activities provide different frameworks for organizing a variety of tasks and problem-solving processes, including, but not limited to, needs assessment, data analysis, action plan development and implementation, and evaluation. Formats for the delivery of TA include meetings, face-to-face site visits with individuals and groups, phone calls, e-mails, webinars and other opportunities for online learning and communication, workshops, seminars, and courses.

How is TA Different from Consultation, Coaching, and Mentoring?

TA is different from other methods of giving help in that it provides a broad scope of services that can be customized, coordinated, and integrated to address a range of organizational and system concerns. As noted earlier, the TA system ideally designs services with the developmental needs of client programs in mind, and, when services are delivered by qualified TA providers and are accessed by informed consumers, the TA system constitutes a dependable infrastructure of support with the potential to promote and sustain program quality. This includes the capacity to help programs that may enter the TA process with very low quality or urgent needs.

Consultation is a specific type of TA service that uses a systematic, face-to-face, problem-solving process to assist either individuals or groups to clarify and address their concerns (Buysse & Wesley, 2005). When a collaborative approach is used, the consultant is not responsible for implementing the intervention strategies but rather supports the consultee to do so, with the goal to empower and equip the consultee program to sustain changes and deal with similar problems in the future. Consultation typically follows predictable stages, including entry, assessment, goal and strategy development, implementation, and evaluation. It has the potential to affect knowledge, skill, and attitudes and may respond to child-specific, practitioner, or program issues (Buysse & Wesley, 2005). This last point is important to distinguish consultation from TA. TA that is established as a continuous and external network of services has the potential to address the ongoing systemwide needs of the receiving organizations that want to change. Consultation, on the other hand, is a temporary process that typically targets a specific aspect of that change process in a particular setting.

Coaching is an adult learning strategy that focuses on an individual's competencies in a specific skill area and is often used to support implementation of new practices. Coaching also can be used to improve existing abilities, including the learner's ability to determine the effectiveness of a practice and to refine it (Rush & Shelden, 2005). Coaching is an interactive and iterative process involving questioning and listening in combination with observation, reflection, and action (Crane, 2002). Coaches use modeling, prompting, and sharing feedback to help a learner incorporate new skills into practice (Hanft, Rush, & Shelden, 2004; Joyce & Showers, 1996). Coaching may be offered as a follow-up component of professional development and is one of many strategies that can be used during the implementation stage of consultation when the consultee program may be adding or refining job skills.

Mentoring is used to promote a person's awareness and refinement of his or her own professional development. Although not necessarily so, mentors are often internal to the program and are formally paired with colleagues who have less experience and competence. The mentoring process involves regular, focused, and systematic conversations and activities and draws upon a variety of approaches to challenge and support the recipient's planning ability, practice, and reflection (Evertson & Smithey, 2000; Kyle, Moore, & Sanders, 1997).

GUIDING PRINCIPLES FOR THE DELIVERY OF TA

In his writing about TA for international development, Owen (1950) highlighted three fundamental conditions for its success: 1) the need to have genuine cooperation between those providing and those receiving help to avoid the recipient's feeling of domination by the TA provider; 2) the need to avoid a one-sided approach to solutions of problems that may have proved successful in the TA provider's experience but which may not be compatible with the social and political culture of the recipient; and 3) the need to take a long-term view, as TA will not produce lasting results in a short period of time. As the senior officer principally concerned with the organization of TA to other countries in the early 1950s, Owen's leadership and writing stimulated passionate discussion about the challenge of providing context-appropriate TA and the qualifications of TA providers. Although there was much to be said for the scientific and specialized knowledge needed by a TA provider to convey the expertise of the scientific, industrialized, and socially progressive world, special qualities in addition to technical competence were needed, including patience, a lack of presumption of authority, and a willingness to work in a variety of settings and circumstances (Keenleyside, 1952).

In addition to Owen's fundamental conditions, which reflect basic principles of how to effect lasting change, many values undergirding collaborative consultation are instructive in guiding TA. For the TA provider, these include having insight and knowledge of self and clarity about what is happening in the present; demonstrating an energetic curiosity about all aspects of a situation, including tensions and negative reactions in interpersonal relationships; and engaging in continuous learning and collective reflection with others about the work being done (Buysse & Wesley, 2005). With these in mind, let us consider some guiding principles for TA:

1. TA is empowering and future oriented. It broadens the recipient program's perspective of its own problems and options for building knowledge and skills to address them. TA provides focused guidance and facilitation in handling current issues but also helps a program develop the ability to anticipate. In other words, TA does not just help programs move from short-term decision to short-term decision, but rather it assists them to develop the structures, processes, and skills to see and plan ahead.

2. TA is evidence based and process oriented. The TA system maintains current awareness of the best available research, wisdom, and values related to recommended practices and of initiatives in the larger professional field. TA providers are aware of the evidence supporting both the advice they give and the techniques they use in delivering TA.

3. TA is client driven and is grounded in a culture of collaboration. It recognizes and values the capability of TA recipients to make informed decisions and stimulates networking with others who can offer additional perspectives and supports. TA is shaped by the client's needs and priorities, resources, and circumstances, although the TA provider could provide the tools to analyze and clarify priorities.

4. TA is systematic. It is guided by a written plan that is developed collaboratively by the TA provider and recipient. This plan should include a statement of who receives TA, types of TA (priorities and sequence), who provides the TA and how, methods for determining the effectiveness of TA, the time frame for TA services, who pays for TA (if relevant), what follow-up is expected or needed, who provides the follow-up, and how often changes to the TA plan are anticipated.

5. Effective TA is built on trust, dialogue, and transparency.

A PROMISING NEW DIRECTION

The early childhood field lacks a comprehensive, integrated system of TA to support statewide program quality improvement efforts. In this section, we offer a promising new direction to respond to this need. Figure 7.1 illustrates a framework that identifies types of needs and corresponding categories of TA response. This framework is based loosely on the notion of primary, secondary, and tertiary

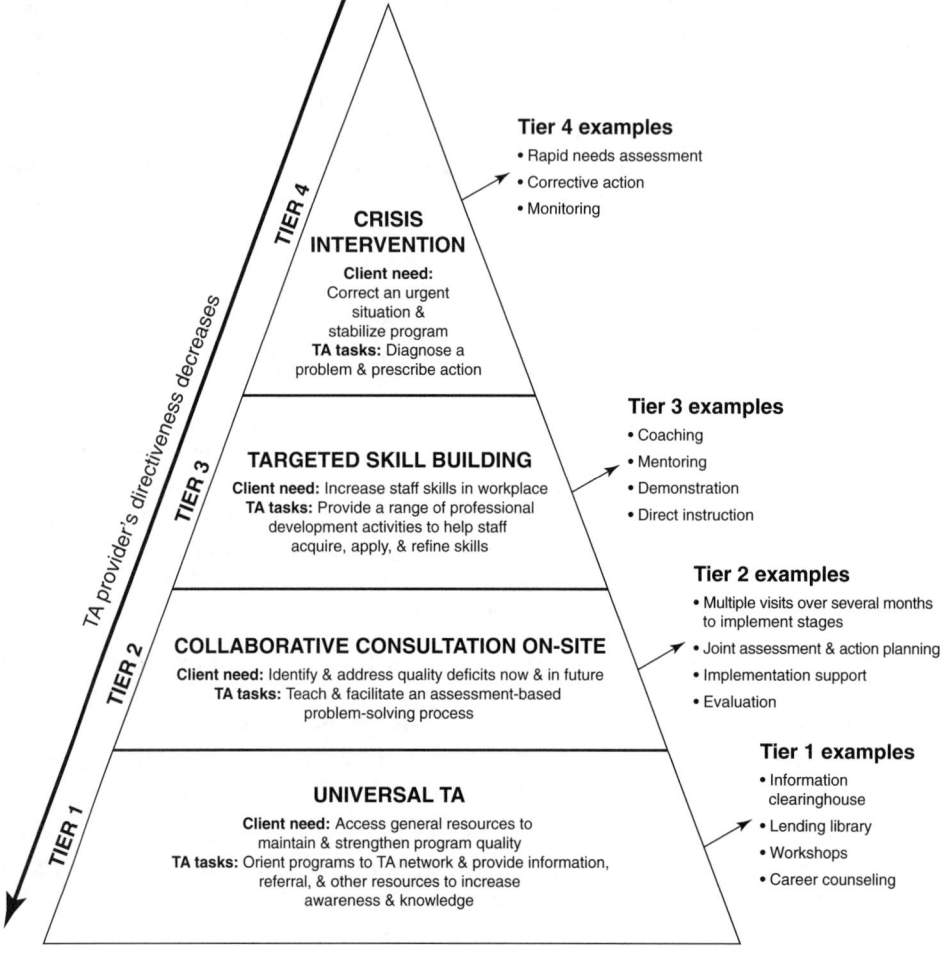

Figure 7.1. Technical assistance (TA) tiers.

prevention in the field of public health and could be used to guide the organization of TA services at the state or local level. Before we describe the figure, let us think about the steps of organizing a TA collaborative at the community level.

First, agencies, organizations, and individuals providing TA in the community would come together to discuss the landscape of TA services and to share information about TA goals, results, supports, challenges, and other issues related to their work in early childhood programs. In some communities it may not be possible for all TA providers to participate in such a collaborative, but at the very least, each agency should identify an administrator, a supervisor, or one lead TA provider who understands and represents TA services and can participate fully in the work of the collaborative. As previously discussed, ongoing joint planning among the TA agencies would ensure opportunities to coordinate their activities and eliminate duplication of services across sectors, share and build on their experiences and resources, coordinate professional development, and maximize evaluation and funding. The collaborating TA providers would use the pyramid of TA tiers illustrated in Figure 7.1 to organize their discussion of existing TA services and TA requests. The group would consider the nature of the needs of TA recipients and develop shared understandings about which TA activities address the various concerns within the tiers. This discussion could expand to consider the numbers of programs needing services at each level and to anticipate future needs for TA.

Early childhood programs and services could request help at any level of the pyramid and move among or combine services from various levels as needs arose. Professionals providing TA in the community would be able to describe services at each level, although they may not all be able to provide services at each level. This understanding of how services are organized would help TA providers and TA recipients think about and plan how they will use TA to increase and maintain high-quality programs.

Tier 1: Universal TA

All early childhood programs would have access to universal TA, a continuous stream of services from which programs could choose. These services would not be intensive or narrowly applied, but rather the TA network would advertise and offer Tier 1 activities broadly for two purposes: 1) to raise awareness about quality and the resources available to build the knowledge and skills needed to maintain or strengthen early childhood program quality and 2) to offer an array of activities and resources that broadly support programs in their efforts to maintain quality. Although Tier 1 TA should include activities that programs of varying levels of quality would find relevant, TA at this level is generic and not designed with the needs of a particular early childhood program in mind. Rather, Tier 1 is an ongoing menu of offerings for the early childhood system as a whole. Services could include workshops, courses, webinars, lending libraries, periodic group meetings of early childhood program administrators, an information clearinghouse (web-based or hotline) to answer various questions (e.g., about subsidy or professional development opportunities), peer linking of similar programs to share resources and ideas, and lunchtime symposiums on new research. Also included in Tier 1 would be the services of career counselors who mentor early childhood teachers and directors to develop and execute a professional development plan to maximize their effectiveness on the job. Although Tier 1 TA typically would not be delivered on site (with the possible exception of visits by a career counselor), a TA provider could make scheduled visits occasionally to maintain positive relationships or to orient a program to the TA network. Tier 1 serves both as an orientation to the network of TA services and as a resource for veteran programs seeking to maintain quality. For most Tier 1 services, a TA provider's approach would be that of a generalist, although for some activities, such as workshops or webinars, knowledge of a particular content area would be required.

Tier 2: On-Site Consultation

Tier 2 involves the delivery of on-site consultation for the purpose of enhancing global program quality or a particular aspect of quality (e.g., program administration, early learning standards, infant-toddler programming, promoting healthy social and emotional development). Consultation has been shown through research to increase program quality in early childhood centers and homes (Bryant et al., 2009; Palsha & Wesley, 1998; Wesley, 1994). It is desirable that, at some point, all early childhood programs would receive Tier 2 services to not only address a particular goal for change that the program has identified but also to equip the program with a problem-solving process to address needs in the future.

Consultation to enhance program quality would involve an assessment-based, collaborative approach, with the ultimate goal of equipping early childhood professionals with the knowledge and skills to identify and address quality deficits in their classrooms and programs. The consultation process would follow predictable stages as follows:

1. The TA provider's thoughtful entry, allowing enough time to build positive relationships and trust

2. Joint assessment by the TA provider and recipients of the program's needs using reliable and valid instruments to address all aspects of quality, including instruction and interactions

3. Analysis of the assessment findings, including discussions of the connection between quality indicators and children's development and learning

4. Collaborative identification of goals and strategies that build on strengths and address areas of weakness indicated in the assessment results

5. Supported implementation of those strategies

6. Mutual evaluation of the consultation outcomes and experience (Bryant et al., 2009; Buysse & Wesley, 2005)

Because intensive consultation of this sort both implements and teaches a problem-solving process in which early childhood staff learn to make informed decisions about their own practices and program, Tier 2 consultation cultivates a constructive climate for continuous reflection about quality. Tier 2 consultation is therefore more demanding than TA at other tiers, making it especially important before implementing it that the TA provider and program director agree that the service matches the program's needs and capacity to participate. Depending on the identified needs and selected TA strategies, early childhood professionals who receive on-site consultation may also participate in activities in other tiers. For example, goals may include building specific instructional skills (Tier 3) or accessing particular resources and networking opportunities (Tier 1).

Tier 2 consultants would possess a range of content expertise, skill, and reliability in the use of assessment tools, and proficient knowledge and experience in a collaborative and empowering consultation process, and in coaching. Tier 2 consultants also should have a comprehensive understanding of the laws and regulations affecting child care programs and of the resources available to support the early childhood workforce.

Tier 3: Targeted Skill Building

At this level, the TA network would offer a range of professional development activities to help early childhood program staff acquire, refine, and apply specific skills in the work setting. It is likely that such services would be short term, would typically occur on site and support teacher staff and/or administrators, and would include consultation, coaching, and mentoring. These services could be offered as a follow-up to more formal training in a given content area (such as a Tier 1 course) or in response to an early childhood program's request to refine instructional or administrative practices. For example, a program could request short-term consultation to identify and incorporate strategies to include a child with significant physical disabilities. Teachers in a 3- to 4-year-old classroom who had received training in an early literacy curriculum that they were now implementing could receive on-site instruction and feedback from a literacy coach. An administrator who wished to refine her skills in budgeting or time management would request assistance from a mentor.

Tier 3 needs could be identified during the Tier 2 consultation process to identify program quality goals, and it is possible that an early childhood program could receive both Tier 2 and Tier 3 services at the same time. For example, during the implementation stage of Tier 2 consultation, the TA provider and recipient might identify the need for coaching to support the application of a new skill in the classroom. At this point the TA provider could initiate Tier 3 services by linking the program with a coach or providing the service herself or himself.

Tier 4: Crisis Intervention

Programs experiencing an urgent need would receive crisis intervention. Services would be immediate, direct, short term, often technical, and delivered for the purpose of correcting or returning a situation to normal as soon as possible. Tier 4 services could be requested through a cry for help from the program itself—for example, an emergency request to address a problem with a child's harmful behavior. They also could be imposed from without, triggered by concerns such as a program's noncompliance with regulations, an abuse/neglect referral, or a sudden health issue. In this case, Tier 4 services would involve state licensing agents or other regulatory professionals.

It is possible that all programs could have a need for services at this level from time to time. Ideally, Tier 4 services could open the door for the problem-solving process, addressing global quality that is provided through Tier 2 consultation or targeted skill building as highlighted in Tier 3. TA providers at Tier 4 would be specialists and possess process skills including rapid needs assessment and action planning, followed by directed implementation.

More About Tiered TA

The tiered TA model proposed here reflects the breadth of client needs and provides a framework for organizing the TA network's various services and activities in response to those needs. The tiers are not intended as ironclad categories that artificially compartmentalize TA activities but rather as broad concepts to guide the organization and marketing of TA services. It is conceivable that a given program could find itself accessing services at all levels at the same time, although this is not likely. More likely, programs would enter the TA network through Tier 1 activities (which would continue to be available to them) and move through Tiers 2 and 3 over time, with the emergency services of Tier 4 always available to them if needed.

The tiered TA model has implications for how TA providers are assigned and supervised. While all TA providers would have the knowledge, skills, and dispositions to provide universal TA, Tier 1 could be a comfortable entry experience for novice TA providers. Tier 2 consultants would need thorough knowledge of all dimensions of program quality and be proficient in on-site, collaborative consultation. Like TA providers at all tiers, they would possess effective interpersonal and communication skills and be versed not only in adult learning theory but also in change principles. Tier 3 TA providers would include those with focused knowledge and skills in critical content areas related to children's early development and learning and teachers' instructional practices. Tier 4 TA providers playing a crisis intervention role would need specific expertise in areas such as child health and safety and expert knowledge of laws and regulations governing child care. Systematic documentation of the number and typical needs of programs at the various levels of the tiered model each year could also become a helpful ongoing tool as the TA system planned for the recruitment, development, and retention of the TA provider workforce. Likewise, the tiered TA model could provide a framework for periodically assessing the needs of early childhood programs across the community and appraising services against those needs (who needs what services at which tiers?), for identifying funding priorities and leveraging resources (how to allocate resources to support each tier), and for delineating agency responsibilities (which agencies provide what services at which tiers?).

Applying the Tiered Model to Rainbow Child Care

Let us recall the case of Rainbow Child Care and the TA activities in which staff are engaged, and consider which tier they represent. Center staff participate in local workshops on early childhood issues, an activity under Tier 1's universal TA. Imagine also that the director attends quarterly meetings of directors held at the local CCR&R, also a Tier 1 resource. In addition, three TA providers deliver services that they hope will ultimately improve professional practices at Rainbow Child Care. However, because they are not all equipping their TA recipients with problem-solving strategies or an understanding of the various dimensions of program quality, it is unlikely that program quality gains will be sustained. As we will see, the prescriptive approach of two of the three TA providers is more typical of the Tier 4 level of crisis intervention.

A quality enhancement specialist is visiting the program regularly to track progress on an action plan that she has created based on the results of an assessment instrument that she has administered. The strategies she is using are prescriptive rather than collaborative—that is, she alone assesses needs and identifies goals and strategies to raise quality. Her approach does not enhance the TA recipients' competencies or provide them with the ability to assess and address quality deficits in the future. The activities in which she engages (rapid needs assessment, prescribed action, monitoring) currently are more aligned with the Tier 4 crisis orientation than the Tier 2 focus on empowerment.

A behavior specialist provides TA to Rainbow Child Care for the purpose of helping staff reduce the challenging behavior of a particular child in the toddler classroom. Along with recommending specific strategies to the teachers based on his assessment of the child's behavior, he hopes to encourage Rainbow's staff to attend the training sessions on positive behavioral supports that he provides periodically through the CCR&R. Similar to the quality enhancement specialist's approach, the behavior specialist's on-site services to address staff needs reflect an expert approach to diagnosis and problem resolution that is found in Tier 4. The training sessions he offers in the community would be considered part of universal TA at Tier 1. Were the behavior specialist to begin providing on-site opportunities for the staff to see him demonstrate classroom strategies and to receive feedback as they implement them, then this would reflect the Tier 3 skill-building focus and range of activities. Were he to engage staff in a collaborative problem-solving process to assess and improve the program's strategies for promoting children's social and emotional development, then this would be Tier 2 consultation and would hold the most promise for staff to be able to prevent challenging behaviors in the future.

Finally, a literacy coach provides a range of TA to enhance a particular dimension of program quality, promoting early language and literacy. She uses various assessment tools to help the teachers identify their needs and collaborates with them to identify strategies for improvement—all activities described under Tier 2. She also provides opportunities for them to practice using storybook strategies in the classroom and provides feedback to help them refine their skills, a Tier 3 approach.

Now that we have categorized the existing TA services according to the tiers, let us reframe this scenario, beginning with the program's request to participate in the quality enhancement program, which the CCR&R director shares with members of the TA collaborative. The TA collaborative discusses any current TA activities in which Rainbow Child Care is engaged and the following steps unfold:

1. Before initiating on-site TA from the quality enhancement specialist, a meeting is held including the behavior specialist, the literacy coach, Rainbow Child Care's director, and the quality enhancement specialist to discuss current professional development needs and TA goals at Rainbow Child Care. In this meeting, it is recognized that staff at Rainbow Child Care have not had an opportunity to assess their program's global quality needs and may not realize what dimensions constitute high-quality care and education.

2. After determining the program's interest and ability to participate, the quality enhancement specialist provides comprehensive and collaborative on-site consultation through which the director and teachers learn how to assess their program's needs using a variety of instruments, select goals to enhance quality, implement strategies with the support of the quality enhancement specialist, and access ongoing resources to enrich and sustain their achievements (Tiers 2 and 1). The entire consultation process takes 10 months and involves multiple visits.

3. The quality enhancement specialist and director share the steps of the consultation process with the literacy coach and behavior specialist, and together they identify areas where they can participate. For example, the literacy coach participates in the discussion of environment rating scale items addressing language and reasoning, sharing examples of strategies that are being implemented in the prekindergarten class.

4. One goal on the action plan developed by the quality enhancement specialist and staff is to increase and improve the interactions between teachers and infants and toddlers attending Rainbow Child Care. The director shares this goal with the behavior specialist, and all agree on a strategy to provide

on-site opportunities for staff to observe each other's interactions with the children and provide feedback, based on guidelines that the behavior specialist will share during an on-site training session (Tier 3).

5. The three TA providers maintain communication during the period in which they are all working in Rainbow Child Care to schedule visits without overwhelming staff, share resources, enhance the consistency of their recommendations, and address TA challenges. Although only the quality enhancement specialist attends meetings of the TA collaborative, the TA providers and their supervisors, who do attend, communicate about key TA issues, needs, and resources.

Many questions remain about how best to organize and implement tiered TA services at the local level. Decisions about leadership within the TA collaborative will be important, as no one agency is responsible for all TA or has the funding to steer this effort. There are also questions about portal of entry and how early childhood program needs can best be conveyed to the collaborative, as agencies providing TA receive their "own" requests for TA, may have their "own" clients, and must do what is necessary to meet their "own" guidelines and funding requirements. There may be a temptation to refer to early childhood programs by the tier of services in which they are engaged—for example, as "a Tier 2 program" or "a Tier 4 program." The tiered TA model is not intended to label programs in this way but rather to provide a coherent framework for thinking about TA services. It is likely that these and other concerns will best be resolved community by community, as TA providers begin to communicate about increasing the quality and efficiency of TA services.

TA PROVIDER QUALIFICATIONS AND COMPETENCIES

In his guide to the profession of management consulting, Kubr makes the point that few professions start out being professional, that professional awareness and behavior develop only after "the early juggling with a little knowledge gives way to skilled application of a generally accepted body of knowledge according to accepted standards of integrity" (2002, p. 129). Many professions—such as medicine, law, management consulting, and the applied sciences—have developed in this way, and early childhood education is no different. Although TA within the field of early childhood education is not considered a profession in and of itself, it is important for agencies providing TA to come to agreement about the competencies necessary for TA providers. This is the first step to recognizing, sharing, and applying a set of norms to the activity.

In considering TA qualifications and competencies, it may be productive to start with the TA relationship in mind. Although there may develop an institutional relationship between the TA network and the community of early childhood programs it serves, TA is likely to be most effective when the provider–recipient relationship is personalized. Services are delivered through direct contact between people from the TA network (who may work for different agencies) and people who work at the early childhood program receiving TA. A productive relationship will depend not on the formal understanding or agreement between organizations but on the abilities and attitudes of the people involved. At this point in the development of early childhood TA, however, virtually anyone can call himself or herself a technical assistant or consultant and offer services without any diploma, certificate, license, credentials, professional recommendations, or registration.

As illustrated in the tiered model, TA should include a variety of approaches, activities, and tasks that respond to differing client needs and that vary in terms of the nature and scope of the work, the role of the TA provider, and the time involved with the client program. Even so, there are generic professional competencies that all TA providers would benefit from possessing. These competencies encompass a range of knowledge, skills, and attitudes that ensure the TA provider's proficiency in the technical aspects of the early childhood field and his or her ability to develop a collaborative relationship with clients and identify and gather information about all aspects of a referring problem to facilitate practical improvements. One way to organize TA competencies is to cluster them under four domains:

1. Personal Effectiveness (e.g., interpersonal skills, ethical and professional behavior, willingness to learn)
2. Day-to-Day Functioning (e.g., basic literacy/numeracy skills, written and oral communication, comfort with tools and technology, critical thinking)
3. Job-Specific Knowledge (e.g., child development; early childhood recommended practices, laws and regulations, and resources; adult learning theory and professional development methods; consultation stages)
4. Job-Specific Skills (e.g., communication and collaboration, data collection and analysis, action planning, measuring and analyzing results)

Table 7.2 presents one example of TA provider competencies that could serve as a starting point for discussion. Currently at least three states have developed competencies for TA positions, and the topic is under discussion in many others. It has been our experience that early discussions of TA competencies in states reflect a view of the TA provider in a limited role—that of adult educator. In contrast, the competencies in Table 7.2 address additional TA principles, including theories of empowerment, change, and consultation.

Whether seen through the eyes of an administrator, teacher, or TA provider, it is clear that current approaches to enhance and sustain program quality, though well intended, could be planned, organized, delivered, and evaluated differently to maximize their effectiveness. In many ways, this reflects the disjointed collection of individual services that compose the early childhood system as a whole. It is a daunting challenge to coordinate and innovate services that are provided under the heading of TA by numerous different agencies in a state or even in a community. Equally daunting is the task of conceptualizing a TA network that possesses the competence to address the needs of diverse early childhood programs and market itself in a way that demonstrates its relevance to each. A starting point is to identify the types of needs that early childhood programs have and to tailor TA approaches to meet those needs.

Table 7.2. Possible technical assistance (TA) provider competencies

A. Personal Effectiveness

1. Demonstrates effective interpersonal skills
   - Shows respect and authenticity in relationships
   - Puts other people at ease through conversation and warmth
   - Establishes and maintains rapport and mutual trust with others

2. Demonstrates ethical and professional behavior
   - Is dependable and honest
   - Values the unique cultural experiences of others and the role cultural differences play in the identification and resolution of problems
   - Monitors and attempts to understand all aspects of the TA relationship, including tensions and negative reactions in interpersonal relationships
   - Adheres to accepted guidelines for professional behavior (e.g., follows confidentiality policy, submits appropriate and timely documentation)
   - Able to articulate and clarify personal and professional values (e.g., the value of children's emotional and social development as a foundation for later school success; of practices that are culturally sensitive and respectful; of reciprocal and collaborative relationships with TA recipients; of experiential and research-based knowledge as a foundation for practice)
   - Aware of own professional limits as evidenced by knowing when to say no, when to seek support, and when to refer a TA client to another resource
   - Establishes and maintains clear professional boundaries by knowing the difference between own personal feelings and needs and the professional needs, concerns, and feelings of the TA recipient
   - Aware of potential conflict between TA recommendations and a program's regulatory standards and of the potential impact of changes on internal program policies or initiatives

3. Demonstrates a willingness to learn
   - Takes stock of own effectiveness, knowledge, skills, and attitudes and pursues personal and professional growth as needed
   - Seeks and accepts feedback from others
   - Systematically incorporates new research findings that support specific interventions into practice

B. Day-to-Day Functioning

1. Communicates clearly and effectively in oral and written form
2. Reads and understands procedures, policies, budgets, and other job-related documents
3. Effectively uses all relevant workplace tools and technology (e.g., office equipment, communication devices, computers and software)
4. Engages in appropriate problem-solving steps, involving others in collaboration when necessary
5. Seeks assistance and supervision to support optimal performance

C. Job-Specific Knowledge

1. Child development theory: Understands major theories about how children learn and develop and implications for TA delivery
2. Special needs: Understands causes of disabilities and impact of disabilities on development and implications for TA delivery
3. Early childhood recommended practices
   - Possesses working knowledge of effective early childhood practices as reflected in NAEYC and DEC (Division of Early Childhood of the Council for Exceptional Children) Recommended Practices documents
   - Aware of current issues and research in the early childhood field (e.g., links between quality and child outcomes; emphasis on school readiness; recognition and response interventions; interagency collaboration; outcomes of early childhood inclusion)
   - Knowledgeable about the use of various instruments and methods to assess aspects of high-quality programs and global program quality (e.g., checklists, surveys, interviews, environment rating scales)

4. TA principles and methods
   - Understands theories of empowerment and change
   - Knows adult learning theory and effective approaches to professional development
   - Knows consultation stages and strategies
   - Understands the different levels of TA services (focus, tasks, purpose) and the various activities provided through a tiered TA model
   - Has knowledge of strategies to evaluate TA

5. Child care laws and regulations
   - Has knowledge of licensure and accreditation standards for early childhood programs
   - Has knowledge of state early learning standards
   - Is familiar with relevant legislation (child abuse/neglect laws, Individuals with Disabilities Act [IDEA], Americans with Disabilities Act [ADA])

6. Local, state, national resources
   - Knows about local early childhood services and the state early childhood system
   - Knows about local early intervention services and the state early intervention system, including procedures for referring a child suspected of having special needs for evaluation and educational planning
   - Aware of local, state, and national resources supporting professionals and families of young children with and without special needs and how to link others to them (e.g., professional organizations, advocacy groups, interagency coalitions)
   - Familiar with local, state, and national resources supporting high quality in early childhood programs and supporting TA to enhance quality

D. Job-Specific Skills

1. Guides TA process
   - Discusses TA process and communication logistics with clients and clarifies mutual roles and expectations
   - Is organized and thoughtful in preparing for and facilitating meetings
   - Completes and uses written documentation as a framework for process (e.g., contact summary forms, action plans, evaluation forms)

2. Selects communication strategies to maximize trust, implementation, and empowerment
   - Uses nonverbal behaviors (e.g., physical posture, eye contact) to demonstrate interest and concern, and is aware of congruency between nonverbal and verbal messages, and is aware of nonverbal messages of others
   - Communicates in a helpful, nonthreatening manner; is able to express own ideas without being overpowering
   - Listens responsively by reflecting content and feelings
   - Seeks consensus and verifies information by questioning, clarifying, and summarizing
   - Uses balance in sharing personal and professional experiences and perspectives to both establish rapport and minimize perceptions of power
   - Respects divergent points of view and is able to suspend or reframe own perceptions to conceptualize situations from multiple perspectives
   - Chooses among many methods of communication between visits, such as phone, e-mail, mail, and group meetings, keeping in mind TA recipient's preferred mode

3. Uses a variety of valid and reliable assessment strategies and tools to gather objective, complete, and relevant information that can be used to clarify program concerns
   - Selects assessment strategy to match desired outcomes with TA recipient input
   - Skilled in observation and questioning; able to synthesize information from multiple sources
   - Able to administer various instruments and processes to assess aspects of early childhood programs, such as administration, instruction, interactions (e.g., surveys, checklists, interviews)
   - Able to administer and score instruments to assess global program quality (e.g., environment rating scales such as ECERS-R, ITERS-R, FCCERS, CLASS)
   - Able to train TA recipients in proper use of various assessment strategies and tools

4. Analyzes data to inform action planning
   - Uses a variety of data to identify, assess, and clarify needs (e.g., from formal and informal observations, interviews, assessment instruments)

(continued)

Table 7.2. Possible TA provider competencies (*continued*)

- Is objective in gathering and interpreting information, identifying responsive interventions, and predicting ramifications
- Formulates and shares hypotheses about root causes of problems before engaging in problem-solving process
- Assesses resources and engages in collaborative planning to generate goals for change

5. Draws upon a variety of roles and methods to support implementation
   - With TA recipient, anticipates, discusses, and prepares for obstacles
   - Uses coaching skills to support TA recipient's use of new approaches and skills (e.g., modeling, reflecting, observing, giving feedback)
   - Helps TA recipient to clarify and understand situations by balancing the need to be clear and honest with the need to avoid blaming others when snags arise
   - Skillfully solves problems, resolves conflict, and manages resistance

6. Evaluates TA outcomes and relationship
   - Requests input about TA process as it unfolds
   - Monitors and discusses TA outcomes
   - With TA recipient, examines relationship and makes adjustments as needed
   - Asks recipient to evaluate TA provider's knowledge, skills, and responsiveness

REFERENCES

Bennis, W., Benne, K., & Chin, R. (1969). *The planning of change* (2nd ed.). New York: Holt, Rinehart, and Winston.

Blase, K. (2009). *Technical assistance to promote service and system change: Roadmap to effective intervention practices #4*. Tampa: University of South Florida, Technical Assistance Center on Social Emotional Intervention for Young Children.

Bromer, J., & Henly, J.R. (2004). Child care as family support? Caregiving practices across child care providers. *Children and Youth Services Review, 26,* 941–964.

Bryant, D., Bernier, K., Maxwell, K., & Peisner-Feinberg, E. (2002). *Smart Start and child care in North Carolina: Effects on quality and changes over time.* Chapel Hill: University of North Carolina, FPG Child Development Institute.

Bryant, D., Burchinal, M.R., Lau, L., & Sparling, J.J. (1994). Family and classroom correlates of Head Start children's developmental outcomes. *Early Childhood Research Quarterly, 9,* 289–309.

Bryant, D.M., Maxwell, K.L., & Burchinal, M. (1999). Effects of a community initiative on the quality of child care. *Early Childhood Research Quarterly, 14,* 449–464.

Bryant, D., & Ponder, K. (2004). North Carolina's Smart Start Initiative: A decade of evaluation lessons. *Evaluation Exchange, X,* 7–8.

Bryant, D., Wesley, P.W., & the QUINCE Study Team. (2009, July). *The QUINCE-PFI Study: An evaluation of a promising model and delivery approaches for care provider training. Final report to the ACF/Child Care Bureau.* Chapel Hill: University of North Carolina, FPG Child Development Institute.

Budde, J.F., & Summers, J.A. (1991). Consultation and technical assistance. In J.L. Matson & J.A. Mulick (Eds.), *Handbook of mental retardation* (2nd ed., pp. 489–502). New York: Pergamon Press.

Buysse, V., & Wesley, P. (2005). *Consultation in early childhood settings.* Baltimore: Paul H. Brookes Publishing Co.

Child Care and Early Education Research Connections. (2007). *Early childhood comprehensive systems: A key topic resource list.* Retrieved December 8, 2009, from www.researchconnections.org

Clifford, R.M., & Trohanis, P. (1980). *Technical assistance in educational settings.* Columbus: Ohio State University.

Cost, Quality, & Child Outcomes Study Team. (1995). *Cost, quality, and child outcomes in child care centers:* Final report. Denver: University of Colorado, Economics Department.

Crane, T. (2001). *The heart of coaching.* San Diego: FTA Press.

Dinnebeil, L.A., & McInerney, W.F. (2000). Supporting inclusion in community-based settings: The role of the "Tuesday morning teacher." *Young Exceptional Children, 4*, 19–26.

Domergue, M. (1968). *Technical assistance: Theory, practice, policies.* New York: Praeger.

Espinsosa, L.M. (2002). High-quality preschool: Why we need it and what it looks like. *NIEER Preschool Policy Matters, 1.* New Brunswick, NJ: National Institute for Early Education Research, Rutgers University.

Evertson, C., & Smithey, M. (2000). Mentoring effects on protégés' classroom practice: An experimental field study. *Journal of Educational Research, 93*, 294–304.

Fixsen, D.L., Naoom, S.F., Blasé, K.A., Friedman, R.M., & Wallace, F. (2005). *Implementation research: A synthesis of the literature* (FMHI Publication #231). Tampa: University of South Florida. Louis de la Parte Florida Mental Health Institute. The National Implementation Research Network.

Fuchs, D., Fuchs, L.S., Dulan, J., Roberts, H., & Fernstorm, P. (1992), Where is the research on consultation effectiveness? *Journal of Educational and Psychological Consultation, 3*, 151–174.

Gallaher, J.J., Danaher, J., & Clifford, R.M. (2009). The evolution of the National Early Childhood Technical Assistance Center. *Topics in Early Childhood Education, 29*, 7–23.

Hanft, B.E., Rush, D.D., & Shelden, M.L. (2004). *Coaching families and colleagues in early childhood.* Baltimore: Paul H. Brookes Publishing Co.

Harms, T., Clifford, R.M., & Cryer, D. (1998). *Early Childhood Environment Rating Scale: Revised edition.* New York Teachers College Press.

Harms, T., Cryer, D., & Clifford, R.M. (2003). *Infant/Toddler Environment Rating Scale: Revised edition.* New York: Teachers College Press.

Harms, T., Cryer, D., & Clifford, R.M. (2007). *Family Child Care Environment Rating Scale: Revised edition.* New York: Teachers College Press.

Havelock, R. (1973). *The change agent's guide to innovation in education.* Englewood Cliffs, NJ: Educational Technology Publications.

Howes, C., Phillips, D.A., & Whitebook, M. (1992). Thresholds of quality: Implications for the social development of children in center-based care. *Child Development, 63*, 449–460.

Joyce, B., & Showers, B. (1996). The evolution of peer coaching. *Educational leadership, 53*, 12–16.

Keenleyside, K. (1952). Administrative problems of technical assistance administration. *Canadian Journal of Economics and Political Science, 18*, 345–357.

Knowles, M. (1978). *The adult learner: A neglected species* (2nd ed.) Houston: Gulf.

Knox, A.B. (1980). Proficiency theory of adult learning. *Contemporary Educational Psychology, 5*, 378–404.

Kubr, M. (2002). *Management consulting: A guide for the profession* (4th ed.). Geneva: International Labour Office.

Kyle, D., Moore, G., & Sanders, J. (1999). The role of the mentor teacher: Insights, challenges, and implications. *Peabody Journal of Education, 74*, 109–122.

Lamb, M.E. (1998). Nonparental child care: Context, quality, correlates, and consequences. In W. Damon (Editor-in-Chief) & I.E. Siegel & K.A. Renninger (Vol. Eds.), *Handbook of child psychology: Vol. 4. Child psychology in practice* (5th ed., pp. 75–117). New York: Wiley.

LeBuffe, P.A., & Naglieri, J.A. (1999). *Devereaux Early Childhood Assessment.* Lewisville, NC: Kaplan Press.

Lippitt, G. & Lippitt, R. (1986). *The consulting process in action* (2nd ed.). San Diego: University Associates.

McKenna, C.D. (1995, fall). The origins of modern management consulting. *Business and Economic History, 24*, 51–58.

National Association of Child Care Resource and Referral Agencies. (1996). *Making child care work: A study of child care resource and referral in the United States.* Arlington, VA: Author.

National Association of Child Care Resource and Referral Agencies. (2007a, March). *Child care resource and referral staff qualifications and compensation* (Report 200-0103). Arlington, VA: Author.

National Association of Child Care Resource and Referral Agencies. (2007b). *NACCRA's 12-point plan for improving our nation's training* (Report 230-0109). Arlington, VA: Author.

National Institute for Child Health and Human Development (2005). *Opening the door to quality: Centers.* Arlington, VA: Author.

National Research Council. (2008). *Early childhood assessment: Why, what, and how.* Committee on Developmental Outcomes and Assessments for Young Children, C.E. Snow & S.B. Van Hemel (Eds.), Board on Children, Youth, and Families, Board on Testing and Assessment, Division of Behavioral and Social Sciences and Education. Washington, DC: The National Academies Press.

Osborne, D., & Gaebler, T. (1993). *Reinventing government: How the entrepreneurial spirit is transforming the public sector.* New York: Plume.

Owen, D. (1950). The United Nations program of technical assistance. *Annals of the American Academy of Political and Social Science 270,* 109–117.

Palsha, S., & Wesley, P.W. (1998). Improving the quality in early childhood environments through on-site consultation. *Topics in Early Childhood Special Education, 18,* 243–253.

Peisner-Feinberg, E.S., Burchinal, M.R., Clifford, R.M., Culkin, M.L., Howes, C., Kagan, L.S., et al. (2001). The relation of preschool child-care quality to children's cognitive and social developmental trajectories through second grade. *Child Development, 72,* 1534–1553.

Pianta, R.C., La Paro, K.M., & Hamre, B.K. (2008). *Classroom Assessment Scoring System Manual.* Baltimore: Paul H. Brookes Publishing Co.

RAND Corporation. (2008). *Report on child care quality rating and improvement systems in five pioneer states.* Santa Monica, CA: Author.

Richman., H., & Clifford, R.M. (1980). Toward a model of technical assistance. In R.M. Clifford & P.L. Trohanis (Eds.), *Technical assistance in educational settings* (pp. 13–18). Columbus: Ohio State University.

Rogers, E., & Shoemaker, F.F. (1971). *Communication of innovations: A cross-cultural approach* (2nd ed.). New York: The Free Press.

Rush, D.D., & Shelden, M.L. (2005). *Evidence-based definition of coaching practice.* Center for the Advanced Study of Excellence in Early Childhood and Family Support Practices. Retrieved December 8, 2009, from http://www.fippcase.org/caseinpoint/caseinpoint_vol1_no6.pdf

Ryan, B., & Wesley, P.W. (2006). *Technical assistance providers survey report.* Chapel Hill: University of North Carolina, Frank Porter Graham Child Development Institute.

Scheuring, A.F. (1988). *History and foundation of the Cooperative Extension.* Retrieved July 1, 2009, from http://are.berkeley.edu/~norwong/bkground.html

Smith, M.W., Brady, J.P., & Anastasopoulos, L. (2008). *Early Language and Literacy Classroom Observation Tool.* Baltimore: Paul H. Brookes Publishing Co.

Sturgeon, S., Tracy, M.L., Ziegler, A., Newfeld, R., & Wiegerink, R. (1977). *Technical assistance: Facilitating change.* Bloomington: Developmental Training Center, Indiana University.

Sullivan, W.P. (1991). Technical assistance in community mental health: A model for social work consultants. *Research on Social Work Practice, 1,* 289–305.

Sylva, K., Siraj-Blatchford, I., Taggart, B., Sammons, P., Melhuish, E., Elliot, K., Totsika, V. (2006). Capturing quality in early childhood through environmental rating scales. *Early Childhood Research Quarterly, 21,* 76–92

Trohanis, P.L. (1982). Technical assistance and the improvement of services to exceptional children. *Theory into Practice, 21,* 119–128.

United Nations Development Programme. (2008). *Practice note, 2008.* Retrieved December 8, 2009, from http://www.undp.org/oslocentre/docs08/sofia/CD%20PN%20May%202008.pdf

U.S. General Accounting Office. (2002, September 6). *Child care: States have undertaken a variety of quality improvement initiatives, but more evaluations of effectiveness are needed* (GAO-02-897). Washington, DC: Author.

Vandell, D.L. (2004). Early child care: The known and the unknown. *Merrill-Palmer Quarterly 50*(3), 387–414.

Wesley, P.W. (1994). Providing on-site consultation to promote quality in integrated child care programs. *Journal of Early Intervention, 18,* 391–402.

Wesley, P., & Buysse, V. (1996). Supporting early childhood inclusion: Lessons learned through a statewide technical assistance project. *Topics in Early Childhood Special Education, 16,* 476–499.

Wesley, P.W., Buysse, V., & Skinner, D. (2001). Early interventionists' perspectives on professional comfort as consultants. *Journal of Early Intervention, 24,* 112–128.

Wilson, G. (2007). Knowledge, innovation and reinventing technical assistance for development. *Progress in Developmental Studies, 7,* 183–199.

CHAPTER 8

Early Childhood Policy and Implications for Quality Initiatives

Beth Rous and Kim F. Townley

In 1976, the chair of the National Commission on Manpower Policy, Eli Ginzberg, made a striking observation that the influx of women in the job market was one of the most notable changes of the century (Ginzberg, 1976). By 1977, the number of mothers in the workforce was three times higher than it had been in 1948 (Grossman, 1978). This change in the makeup of the labor market has since affected the lives of many who have or work on behalf of young children in the United States. Since that time, there have been numerous policies and programs that have attempted to provide support to families of young children as they balance their work and family obligations. As the field of early childhood has learned more about the importance of the early years to the overall success of children in school and life, these policies and programs have increasingly focused on ensuring that young children have access to settings outside the home that are of high quality and hold the best promise of supporting and maximizing their growth and development.

Before discussing these policies, it is important to define what we mean by policy and clarify the role of policy in early care, intervention, and education initiatives and programs. Traditionally, policy has served as the foundation for a course of action to be taken at the federal, state, or local level; however, definitions of policy and policy making vary greatly in the fields of human services and education (e.g., Fowler, 2000; Gallagher, 1994). Across these definitions, there are consistent components of policy making that apply across levels (e.g., federal, state, local). First, policy involves formal processes such as executive orders, legislation, rules/regulations, policy memos/directives, guidelines/standards, and court decisions. Second, policies are designed to address social needs or public issues of consequence. Third, policies are generally developed through a series of decision-making processes that include key stakeholders at the development and/or comment level. Fourth, policies are based on a set of shared values.

While policy making generally includes these key components, in the area of early care, intervention, and education, policy decisions are more often based on a rationalist tradition (Scribner, Aleman, & Maxcy, 2003), which recognizes the impact of economic implications on policy makers' decisions about whether to support or push a policy. Policies are generally designed to be flexible and provide guidance while allowing for specificity in implementation based on state or local context.

As it relates to policy and quality, research has helped to identify specific dimensions of quality, which have been detailed in Chapters 1–3 of this book. Across these dimensions of quality, policy makers have traditionally used a patchwork approach to address quality, in part due to the multiple federal agencies involved in early care, intervention, and education and state-by-state differences in implementation of these programs. The remainder of this chapter provides a brief historical overview of national policies and influences on policy development and implementation with regard to quality, including examples of state efforts to support quality initiatives. This is followed by a discussion of current issues in the area of quality for early childhood. The chapter ends with recommendations for a national agenda to improve the quality of settings and services for young children.

HISTORY OF EFFORTS TO IMPROVE QUALITY

While it is impossible in this chapter to provide a complete history of efforts to improve quality in the area of early childhood, examples of the types of efforts that have occurred are important in setting the context for how we can move closer to agreeing on key dimensions of quality that are important to address at the national level. In light of Winston Churchill's famous quote, "Those that fail to learn from history are doomed to repeat it," it is critical that we understand previous efforts to enhance quality and build upon efforts that have been successful.

Kindergarten, inspired by a German educator named Friedrich Froebel, was one of the earliest early childhood initiatives in the United States, emerging in the mid-19th century. The first public school kindergarten opened in 1870 in St. Louis and served three 6-year-old children. While kindergarten looks different from state to state, 43 states mandate that districts offer at least a half-day program, 9 states require that districts offer full-day kindergarten, and 14 states require children to attend kindergarten (Education Commission of the States, 2005).

On a more contemporary level, one important time period in the quest for quality in early childhood was during the rapid growth that occurred in programs for young children in the 1970s, which, as stated previously, was primarily attributed to the increased numbers of mothers entering the labor market. During this same time period, concerns about quality of the settings in which children spent time were raised through numerous reports, such as *Windows on Day Care* (Keyserling, 1972), the *President's Commission on School Finance Report* (Piele, 1972), and *A Nation at Risk: The Imperative for Educational Reform* (National Commission on Excellence in Education, 1984). As more attention focused on the quality of care for young children, research reports such as *Changed Lives: The Effects of the Perry Preschool Program on Youths Through Age 19* (Berrueta-Clement, Schweinhart, Barnett, Epstein, & Weikart, 1984) surfaced to provide an evidence base for national efforts toward quality enhancement.

Professional organizations have also had significant influence on the call for quality enhancements and funding for early care, intervention, and education, including organizations at the international (e.g., Association for Childhood Education International [ACEI]), national (e.g., National Association for the Education of Young Children [NAEYC], National Association of Child Care Resource and Referral Agencies [NACCRRA], Division for Early Childhood [DEC] of the Council for Exceptional Children [CEC]), and regional levels (e.g., Southern Association on Children Under Six, now the Southern Early Childhood Association).

Through these professional organizations, numerous initiatives, positions, papers, and research findings have been developed and disseminated and influenced how both early childhood professionals and government officials at the state and national level have attempted to support higher quality. A few notable examples include the *Early Childhood Education Teacher Education Guidelines* (NAEYC, 1982), *Developmentally Appropriate Practice in Early Childhood Programs Serving Children from Birth Through Age 8* (Bredekamp, 1987), *The Right to Quality in Child Care* (Gotts, 1988), the *Child Development Associate (CDA) program* (1971) through the Council for Early Childhood Professional Recognition (formerly the Child Development Consortium), *Unacceptable Trends in Kindergarten Entry and Placement* (National Association of Early Childhood Specialists in State Department of Education [NAECS-SDE], 1987), and *Right from the Start* (Schultz & Lombardi, 1989).

While the initiatives and publications of professional organizations were geared toward educating and supporting high-quality early childhood programs, a number of organizations also emphasized the policy needs related to establishing a national agenda to support our youngest citizens in accessing safe, high-quality early learning experiences. For example, in 1980 the National Campaign for Child Day Care for Working Families developed a political platform emphasizing the need for working families to be able to access quality child care at affordable rates. Specific policy alerts and briefs were initiated through organizations such as NAEYC, the Yale Bush Programs in Child Development and Social Policy, the Children's Defense Fund, and the Society for Research in Child Development (SRCD). These reports provided information on policy issues and recommendations that could be used at the national, state, and local level.

Federal agencies have also initiated efforts to improve quality in early childhood settings. In 1969, Edward Zigler headed the first federal office devoted to early childhood, the Office of Child Development (renamed the Administration for Children, Youth and Families in 1977), which followed funding for Head Start in 1965. To date, Head Start represents the first and longest-standing national program designed to support a preschool program to address the emotional, social, health, nutritional, and psychological needs of children from low-income families. In 1994, after numerous efforts, the Early Head Start program was established to support prevention and promotion of healthy development in infants and toddlers.

Another success story for the federal government was the establishment in 1976 of the Preschool Incentive Grants program, which provided $12.5 million to states to provide services for children 3–5 years of age with disabilities. This was followed over a decade later with the passage of PL 99-457, which added incentive grants to states to serve infants and toddlers (up to age 3) with disabilities and their families. These programs, which are still in existence today, were part of the Education of the Handicapped Act (EHA) of 1970 (PL 91-230), later renamed the Individuals with Disabilities Education Act (IDEA), through the U.S. Department of Education.

While there are successes at the national level for providing prevention and intervention services to children from targeted populations, efforts to support a

Table 8.1. Key child care legislation and actions (1970–1989)

Year	Bill	Key purpose	Action
1971	Universal Child Care and Child Development Act	Establish a comprehensive system of child care	Vetoed by President Nixon
1975	Child and Family Services Act	Federal Interagency Day Care Requirements included standards, specifically adult–child ratios	Vetoed by President Ford
1987	An Act for Better Child Care	Subsidies for low- to moderate-income families, health and safety standards, ratios, and professional development funds	Action halted due to impasse in Congress, which voiced multiple concerns, including how to provide funds to states

national agenda for universal supports for young children and their families are still lacking. For many years, Title XX of the Social Security Act, which merged with Social Services Block Grant in 1981, provided the largest federal support for child care across the country. Efforts to increase funding were many, such as a Child Care Bill in 1971, the first of a long line of requests (see Table 8.1) to provide comprehensive child care to address the social, emotional, physical, and cognitive development of children in the United States. All failed to be enacted in full, most often due to funding concerns by Congress or the administration.

In 1990, there was passage of a child care bill, the Child Care and Development Block Grant. This bill required states to establish a lead agency, set health and safety standards for care, and provide choices in child care for families receiving federal funds for child care services. Changes have been made to the Child Care Block Grant program since its inception, including changes in funding for research, technical assistance to states, and increases in funding to support low-income families in accessing child care while they work. The newest efforts to increase support for early care, intervention, and education programs comes through President Obama's American Recovery and Reinvestment Act (ARRA) of 2009. These stimulus dollars have provided an infusion of funds to support programs for children and working parents, including additional funding for child care, with an emphasis on improving quality and support services for infants and toddlers.

As early childhood advocates began to understand just how difficult it was going to be to move a national agenda, no matter how specific or small, state early childhood efforts have become the predominant method implemented to make progress on quality issues in early care, intervention, and education. Again, while it is impossible to outline all the efforts by states to enhance quality, it is worthwhile to provide some key examples of the types of efforts states have undertaken. For example, North Carolina governor James Hunt (1993–2001) led one of the earliest efforts with the implementation of Smart Start, in 1993. The early mission was "to ensure that every child in the state begins school healthy and prepared to succeed" (Dombro, 1999, p. 2). Since that time, almost all states have implemented early childhood efforts at some level, thus becoming laboratories for innovative statewide or targeted programs or combinations of programs. More recently, Governors Rendell (PA) and Bredesen (TN) have led and passed major early childhood initiatives in their states. These state efforts can generally be categorized into 1) statewide or geographic-specific initiatives; 2) state-funded initiatives for preschool or prenatal to 3 years of age; 3) educational or health initiatives; or 4) state-funded, private-funded, or public–private partnership initiatives.

One approach states are increasingly taking to improve quality is the implementation of quality rating and improvement systems (QRISs). These systems are diverse and range from those that are voluntary (e.g., KY) to mandatory (e.g., TN) and statewide (e.g., OK) to local (e.g., Miami, FL). States are also continually changing the quality rating systems based on new research or statewide evaluation efforts. For example, Indiana's system existed in only a few counties until 2007, when Governor Daniels expanded the program statewide (National Child Care Information Center [NCCIC], 2009).

Another example of increasing quality can be seen in the increase in state-funded public programs. While 38 states currently fund some form of preschool (Barnett, Epstein, Friedman, Boyd, & Hustedt, 2008), only recently have states begun to allocate state funds to programs that serve children prenatally through 3 years of age. For example, in 2000, Kentucky became one of the first states to implement a statewide home visitation program for at-risk families beginning at the time of diagnosis of pregnancy until the baby's second birthday. More recently, Illinois designated 10% of the early childhood state funds to infant and toddler programs. Congruent counties in West Virginia, Kentucky, and Ohio have implemented "Brain Under Construction Zones" to help prepare new parents and caregivers for the early years.

While early childhood educators may be most familiar with the educational efforts just mentioned, some states have taken a more global approach that targets the whole child within the family and community context. The most common examples across states are those that support the overall health of young children, such as providing folic acid to women of child-bearing age to reduce the number of children born with spina bifida, early hearing detection and intervention programs now legislated in 42 states, and oral health programs, which help reduce illness and long-term health conditions in children and youth.

Other states have been able to garner the support of public–private partnerships to move the early childhood agenda forward. For example, in 2007, Mississippi Power funded the Mississippi State University Early Childhood Institute to improve the quality of center-based care for young children in the company's service areas that were affected by Hurricane Katrina. Nebraska's Early Childhood Education Endowment Grant Program represents a public–private partnership funded with $40 million from state funds and an additional $20 million raised from the private sector aimed at helping school districts cooperate with other community-based organizations to provide programs and services for infants and toddlers who are at risk of school failure.

CURRENT ISSUES

Over time, there have been consistent themes in the quest for quality in early care, intervention, and education, most notably efforts to 1) support a workforce that has the skills and competencies to provide high-quality services, 2) provide guidance on what a quality environment looks like and supports needed for changing practice, and 3) reach populations that most need access to high-quality environments. At the same time, there have been changes in the focus of our work to advocate for more public investment in young children. From a state and federal policy perspective, there are several pressing issues to be addressed as a field. These issues cross three broad areas: 1) responding to increased calls for accountability in the use of federal and/or state funds targeted toward early care and education, 2) defining quality, and 3) supporting a high-quality workforce. Across these three issue areas, specific considerations are proposed.

Responding to the Call for Accountability

One of the most notable changes in the last decade across both the private and public sectors is the call for greater accountability. For programs funded and supported by the federal government, reporting requirements through the 1993 Government Performance and Results Act (GPRA) of 1993 (PL 103-62) changed the process by which federal programs were deemed effective (Harbin, Rous, & McLean, 2005). This was followed in 2003 by the Program Assessment Review Tool (PART) designed by Office of Budget and Management to link GPRA findings with budget decisions. The implementation of these federal accountability programs has resulted in direct changes in the type of data collected in early care, intervention, and education programs and thus has resulted in changes in practices at the state and local levels (Meisels, 2007).

Another key influence on the move to greater accountability was the passage of the No Child Left Behind Act (NCLB) of 2001 (PL 107-110) and Good Start, Grow Smart (GSGS), an early childhood initiative launched by President and Mrs. Bush in 2002. These federal initiatives have required considerable attention to the development of standards at the state level and in pushing states to measure progress against those standards. Evidence of the long-reaching arm of accountability through NCLB and GSGS can be seen in everything from the use of evidence-based practice, to the development of child learning guidelines, to the ways in which we train professionals in the field, and how states report outcomes of federally funded or supported programs.

This is especially true for early childhood programs that have a primary focus on either prevention or intervention services targeted at children and/or families, particularly those with program goals that indicate they affect child and/or family outcomes. An example is the mandate from the Office of Special Education Programs (OSEP) that now requires all states to provide aggregate level-state data on child outcomes at program exit across three areas (i.e., positive social-emotional skills, acquisition and use of knowledge and skills, and use of appropriate behaviors to meet their needs) for all children who receive services through early intervention (Part C of the Individuals with Disabilities Education Improvement Act of 2004 [IDEA 2004, PL 108-446] or early childhood special education (Part B, Section 619, of IDEA 2004) (Hebbeler & Barton, 2007). These types of mandates on programs receiving federal funds aimed at improving the quality and outcomes for the populations they serve are not likely to go away. Indeed, given the current and potential investments of the federal government in early care, intervention, and education services, one can project there will be an increase in the type of outcome data required by states and programs.

Another example of the influence of the accountability movement is the renewed and expanded interest in the development and implementation of standards. In the United States, professional organizations have traditionally played a role in developing standards. For example, both the NAEYC and the

DEC have developed personnel standards that have been incorporated into national accreditation processes, such as National Council for Accreditation of Teacher Education (NCATE), which accredits schools, colleges, and departments of education. More recently, due to the influence of GSGS and NCLB, states have used these standards as a foundation to build state-specific standards and guidelines, many times in ways that extend the standards to cross multiple dimensions and programs.

Dimensions of Quality

Over the last three decades, great progress has been made in defining specific aspects of quality that are important to the field of early care, intervention, and education and thought to contribute positively to children's overall development. Broad aspects of quality systems addressed in the literature include specific aspects of the environment in which children spend time, the program structure (e.g., National Associate for the Education of Young Children [NAEYC], 2005; Philips & Howes, 1987), and the interactions children experience within those environments (e.g., Pianta & Hamre, 2009).

From a policy perspective, there have been numerous recommendations related to aspects of quality used by state policy makers as they design and implement systems to address the quality of early care, intervention, and education environments. These include early recommendations from the American Public Health Association and the American Academy of Pediatrics (2002) related to national health and safety standards for child care programs; standards put forth via NAEYC position statements such as *Guiding Principles for the Development and Analysis of Early Childhood Public Policy* (1992) and *Where We Stand: Preparing Early Childhood Professionals: NAEYC's Standards for Programs* (2009); and standards put forth for public prekindergarten programs through the National Institute for Early Education Research (NIEER; Barnett, Hustedt, Robin, & Schulman, 2004).

Critical needs for the future include the development of more discrete measures of quality that can be used to 1) refine the dimensions of quality currently identified and 2) support the integration of measures into state systems. Much work is currently underway in this area, as evidenced by the development of a compendium of quality measures (Halle & Vick, 2007) commissioned by the Child Care Bureau. As this type of work continues, there are three major steps that can help ensure that the work meets the needs of the diverse providers, families, and children served through the current early care, intervention, and education system. First, it is critical that attention is given to developing measures that address all dimensions of quality (e.g., structural, environmental, interaction), across all environments in which children spend time (e.g., home based, center based, part day, full day), and acknowledging the diversity of children (e.g., ability, primary language, culture) and families (e.g., income level, language, culture). Second, an iterative process will be required that allows for continued discussions and cross-pollination between policy makers, researchers, and providers so we can develop measures that take into consideration the needs of policy makers related to the costs, large-scale implementation, and data to support program improvement, as well as justification of expenditures. Third, the development of measures should be coordinated at the federal level to reduce unnecessary duplication of effort across programs (e.g., Head Start, child care, programs for children with special needs). For example, measures of structural quality need to be developed to help ensure the specific needs of children with disabilities are addressed in explicit ways (Buysse & Hollingsworth, 2009). This is especially important as states continue to work toward more coordinated services for children and families across the early years.

Supporting the Workforce

Professionals who care for our young children are as diverse as the programs under which they provide services. A great deal of attention has been given to supporting providers in obtaining the education and training they need to be effective in their work and to provide guidance to states in developing comprehensive professional development systems (e.g., NCCIC, 2007). Along with professional organizations, both GSGS and NCLB have been influential in shifting and strengthening the focus on developing and maintaining a high-quality workforce. Specifically, as states began to articulate what children should know and be able to do through the development of early learning guidelines or standards as required by GSGS, they also began to seriously consider the skills and competencies professionals need to ensure that children are provided with experiences to help them meet those standards. Another strong influence has been the introduction of the term *highly qualified* in NCLB. While NCLB pertains specifically to public schools, it has greatly influenced the way the field thinks about the preparation of all professionals who work with children and who are expected to help them achieve at high levels.

From a policy perspective, the call for high-quality professionals combined with the need to ensure there is an ample workforce presents a challenge to state and local policy makers. These challenges include differential expectations for professionals across early care, intervention, and education systems. For example, while Head Start has emphasized the need for teachers to become more educated through the obtainment of Child Development Associate credentials, associate degrees, or higher, public school programs are determining how to set and meet "highly qualified" requirements of NCLB, and child care programs struggle to provide compensation packages that allow them to retain staff once they have obtained a degree or credential. Scholarship programs have been effective in helping build a more educated workforce, yet articulation across 2- and 4-year institutions of higher education is sometimes an arduous process and remains difficult in many states.

There has also been tremendous movement in the design and implementation in professional development opportunities. The use of evidence-based practice at the program or classroom level includes the selection of direct instructional and intervention strategies based on research. In addition, the consideration of evidence-based practice has also extended to the design and delivery of professional development opportunities at both the preservice and in-service level. For example, the Institute of Education Sciences includes specific language in its funding priorities related to research that evaluates the efficacy of professional development programs, specifically how they improve practice and thus student learning. The field is at the beginning stages of understanding and building this evidence base for choosing the best methods to support both knowledge acquisition and knowledge utilization in the workplace, including the role of training and technical assistance through formats such as mentoring and consultation (Fixsen, Naoom, Blase, Friedman, & Wallace, 2005). As new information is gathered on research-based professional development strategies, it can fundamentally change the ways in which professionals are trained by both training organizations and higher education entities, including how to use new technology to support professional development.

The changing landscape of how professional development is provided offers opportunities and challenges for policy makers as they determine key components of quality initiatives in which to invest resources. However, consistent with quality, the investment in professional development at the state and local level must be balanced with the critical need in the field for developing consistency in how professional development is defined and measured (Maxwell, Field, & Clifford, 2006). This is especially important given that policy decisions related to quality initiatives currently being implemented in states have been based on early research linking education and training to higher quality and better child outcomes.

FUTURE DIRECTIONS

The good news for early childhood is that states are continuing to invest in early care, intervention, and education efforts. According to the National Conference of State Legislators, states continued to invest in a number of early childhood efforts in 2009, in spite of tough economic situations. For example, state appropriations in child care access and quality (17 states), prekindergarten expansion (21 states), and other early learning initiatives (e.g., parent education, Head Start, teacher scholarships) actually increased between 2008 and 2009 (Poppe & Clothier, 2009). However, while states are investing in early childhood, a recent report from the Organisation for Economic Co-operation and Development (OECD; 2009) found that public spending in the United States lags way behind the other 30 countries included in the study, with the United States spending $20,000 per child up to age 6 compared with the average of $30,000 (OECD, 2009).

One thing is clear from a review of past efforts and current issues in supporting high-quality early care, intervention, and education settings: There is a strong need for a national policy agenda. In the words of Kolker, Osborne, and Schnurer (2004) in a paper from the Center for National Policy:

> Early care and education should be an important focus of national policy: Whether children succeed at school, and eventually at work and as contributing members of society, is greatly influenced by whether they are provided adequate high-quality early childhood care and education. Adequate ECE therefore also can have a dramatic effect on future public social spending, the future productivity of the nation's workforce, and a broad range of social costs such as income dependency, crime, and health care. Yet, despite all this, the country lacks a comprehensive policy for ECE. (p. 14)

A review of the recommendations from key agencies and authors related to a national policy agenda reveals common recommendations that cross authors and sources (e.g., Greenberg, 2007; Kolker et al., 2004; Lombardi, 2003; National Association of Child Care Resource and Referral Agencies, 2009; NAEYC, 2000), which can help bring focus to critical issues that face early care, intervention, and education and should be the target of joint efforts to support a national policy agenda. These areas include 1) coordinated and integrated system of early childhood services; 2) access to high-quality, affordable early care, intervention, and education; 3) high-quality workforce; and 4) an evidence base to support best practice. A summary of the major recommendations across the sources reviewed is included in Table 8.2.

Table 8.2. Example of national policy agenda recommendations from key sources

Source	Major recommendations	Coordinated and integrated system	Access	High-quality personnel	Evidence base to support practice
Greenberg (2007)	• Every parent who needs child care to get or keep work should be able to afford care without having to leave children in unhealthy or dangerous environments. • All families should be able to place their children in settings that foster education and healthy development. • Parental choice should be respected. • A set of good choices should be available.		✓		
Lombardi (2003)	• Care and education should be integrated. • Parents should have access to quality options. • All adults caring for children should have the support needed to be successful.	✓	✓	✓	
Kolker et al. (2004)	• We need a national debate on early care and education. • Policy makers and society should care enough to fund early care and education. • Coordinate education and social services for young children and services to help their parents in the workforce. • Provide adequate training for provider and directors. • Disseminate research and best practice. • Disseminate and enforce national quality standards.	✓	✓	✓	✓
NACCRRA (2009)	• Ensure that children and families have access to affordable, healthy, and safe care. • Improve quality to promote early learning. • Improve and expand care for infants and toddlers. • Provide needed research and technical assistance.		✓	✓	✓
NAEYC (2000)	• All young children deserve excellent early care and education. • High-quality early experiences make a difference in children's lifelong academic and social success. • These programs must be accessible to all families. • Early childhood professionals must have excellent preparation, ongoing professional development, and compensation commensurate with their qualifications and experience. • Effective early education must be both challenging and appropriate to young children's ages, individual needs, and cultures. • Everyone needs to work together to build a successful future for our youngest children.	✓	✓	✓	✓

Coordinated and Integrated System of Early Childhood Services

There is a need to support state and local programs in coordinating and integrating early childhood services. The field of early childhood has made a gradual shift from a focus on providing care for children to a focus on supporting children's growth and development, primarily as a result of research into the critical importance of the early years on children's long-term success (e.g., Peisner-Feinberg et al., 1999; Shonkoff & Phillips, 2000). Most would agree that the current system of services in the United States for early care, intervention, and education services for young children is diverse and includes multiple types of programs, including prevention (e.g., Head Start), intervention (e.g., early childhood special education services) and service (e.g. child care).

This myriad of programs requires coordination and collaboration across these sectors. To address this issue there have been recommendations, and indeed states, that have focused on the "structure" of early childhood services by combining programs into one early childhood cabinet or division (e.g., in the state of Georgia). While it is too early to gauge the overall success of this approach, similar approaches used for other early childhood programs can provide insights for policy makers. For instance, for infants and toddlers with special needs, states were able to choose the lead agency to design and implement services through IDEA, Part C, when the program was first initiated in 1987. Some states opted for departments of education, others for health or human services. Almost two decades into the program, a review of the annual state profiles published through the National Early Childhood Technical Assistance Center (NECTAC) indicate that the lead agency for the program has often shifted in states, in some cases multiple times. One recent study found that coordination and collaboration between Part C and preschool special education services (Part B, Section 619), even for those that are both housed in departments of education, remains a significant challenge in many states (Harbin, Rous, Gooden, & Shaw, 2008). In the case of these state-level programs, regardless of the agencies that house the programs, the relationships between agency staff and communication across the programs were found to be critical ingredients to more coordinated services.

There is also a strong literature base for considering aspects of coordination of services, such as a focus on continuity in the philosophy and standards that guide services (e.g., Harbin et al., 2008; Kagan & Cohen, 1997). An area that has received limited attention in the field of early childhood is leadership within the specific programs at both the state and local level. The education literature provides clear evidence of the role of leadership by school personnel, including their philosophical approach related to collaboration and relationship building across team members and on school improvement and student achievement (e.g., Leithwood, Louis, Anderson, & Wahlstrom, 2004; Waters & Marzano, 2006). However, while there have long been efforts to move a research agenda and practice forward with respect to early childhood leadership (e.g., Bloom & Sheerer, 1992), and with promising findings related to connections between the leadership and quality (e.g., Rous, Grove, Cox, Townley, & Crumpton, 2008), little attention has been given to national efforts to support and grow early childhood leaders, specifically at the state level. As we continue to shape a national agenda to support improved quality in early care, intervention, and education services, it will be critical to focus not only on the structure and location of programs but also on the philosophy that undergirds services and the leadership within the programs at the state level that can make coordination happen.

Access to Early Education and Care

We need to ensure that families have access to high-quality, affordable services to meet their needs. Most often, services designed for prevention (e.g., Head Start) or intervention (e.g., early childhood special education) are provided at little or no cost to families. However, programs that fall under the service sector, such as child care, are open to the influence of the current market rate and often are undersupported in their efforts to provide services to low-income families, especially as they attempt to engage in efforts to increase the quality of their programs (Cohen, 1996; Peisner-Feinberg et al., 1999).

While affordability is a key issue, it is also important to support access of services to a wide range of families and children. This includes addressing longstanding concerns in the United States about the availability of quality care for diverse populations, including infants and toddlers (e.g., Kreader, Ferguson, & Lawrence, 2005; NACCRRA, 2009), low-income families and children (e.g., U.S. Department of Health and Human Services, 1999), children with special needs (e.g., Shaw et al., 2001), and children from diverse cultures (e.g., Capps, Fix, Ost, Reardon-Anderson, & Passel, 2005; U.S. Government Accountability Office, 2006).

Finally, children have a right to receive services in safe and healthy environments that support their growth and development. Clear evidence exists linking poor child health with environmental hazards, such as airborne pollutants and child asthma, and as do connections between lead and intellectual impairments and behavioral issues in children (Lanphear, Paulson, & Beirne 2006). Too often, early childhood services are provided in inadequate facilities, at times in older buildings and homes that may be prone to more environmental toxins, lacking well-designed spaces that better support implementation of high-quality practices. There has been a significant amount of research to provide information on what we need to do to ensure that environments are of high quality but historically less focus on how we can actually fund it (Cohen, 1996). We need national cost analyses studies that focus on strategic ways in which the United States can fund efforts to increase the quality of early care, intervention, and education services. These national efforts must take into consideration the multiple sectors that provide services. In addition, efforts should take care to build on what states have already done to enhance access and quality to ensure that new efforts do not undermine state efforts by making policy and program decisions that require more progressive states to step back from the initiatives in which they have invested.

High-Quality Workforce

We need to ensure that early care and education services are provided by highly qualified professionals. Like all professionals, those who work in the field of early care, intervention, and education need ongoing professional development to help them stay current on new practices and interventions that produce the most positive outcomes for those they serve. Continued efforts to help ensure that the workforce has the key skills and competencies they need to be effective are critical. Supports and incentives are needed for states to develop core content for early childhood professionals, as are career ladders that support professionals in articulating from credential-bearing programs to degree-bearing programs.

While we can improve the education and training of early childhood professionals, we must recognize and address the fact that those who work with young children and families are often underpaid and underappreciated. There are significant gaps and inequities in the compensation provided to the early childhood workforce across sectors. Most often, those who work in the public sector are compensated at higher levels than those in the private sector, such as child care. While raising the compensation rates to equitable levels may seem impossible given the current structure of early care, intervention, and education services in the United States, a national public relations campaign can help raise awareness of the importance of the early years as part of the broader educational system and begin to build the foundation for professionalizing the field. In the increasing age of technology, agenda-setting theory (McCombs & Shaw, 1972), which focuses on influencing the public view on issues of critical importance through the use of mass media, provides a framework for thinking about how to raise public demand for high-quality services provided by a high-quality and appropriately compensated workforce.

New technologies also provide opportunities to support the workforce in becoming a true community of learners, regardless of where they live and work. We need to find ways to link providers across sectors and help them engage in meaningful dialogue around relevant issues that improve quality across sectors. While there will always be a need for sector- and population-specific supports, professional development, and initiatives, the sharing of ideas across early childhood sectors can help move the field forward in understanding the issues for diverse families and children, rather than continuing to ask questions after the fact of how a specific policy, program, or initiative will work with a different population.

Evidence Base to Support Practice

We need to develop a national research agenda to move us forward in providing effective services to young children and families. As a field, we must identify key issues for which we need new knowledge that crosses sectors (e.g., health, mental health, child care, education). This includes an emphasis on research related to policy and the impact of state and federal policies on the implementation of specific practices in local programs (Wesley & Buysse, 2006). An example is the *National Goals and Research for People with Intellectual and Developmental Disabilities* (Lakin & Turnbull, 2005), which grew out of a collaborative initiative between 10 federal agencies, 9 professional and advocacy organizations, and numerous academic organizations, all of which had programs or services that focused on and impacted the lives of people with disabilities.

As part of this national research agenda, there is a substantial need to identify and develop reliable and valid measures that truly represent and capture the full continuum of children and families served in early childhood settings, as well as the diverse administrators and providers who work with them. A key component of this research should be on appropriateness of using the same measures for research and as part of state quality initiatives. At the state level, measures are needed to support the evaluation of quality in both the design and delivery of programs, including research related to the full costs of implementation of measures within a state system. This is critical, as both the design and interpretation of research and evaluation findings must provide an evidence base upon which states can make informed policy decisions that are responsive to their state context. In other words, our research findings are only as good as our measures.

The work that has occurred to date provides us with a starting point in identifying future directions in terms of the development of quality measures. Significant efforts are currently underway to develop measures of quality for center-based and home-based environments (Halle & Vicks, 2007), yet a gap currently exists in reliable and valid measures for services provided within an itinerant or home-based model. Work is also needed in the development of measures to capture child progress and outcomes at the infant-toddler level and for children who have significant disabilities. As mentioned previously, additional measures of the full continuum of professional development activities are needed (Maxwell, Field, & Clifford, 2006), as measures of administrative functions within early care and education organizations and the impact of leadership dimensions on quality and outcomes are sparse.

SUMMARY

The field of early care, intervention, and education has made great strides over the last 3 decades. Families and children across the United States have access to more programs and services than ever before. There is increased attention to the importance of the early years across multiple sectors, including the recognition that investments in young children can help us move toward our national goal of ensuring that we have an educated, skilled, and productive workforce.

At the center of our quest to improve quality are the policies that guide the implementation of practices within individual programs, classrooms, and settings. Given the array of services and supports available, additional investments are needed at the federal and state level to ensure that we provide coherent and coordinated guidance to states and localities. At the same time, policies must be developed that are comprehensive yet allow for flexibility so programs are not hampered in using creative approaches to meeting the specific needs of the diverse families and children they serve.

REFERENCES

American Academy of Pediatrics, American Public Health Association, and National Resource Center for Health and Safety in Child Care and Early Education. (2002). *Caring for our children: National health and safety performance standards: Guidelines for out-of-home child care programs* (2nd ed.). Elk Grove Village, IL: American Academy of Pediatrics, and Washington, DC: American Public Health Association. Also available at http://nrckids.org

Barnett, W.S., Epstein, D.J, Friedman, A.H., Boyd, J.S., & Hustedt, J.T. (2008). *The state of preschool: 2008 state preschool yearbook.* New Brunswick, NJ: National Institute for Early Education Research.

Barnett, W.S., Hustedt, J.T., Robin, K.B., & Schulman, K.L. (2004). *The state of preschool: 2004 state preschool yearbook.* New Brunswick, NJ: National Institute for Early Education Research, Rutgers University.

Berrueta-Clement, J., Schweinhart, L.J., Barnett, W.S., Epstein, A.S., & Weikart, D. (1984). *Changed lives: The effects of the Perry preschool program on youths through age 19.*

Ypsilanti, MI: High/Scope Educational Research Foundation. (ERIC Document Reproduction Service No. ED313128).

Bloom, P.J., & Sheerer, M. (1992). The effect of leadership training on child care program quality. *Early Childhood Research Quarterly 7*(4), 579–594.

Bredekamp, S. (1987). *Developmentally appropriate practice in early childhood programs serving children from birth through age 8* (Expanded edition). Washington, DC: NAEYC.

Buysse, V., & Hollingsworth, H.L. (2009). Program quality and early childhood inclusion: Recommendations for professional development. *Topics in Early Childhood Special Education 29*(2), 119–128.

Capps, R., Fix, M., Ost, J., Reardon Anderson, J., & Passel, J.S. (2005). *The health and well-being of young children of immigrants.* Washington, DC: Urban Institute. Retrieved September 2009 from http://www.urban.org/UploadedPDF/311139_ChildrenImmigrants.pdf

Cohen, A. (1996). A brief history of federal financing for child care in the United States. *Future of Children, 6*(2), 26–40.

Dombro, A. (1999). *Getting started: How Smart Start began.* New York: Families and Work Institute.

Education Commission of the States (2005). *Full-day kindergarten: A study of state policies in the United States.* Denver, CO: Author.

Fowler, F.C. (2000). *Policy studies for educational leaders.* Upper Saddle River, NJ: Prentice Hall.

Fixsen, D.L., Naoom, S.F., Blase, K.A., Friedman, R.M., & Wallace, F. (2005). *Implementation research: A synthesis of the literature* (FMHI Publication #231). Tampa: University of South Florida, Louis de la Parte Florida Mental Health Institute, National Implementation Research Network.

Gallagher, J. (1994). Policy designed for diversity: New initiatives for children with disabilities. In D. Bryant & M. Graham (Eds.), *Implementing early intervention* (pp. 336–350). New York: Guilford.

Ginzberg, E. (1976). *The human economy.* New York: McGraw-Hill.

Gotts, E.E. (1988). *The right to quality child care.* Onley: MD: Association for Childhood Education International. Retrieved March 2009 from http://www.acei.org/childcare.htm

Greenberg, M. (2007). Next steps for federal child care policy. *Future of Children, 17*(2), 73–96.

Grossman, A.S. (January, 1978). Children of working mothers: Special labor force report 217. *Monthly Labor Review:* 30–33. (ERIC Document Reproduction Service No. ED176886)

Halle, T., & Vick, J.E. (2007). *Quality in early childhood care and education settings: A compendium of measures.* Washington, DC: Prepared by Child Trends for the Office of Planning, Research and Evaluation, Administration for Children and Families, U.S. Department of Health and Human Services.

Harbin, G., Rous, B., Gooden, C., & Shaw, J. (2008). *State infrastructures to support young children with disabilities* (Technical Report #4). Lexington: University of Kentucky, Human Development Institute, National Early Childhood Transition Center.

Harbin, G., Rous, B., & McLean, M. (2005). Feature article: Issues in designing state accountability systems. *Journal of Early Intervention 27*(3), 137–164.

Hebbeler, K., & Barton, L. (2007). The need for data on child and family outcomes at the federal and state levels. *Young Exceptional Children Monograph Series, 9,* 1–15.

Kagan, S.L., & Cohen, N.E. (1997). Not by chance: Creating an early care and education system for America's children. (ERIC Document Reporoduction Service No. ED417027)

Keyserling, M. (1972). *Windows on day care: A report on the findings of members of the National Council of Jewish Women on day care needs and services in their communities.* New York: National Council of Jewish Women. (ERIC Document Reproduction Service No. ED063027)

Kolker, J., Osborne, D., & Schnurer, E. (2004). *Early child care and education: The need for a national policy.* Washington, DC: Center for National Policy.

Kreader, J.L., Ferguson, D., & Lawrence, S. (2005). *Infant and toddler child care quality.* New York: National Center for Children in Poverty.

Kreader, J.L., Ferguson, D., & Lawrence, S. (2005). *Impact of training and education for caregivers of infants and toddlers.* New York: National Center for Children in Poverty, Columbia University Mailman School of Public Health.

Lakin, K.C., & Turnbull, A. (2005). *National goals and research for people with intellectual and developmental disabilities.* Washington, DC: American Association on Mental Retardation.

Lamphear, B.P., Paulson, J., & Beirne, S. (2006). Trials and tribulations of protecting children from environmental hazards. *Environmental Health Perspective, 114*(10), 1609–1612.

Leithwood, K., Louis, K.S., Anderson, S., & Wahlstrom, K. (2004). *How leadership influences student learning.* Minneapolis: University of Minnesota.

Lombardi, J. (2003). *Time to care: Redesigning child care to promote education, support families and build communities.* Philadelphia: Temple University Press.

Maxwell, K.L., Field, C.C., & Clifford, R.M. (2006). Defining and measuring professional development in early childhood research. In M. Zaslow & I. Martinez-Beck (Eds.), *Critical issues in early childhood professional development* (pp. 21–48). Baltimore: Paul H. Brookes Publishing Co.

McCombs, M.E., & Shaw, D.L. (1972). The agenda-setting function of mass media. *Public Opinion Quarterly, 5*(36), 176–187.

Meisels, S.J. (2007). Accountability in early childhood: No easy answers. In R.C. Pianta, M.J. Cox, & K. Snow (Eds.), *School readiness, early learning and the transition to kindergarten* (pp. 31–47). Baltimore: Paul H. Brookes Publishing Co.

National Association of Child Care Resource and Referral Agencies. (2009). *2009/2010 public policy agenda.* Retrieved July 14, 2009, from http://www.naccrra.org/policy/policy-agenda

National Association of Child Care Resource and Referral Agencies. (2009). *High-quality infant & toddler care matters.* Retrieved August 29, 2009, from: http://www.naccrra.org/policy/background_issues/infants-and-toddlers-need-quality-care

National Association of Early Childhood Specialists in State Departments of Education. (1987). *Unacceptable trends in kindergarten entry and placement.* Washington, DC: Author.

National Association for the Education of Young Children. (1986). Position statement on developmentally appropriate practice in programs for 4- and 5-year-olds. *Young Children 41*(6), 20–29.

National Association for the Education of Young Children. (1992). *Position statement on guiding principles for the development and analyses of early childhood policy.* Washington, DC: Author.

National Association for the Education of Young Children. (2000). *A call for excellence in early childhood education.* Retrieved October 14, 2009, from http://www.naeyc.org/about/positions.asp

National Association for the Education of Young Children. (2005). *Position statements of NAEYC.* Retrieved November 11, 2005, from http://www.naeyc.org/about/positions.asp

National Association for the Education of Young Children. (2009). *Where we stand on standards for programs to prepare early childhood professionals.* Washington, DC: Author.

National Child Care Information Center. (2007). *Early childhood professional development systems toolkit.* Fairfax, VA: Author.

National Child Care Information Center. (2009). *Quality rating systems.* Retrieved March 16, 2009, from http://nccic.acf.hhs.gov/topics/topic/index.cfm?topicId=44

National Commission on Excellence in Education. (1984). *A nation at risk: The imperative for educational reform.* Washington, DC: U.S. Department of Education.

Organisation for Economic Co-operation and Development. (2009). *Doing better for children.* Paris: OECD Publishing

Peisner-Feinberg, E.S., Burchinal, M.R., Clifford, R.M., Culkin, M.L., Howes, C., Kagan, S.L., et al. (1999). *The children of the cost, quality, and outcomes study go to school: Executive summary.* Chapel Hill: University of North Carolina at Chapel Hill, Frank Porter Graham Child Development Center.

Pianta, R., & Hamre, B.K. (2009). Classroom processes and positive youth development: Conceptualizing, measuring, and improving the capacity of interactions between teachers and students. *New Directions for Youth Development, 121,* 33–46.

Piele, P.K. (1972, Spring). The president's commission on school finance. *R & D Perspectives,* 5–10. (ERIC Document Reproduction Service No. ED063654)

Poppe, J., & Clothier, S. (2009). *Early care and education state budget actions FY 2009.* Denver, CO: National Conference of State Legislatures.

Rous, B., Grove, J., Cox, M., Townley, K., & Crumpton, G. (2008, September). *The impact of the Kentucky professional development framework on child care, Head Start and public preschool classroom quality and child outcomes.* Lexington: University of Kentucky, Human Development Institute, Professional Development Framework Research Collaborative.

Schultz, T., & Lombardi, J. (1989). Right from the start: A report of the NASB task force on early childhood education. *Young Children* 44(2), 6–10.

Scribner, J., Aleman, E. & Maxcy, B. (2003). Emergence of the politics of education field: Making sense of the messy center. *Educational Administration Quarterly, 39*(1), 10–40.

Shaw, P., Santos, S., Cohen, A., Araki, C., Provance, E., & Reynolds, V. (2001). *Barriers to inclusive child care.* Sacramento: California Children and Families Commission.

Shonkoff, J., & Phillips, D.A. (Eds.). (2000). *From neurons to neighborhoods: The science of early childhood development* Washington, DC: National Academies Press, National Research Council and Institute of Medicine.

U.S. Department of Health and Human Services, Administration for Children and Families. (1999). *Access to child care for low-income working families.* (ERIC Document Reproduction Service No. ED43547)

U.S. Government Accountability Office. (2006). *Report to congressional requestors, child care and early childhood education: More information sharing and program review by HHS could enhance access for families with limited English proficiency.* Retrieved September 2009 from http://www.gao.gov/new.items/d06807.pdf

Waters, J.T., & Marzano, R.J. (2006). *School district leadership that works: The effect of superintendent leadership on student achievement.* Denver, CO: McRel.

Wesley, P., & Buysse, V. (2006). Making the case for evidence-based policy. In V. Buysse & P. Wesley (Eds.), *Evidence-based practice in the early childhood field.* Washington, DC: ZERO TO THREE: National Center for Infants, Toddlers, and Families.

CHAPTER 9

Program Quality Through the Lens of Disruptive Innovation Theory

Virginia Buysse and Patricia W. Wesley

Previous chapters examined the history and evolution of the program quality movement in early childhood. Various chapters offered an in-depth look at each of the multiple facets of program quality (e.g., definitions of quality; quality standards, measures, and accountability systems; and the methods for achieving and supporting program quality through professional development and technical assistance). In addition, Chapter 2 explores the ways in which research has shaped current thinking and recommended practices related to program quality, whereas Chapter 8 addresses the policy implications of program quality. All of these chapters offer new ideas and promising future directions to address current challenges that permeate all aspects of the program quality enterprise. One monumental challenge that represents a recurrent theme throughout this volume is the need to integrate the various components of program quality into a single, coherent system—certainly no small task.

In this chapter, we revisit the challenges raised by chapter authors and consider how the early childhood field could begin to address them in a new way, by viewing program quality reform through the lens of innovation. Before we say more on the subject of innovation, it may be helpful to acknowledge that there are other viable lenses that could have been used to advance understanding on how to improve program quality. For example, program quality can be viewed from the perspective of research. Many efforts aimed at creating reform begin by studying the phenomenon of interest, with the school reform movement being a case in point. Certainly, the merits of advancing knowledge and understanding through scientific research must be acknowledged. At the same time, the nature of scientific research is such that the accumulation of new knowledge occurs incrementally over a long period through "a continual process of rigorous reasoning supported by a dynamic interplay among methods, theories, and findings" (Shavelson & Towne, 2002, p. 2). Furthermore, advancing understanding of program quality through research demands attention to the contexts and conditions under which early childhood programs operate—the diverse settings and the varied characteristics and experiences of practitioners, children, families, and the communities in which they live. All of this means that, despite the urgent need to address current challenges related to program quality in the present, research by its very nature evolves gradually from preliminary studies that describe the phenomena and relationships among variables, to statements of causality and the ability to predict specific factors that can lead to quality improvements and, ultimately, better outcomes for children and families. Even though we elected not to use research as the vehicle for considering ways that the field can leap (as opposed to crawl) forward to improve the current program quality infrastructure, we return to the topic of research at the end of this chapter and offer some ideas on how research needs to change to become more relevant and useful for improving program quality in the future.

Another way of viewing program quality is through the lens of regulation and accountability. As discussed in Chapter 1, the meaning of program quality in the United States resides largely in concepts related to measurement and regulation, along with corresponding methods for managing people and assessment systems to gauge conformity to predetermined norms. Although the language of monitoring and accountability in relation to program quality is widely accepted in the United States, other countries do not operationalize program quality in these terms but approach the meaning of quality in a more philosophical or theoretical way, as is the case in the United Kingdom, where the definition of program quality is continually contested, debated, and refined (Dahlberg & Moss, 2008).

Within the United States there is a danger that the push for accountability and national standards may be viewed as the only way to fix the system (see the following web sites for information on the development of national standards: http://aft.org/news/2008/standards.htm; http://nctm.org/standards; http://ncte.org/standards; http://nces.ed.gov/nationsreportcard). Although reaching consensus on what students should know and be able to do is certainly a laudable goal, it would be a mistake to confuse the establishment of national standards with actual teaching and learning or to think that standards automatically lead to effective classroom practices (Christensen, Horn, & Johnson, 2008). Yet, the push to create standards as one component of school reform often begins and ends with these efforts. Rarely has revising accountability systems resulted in dramatically improved educational systems. The same can be said for the current emphasis and flurry of activity around creating professional competencies, early learning standards, and quality rating and improvement systems (QRISs) in the early childhood field. These competencies and standards in and of themselves will not lead to quality improvements. In this chapter, we maintain that the best ideas for achieving improvements in program quality will come not through increasing our program monitoring and accountability efforts but through innovations that fundamentally change the current structures and ways of thinking about program quality.

Thinking about program quality through the lens of innovation allows us to stand outside the early childhood field to view the problem from a completely different perspective—to peel away the surface explanations to expose fundamental root causes and solutions, to answer the question of why, despite the extent to which research and human resources have been poured into improving program quality, we cannot predict with any precision which factors cluster together to achieve more dramatic results. In our search for a theory that could breathe new life into the quest to improve program quality (and to achieve this goal rapidly rather than incrementally), we discovered a construct that had not been previously used in this way in early childhood—*disruptive innovation*. Clayton

M. Christensen, a leading scholar in this area and a faculty member of the Harvard Business School, along with his colleagues, has applied disruptive innovation theory to solve pressing problems and create innovations in a number of fields, including business, technology, industry, and, most recently, education (Christensen et al., 2008).

The purpose of this chapter is to share ideas that we gleaned from this literature for creating significant, enduring innovations to improve program quality in early childhood—ideas that could both explain current issues and challenges as well as point to promising innovations and solutions in the future. We focus in particular on examples of how disruptive innovation theory has been applied to the field of education, primarily to explain why previous school reform efforts have not produced more dramatic results to date, since this is the closest corollary we could find to issues that we face in the field of early education and intervention. We begin by first explaining what is meant by the term *disruptive innovation*. Next, we examine the specific features of this theory as these apply to the program quality movement, and we describe promising future directions for achieving a consensus for change in this regard. We end by offering ideas for how research on program quality will need to change to advance our understanding of the effects of innovations to improve program quality.

WHAT DO WE MEAN BY DISRUPTIVE INNOVATION?

At first blush, the term *disruptive* is off-putting, particularly within the early childhood field, in which values such as collaboration and consensus building seem more aligned with maintaining the status quo than creating innovations that disrupt existing structures. According to disruptive innovation theory, programs and organizations are constantly improving or attempting to improve the goods and services they offer consumers. However, there are many factors that work against these improvements. Christensen and his colleagues (2008) point to public education as one example of this phenomenon. They note that public schools have made steady progress over the past several decades, yet it is widely acknowledged that the majority of public schools in this country today are not faring well in meeting their accountability goals with respect to educating an increasingly diverse population of students. Why? For one thing, definitions of quality and the goalposts and metrics for achieving positive results keep changing. The authors note that one disruption occurred in 1983 when the *Nation at Risk* report concluded that student achievement as measured by test scores offered better evidence of high-quality instruction than the level of resources and curricula used, which represented a shift (i.e., disruption) from an emphasis on educational inputs to student outcomes (U.S. Department of Education, 1983). The No Child Left Behind Act of 2001 (PL 107-110) is another example of a significant disruption, because a new definition of *annual yearly performance* meant that schools did not look as good as they once did in light of the new requirements to focus on the academic achievement of specific subgroups of students (e.g., students from diverse cultural, racial, linguistic, and ability groups).

The current public education system is based on a factory model in which students are categorized by age, and teaching is standardized and organized accordingly; educators are expected to teach the same subjects in the same ways using the same materials. Innovating within this system would mean disrupting the current education architecture to customize teaching and learning to address individual needs. Innovations around customized learning would stand in direct opposition to standardized methods of teaching and create a demand for new approaches (e.g., technologies) to assist teachers in managing all of the information needed to customize teaching and learning (e.g., monitoring the progress of individual students throughout the year as opposed to annual end-of-grade assessments). Similar disruptions related to customized teaching and learning could be expected to occur at other levels of the education system—for example, among curriculum developers, technologies related to computer-assisted learning, and assessment and accountability systems.

In disruptive innovation theory, these disruptions to the status quo are viewed as a positive force for change and improvement. But it is almost impossible for schools and other organizations to create these types of disruptive innovations within their existing structures, largely because these innovations do not sustain the traditional methods already being used for improvement (but rather represent direct competition to the existing approach to improvement) and because disruptive innovations are often complicated and expensive when first introduced. The challenges of introducing disruptive innovations within existing organizational structures are not unique to public education. Christensen and colleagues observed, "In our studies of disruptive innovation in the private sector, we are not aware of a single instance in which a for-profit company was able to implement successfully the disruptive innovation within its core business" (2008, p. 61). The need for schools to meet current demands (which generally translates to using available resources to sustain current methods for improving education) competes with the need to develop innovations that disrupt the current system and create a paradigm shift. Efforts to sustain existing quality improvement reforms win out over disruptive innovations almost every time. This reality, along with changing definitions and metrics associated with the enterprise of reform, explains why schools have been unable to adopt disruptive innovations, even though they are continually and incrementally improving along a sustainability pathway.

If schools and other organizations cannot possibly achieve disruptive innovations on their own within existing structures, then how do disruptive innovations occur? We delve deeper into this question in the remaining sections, but first we use the previous example of public schools to draw a few parallels in the early childhood field. Just as quality definitions and metrics continually change in the broader field of education, we can find similar disruptions that have changed the meaning of program quality in early childhood. Disruptions to current thinking about child development and learning occurred with the release of two landmark publications. The first, *Eager to Learn: Educating Our Preschoolers* (Bowman, Donovan, & Burns, 2000), put forth the bold assertion that children's early experiences lay the foundation for later development and academic learning, well before formal schooling begins. Further, the report referred to children ranging in age from 2 to 5 years old as "learners," with the expectation that much of what was learned was organized and facilitated by adults in the context of child care and other group care arrangements. If anyone in the early childhood field harbored any outmoded conceptions about child-initiated play and good custodial care as being the most important dimensions of program quality, the *Eager to Learn* report dispelled these notions and reinforced the idea that school readiness was now central to the definition of program quality. It is not difficult to see the connection between the importance of preparing young learners for future school success and the genesis of standards and accountability systems that followed in the wake of this report.

Another disruption occurred in 2000 with the release of *From Neurons to Neighborhoods* (Shonkoff & Phillips, 2000). This publication further elevated the early childhood enterprise by referring to the accumulation of knowledge in this area as the "science" of development and learning. The main premise was that the field should draw on the wealth of scientific findings from neurobiology and the social sciences to make decisions related to designing early learning environments and facilitating children's learning and development in all domains, but particularly in the area of social-emotional development. Although the premise is sound in theory, a closer look at the body of knowledge in early childhood reveals the unevenness of existing scientific evidence, with little or no research on some topics and too much in other areas, and much of this information not directly relevant for practitioners (i.e., inadequate information on what works and how to replicate research-based interventions in practice settings). At the same time, the field was left to ponder an important idea as it relates to the challenge of creating high-quality early learning experiences for young children: We could now turn to science for answers.

There are likely many other examples of disruptions that have changed the field's understanding of program quality, but at least two more recent examples are worth noting. Following on the heels of *From Neurons to Neighborhoods*, in which science was held up as a vehicle for improving early childhood programs and services, the field witnessed the dawn of the evidence-based practice movement. The term *evidence-based practice* was (and continues to be) confusing to practitioners and policy makers alike. Does it mean that certain practices are supported by scientific evidence, whereas others are not? If so, which ones? There have been various attempts to answer these difficult questions, including an edited volume titled *Evidence-Based Practice in the Early Childhood Field* (Buysse & Wesley, 2006). Drawing on constructs from evidence-based medicine, this volume offered a definition of evidence-based practice in early childhood as a decision-making process in which various sources of evidence (research, wisdom, values, and contexts) needed to be taken into account. In our view, the key disruption to the definition of quality that occurred as a result of the evidence-based practice movement was the notion that effective practitioners should not only recognize the wealth of accumulated knowledge on child development within science but should also use these research findings, along with other sources of evidence (including assessment information that practitioners themselves gather), to make sound decisions in practice. In some ways, the evidence-based practice movement reflects a natural evolution from emphasizing practices that are considered developmentally appropriate (see Chapter 1 for a description on how the meaning of this term has changed over time) to practices that are both developmentally appropriate and have been found to be effective through research.

One final example of a recent disruption that has shaped our evolving definition of program quality concerns a renewed interest in professional development. There is now wide consensus that the quality of the workforce is a critical factor—and may be of overriding importance—in determining whether an early childhood program is of high or poor quality (see Chapter 6 for information on the relationship between program quality and professional development). Along with a safe and well-equipped early learning environment, it is the practices of teachers themselves that likely contribute most to the quality of the program and its effectiveness for young children and families (Buysse & Hollingsworth, 2009; Cost, Quality, & Child Outcomes Study Team, 1995). However, within the broader field of education, a report titled *Studying Teacher Education,* published by the American Educational Research Association, offered the unsettling conclusion that "the body of teacher education research that directly addresses desirable pupil outcomes and the conditions and contexts within which these outcomes are likely to occur is relatively small and inclusive" (Cochran-Smith, & Zeichner, 2005, p. 3). It goes without saying, perhaps, that, compared to the broader field of education, the body of knowledge about effective professional development in early childhood is even smaller and less conclusive. With little to guide us beyond the need for an evidence-based orientation to promoting school readiness for every child, the challenge we now face is how to improve existing professional development through methods such as technical assistance, a fundamentally essential step in creating a highly effective early childhood workforce and a key to improving program quality in the future.

With these examples of how the definition of quality has evolved in recent years, we point to three possible, related disruptive innovations that could be adopted to improve program quality in early childhood in the future:

1. Just as in the public schools, there is a similar need in the early childhood field to customize teaching and learning to address the needs of an increasingly diverse population of young children and families. There are a couple of signs that the field is already moving in this direction. One indication of the field's willingness to customize early education is the move to adopt tiered models of instruction, such as Recognition & Response (R&R; Buysse & Peisner-Feinberg, in press; Peisner-Feinberg, Buysse, Ayers, & Soukakou, in press), Building Blocks (Sandall & Schwartz, 2008), and the Teaching Pyramid (Hemmeter, Ostrosky, & Fox, 2006). These tiered models organize instructional approaches by level of intensity to reflect how directive and involved a teacher must be to help every child learn, including those with learning or behavioral difficulties. Other indications that the early childhood field is moving in this direction include efforts to identify the defining features of high-quality inclusive programs that serve children with identified disabilities (DEC/NAEYC, 2009) and recommendations in the literature for ways to differentiate teaching for dual language learners (Castro, Páez, Dickinson, & Frede, in press).

2. Customizing early education can be expected to disrupt current organizational structures and introduce new technologies and approaches to help teachers manage information related to addressing the needs of individual children and monitoring their progress. For example, teachers who customize education for young learners will need to acquire new knowledge and skills to help them link assessment results with instructional approaches (e.g., computer-assisted technology, web-based assessment systems). Further, reliance on research and other forms of evidence will be necessary to ensure sound decisions and desired results related to core instruction and targeted interventions. This will require that we make research-based knowledge more relevant and

accessible to a wide array of consumers of this information, including practitioners, administrators, and families.

3. As the field begins to customize teaching and learning in early childhood, there will be reverberating effects on all aspects of the current program quality infrastructure, creating the need for organizational structures and mechanisms that integrate quality standards, accountability systems, and professional development in ways that cut across all sectors of the early childhood field (e.g., Head Start, child care, public prekindergarten, preschool, early intervention). The result of this innovation, although difficult to envision and achieve, is exactly what is needed to disrupt the current fragmented program quality efforts to produce a single, coherent, cross-sector system. These efforts to create an integrated system must be informed by and coordinated with the specific educational practices (e.g., embedded interventions, differentiated teaching, universal design for learning) that will be promoted and supported through an improved program quality infrastructure.

In the next sections, we further explore the ways in which these disruptive innovations in early childhood might be used to advance program quality and effectiveness for every young child and family who receives early childhood services.

KEY FEATURES OF DISRUPTIVE INNOVATIONS

We now turn our attention to features of disruptive innovations as these apply to improving program quality in early childhood. These features include the importance of modularity, the need for noncompeting contexts, patterns of adoption, and the need for user networks and creating consensus for change (Christensen et al., 2008).

Modularity

In disruptive innovation theory, modularity is a characteristic of the design of a system in which the components fit and work together in well-understood, codified ways. In other words, the components are so well defined that individual components can be developed or modified by anyone who has access to the specifications. Christensen and his colleagues (2008) offered the design of a light bulb as an example of a product that has a modular interface with the light bulb socket in a lamp. We can swap one light bulb for another (or one lamp for another), and the two components will still fit together. By contrast, a product's design is interdependent when the way one component is designed depends on how other components in the system are designed and made, and the other way around. Further, the level of modularity or interdependence found within a product is a function of evolution and maturity, with early prototypes demonstrating an interdependent interface and later versions moving toward modularity. The authors point to public schools as an example of an enterprise exhibiting interdependencies, as opposed to modularity, among components of the system. This means that the interface between any two components is unpredictable in terms of how a change in one part of the system will affect another part, and, even more noteworthy, a change in one part of the system generally requires a complete overhaul or redesign of the entire system (e.g., teachers cannot teach content designed to be taught in third grade if the prerequisites were not covered in second grade, or the physical layout of school buildings and the organization of the school day are not conducive to project-based learning).

To create disruptive innovations to improve program quality in early childhood, it will be necessary to identify the points of interdependency within the current program quality infrastructure and to begin to move toward a modular interface between program quality components. For example, if the goal is to customize teaching and learning, then state- or program-level decisions related to selecting a core curriculum and approaches to intentional teaching should be made in a way that support, rather than undermine, this innovation. Similarly, shifts in teaching practices related to customizing early education should be coordinated with corresponding changes in program standards, practice guidelines, and professional competencies so that all components of the system work together. Currently, because of the nonmodularity that exists within the existing program quality architecture, practitioners too often find themselves trying to implement new practices, such as tiered models, without access to practice guidelines, adequate professional development, and other key supports contained within other parts of the program quality infrastructure. Adopting innovations to improve program quality, therefore, will require careful coordination and planning across all aspects of the system as well as codification of the defining characteristics of the innovation (e.g., defining a practice and specifying how it works in sufficient detail to ensure shared understanding and consistent implementation). In our view, it is a common mistake for well-intended program quality reformers to focus on only one part of the system (e.g., creating or revising professional competencies, creating or revising early learning standards or QRISs) without considering why and how such competencies and standards can be expected to lead to improved practices, how one component relates to another, and what effect changes in one part of the system will have on another. Modularity that expands current ideas around the frequent call for alignment should be a guiding principle in our efforts to improve program quality.

Introducing Innovations in Noncompeting Contexts

Disruptive innovation theory suggests that innovations work best when introduced within noncompeting contexts. A disruptive innovation does not consist of a breakthrough improvement within an existing system (making an airplane fly faster or a battery last longer) but rather represents a new product that disrupts the current system and changes it fundamentally. Christensen and colleagues (2008) offered the Apple IIe as an example of a disruptive innovation, because it eventually replaced (rather than improved) the mainframe computer as the dominant computing model. As mentioned previously, it is almost impossible for existing organizational structures to adopt disruptive innovations on their own, as these innovations conflict with current reform efforts and compete for limited resources. The Apple IIe was first introduced as a toy for young children because the early version could not compete for consumers of mainframe computers. It took almost 10 years before the Apple IIe had evolved into a PC that could compete with the mainframe computer market. Within public education, charter schools were designed to offer an opportunity to create a new model of schooling within a noncompeting context, although the verdict is out on whether this investment will pay off. Other examples of noncompeting contexts to support disruptive innovations in education include advanced placement courses, rural education, home schooling, and schools that have adopted early intervening models such as response to intervention (RTI).

In early childhood, the field will need to consider how innovations to improve program quality might occur initially outside of existing organizational structures, to provide an opportunity to think in new ways and innovate outside of this system. One idea in this regard is for areas of the country that do not yet have a fully developed program quality infrastructure (e.g., QRIS, early learning standards, technical assistance) to begin to build these systems with an eye toward customization and cross-sector integration, as opposed to emulating a system developed by another state that does not contain these features. Alternately, states that already have a quality improvement infrastructure that applies to only one sector of early childhood (e.g., child care) could turn their attention to other sectors as a laboratory for developing quality improvement innovations in these programs (e.g., public prekindergarten, early intervention), with the ultimate goal, of course, of having one integrated, cross-sector system. Another noncompeting context at a different level of the system might be found within special education and early intervention programs. The disability field contains a wealth of knowledge, resources, and technologies related to customizing education for individual children with disabilities and their families. How could specific intervention practices such as embedded instruction, universal design for learning, and other scaffolding strategies (e.g., prompting, modeling, responsive teaching, mand and delay) be used within a general early childhood education context to address the needs of a broader group of young children? This strategy would require harvesting innovations created for a different target group for a different purpose and applying them in a new way as part of a program quality improvement effort.

Patterns of Innovation Adoption

According to disruptive innovation theory, as defined by Christensen and colleagues (2008), motivation is the catalyst for every successful innovation. Without the will or desire to change something, it is virtually impossible to transform a system that is complicated, expensive, or disjointed into one that is accessible, efficient, affordable, and effective. However, disruptions to an existing system rarely manifest as an abrupt shift, as pointed out in the example of the transition in the computing market from mainframes to PCs. The evolution of an innovation generally follows a similar S-curve pattern across two phases of adoption. The S-curve pattern varies, in that sometimes it is steep and other times gradual, but the pattern is generally the same. In the first phase (at the beginning of the S-curve), an innovation is introduced in a noncompeting context. During this phase, the technology (e.g., product, tool, process) is improved and the costs begin to decline (recall that innovations are expensive when first introduced), but the innovation is not disruptive to the existing system. In the second phase, the innovation disrupts the existing system and competes with it, drawing consumers and clients away from the existing system and toward the new approach or technology. At the point at which the innovation has an economic or technological advantage over the old one, the pace at which the new technology substitutes for the old one increases (i.e., with the pattern being initially slow, then quickening dramatically, and finally constituting most of the market). The example of this pattern of innovation adoption offered by Christensen and colleagues is the shift from film photography to digital. It took a decade, but then the digital technology "flipped" the market and more or less put film photography out of business. Witness recent disruptions in the smart mobile phone market that has shifted industry standards to incorporate disparate computing functions related to making phone calls, e-mailing and using other messaging systems, and accessing the Internet, along with seemingly endless other applications, into a single mobile device. These innovations in the cell phone market mean that consumers are skipping the traditional step of purchasing both a cell phone and a PC and are opting instead to have a single mobile device that can be used to download music, watch movies, make phone calls, and access the Internet. Are we witnessing a flip in technology at this moment in which PCs and laptops will no longer be needed? Although we cannot examine this phenomenon in detail here, readers may be interested to learn that innovation theorists have figured out a way to forecast or predict these flips, the points at which an innovation is widely adopted, seemingly out of nowhere.

What are the implications of this for the early childhood field? Simply, that we should expect that change related to innovation will not occur abruptly but rather slowly at first, and then more rapidly, once the technology improves and the costs become more reasonable. Returning to our earlier example of customizing within one aspect of the early childhood sector, we should expect that programs that adopt a tiered model, such as the Teaching Pyramid, R&R, or Building Blocks, would not gain much attention from the broader early childhood community in the beginning; however, as teachers learned new ways of conducting assessments using web-based technology and began linking these results to decisions related to instruction and interventions, and found that these methods were effective in helping every child make developmental gains, the field would take notice. In time, once the new technologies related to implementing a tiered model became less expensive and more accessible and reflected recommended practices, we could expect that the approach would draw consumers and clients away from old technologies and toward the new tiered model. Somewhere in this adoption cycle, if the innovation followed the usual S-curve pattern, we would see a blip on the radar screen in which nearly everyone in the mainstream had adopted it. Based on innovation theory, this is a typical adoption pattern for a disruptive innovation. (It is important to note that the same pattern does not apply to reforms aimed at making incremental improvements to an existing system—e.g., adopting a new curriculum, offering additional professional development, creating professional competencies, increasing program monitoring efforts).

Ongoing Learning and User Networks

One important ingredient in the development and adoption of innovation centers on user networks. To harvest the best thinking in our field and the innovation energies of a larger group of people, innovation theory suggests that we must find ways to connect with one another. Online user networks or user-generated resource libraries create opportunities whereby participants can instruct and learn from each other and inform the development or refinement of the innovation in a synchronous fashion, much as it unfolds within a community of practice framework (Wesley & Buysse, 2006). Contrast this dynamic, energizing environment of learning and innovation with one in which a handful of state agency personnel make key decisions regarding the best ways to improve program quality with little input from consumers. The notion of a community for shared inquiry and learning also has been recommended as a vehicle for contributing to the knowledge base in conjunction with the evidence-based practice movement (Wesley & Buysse, 2006). It is perhaps not too surprising that user networks are important for both purposes—developing innovations and promoting evidence-based practice—and remind us of the vital connection between the two. With respect to program quality, user networks could create opportunities to share innovations related to program quality as these emerge in different parts of the country (and throughout the world). Specific ideas, measures, technologies, QRISs, and methods for creating modularity in program quality infrastructure could be rated by various users, much as recipes and books are rated online, and borrowed, refined, and offered in new formats for further comment and review. An example of an online early childhood community focused on improving professional development related to inclusion can be found at http://community.fpg.unc.edu/.

Creating Consensus for Change

Once a decision has been made to move in the direction of creating a disruptive innovation, and factors such as modularity and noncompeting contexts have been taken into account, another consideration is determining how to forge consensus for change. This isn't to imply that these considerations are steps that happen in a linear fashion, but they rather represent the interplay of factors that influence key decisions along the way. How can people who want to innovate to improve program quality in early childhood convince their constituencies to work with them to achieve this goal for change, given the disruptive nature of what they are proposing? According to disruptive innovation theory, there are a variety of "tools of cooperation" that traditionally have been used to get people on board with reform, ranging from instituting training or standard operating procedures, to offering financial incentives and rewards, to using charisma and diplomacy, to resorting to coercion and threats (Christensen et al., 2008); however, these rarely work with respect to innovations. The authors suggest that these tools of cooperation generally fall into four broad categories: leadership tools such as charisma and social influence, power tools such as hiring and promoting, culture tools such as apprenticeship and tradition or rituals, and management tools such as training and measures or standards. The effectiveness of these tools depends on the extent to which people agree on two dimensions: what they want to achieve and which actions will lead to the desired results. As an example, if there is no consensus on what people want, nor on how to get there, then power tools such as threats, coercion, or control are thought to work best (obviously, this is not something we recommend for promoting consensus on innovations within early childhood). On the other hand, if there is broad agreement on what people want, but no agreement on how to get there, then leadership skills such as envisioning or charisma tend to work best. None of these situations or sets of tools are ideal for reaching consensus, and we are not recommending them with respect to improving program quality, but the framework is a helpful way of thinking about how to assess the current innovation climate and to consider how to begin to shift opinions toward agreement on both dimensions (what needs to change, how to get there).

Drawing again from theory on how innovations occur, there are two vehicles for shifting the balance of a team focused on program quality toward agreement. The first is experiencing some modicum of success on some aspect of the innovation. In the early childhood field, can we find one example in which the innovation or a key component of the innovation appears to be working well? For example, a state that is frustrated in its attempts to create a single, cross-sector professional development system could point to their statewide network of technical assistance (TA) providers as evidence that they are beginning to move in the right direction. The second is a conceptual framework or common language to help frame the problem. Without this common frame, people often talk past each other in describing the current challenges, or they describe one aspect of the problem from their own perspective and based on their own experiences. The *who*, the *what*, and *how* conceptual framework described in Chapters 1 and 6 provides an example of this. This framework helped people use common language to identify pressing challenges and problems related to creating cross-sector systems of professional development, to categorize these as either infrastructure issues or core to delivering professional development in terms of content and methods, and to begin to make connections across these dimensions (Buysse, Winton, & Rous, 2009; National Professional Development Center on Inclusion, 2008). It is important to note that, although conceptual frameworks and common language do not immediately lead to innovations and solutions, they are fundamentally important in reaching consensus on what needs to change, a precursor to figuring out how to reach this goal. Too often in early childhood, the first step in achieving consensus for change is to implement a strategic planning process that involves creating a vision and then developing goals, objectives, and so forth. But, this work can be misguided if common language has not been used to reach consensus on the definition of the problem as well as what needs to change. Merely creating a written vision statement does not mean that there is consensus for change, nor cooperation in how to work together to achieve it. Sometimes what is needed, according to Christensen and colleagues (2008), is a "heavyweight" team structure, particularly when the current team structure cannot adequately move outside of the sphere of the interdependencies (as opposed to modularity) within the current system. The idea of establishing state early childhood advisory councils on early education and care could fulfill this heavyweight function by transcending traditional boundaries across sectors of the early childhood field to create new ways of working together and innovating to improve program quality. In addition, the proposed legislation to establish early learning challenge grants offers a unique opportunity for states to compete for additional resources (up to $1 billion per year) to strengthen their early learning systems for children birth through 5 years of age through innovations in program quality (see, e.g., http://www.ed.gov/about/inits/ed/earlylearning/elcf-factsheet.html).

NOTES ON FUTURE RESEARCH ON PROGRAM QUALITY INNOVATIONS

As discussed earlier in this chapter, research is a valued enterprise in the early childhood field for advancing knowledge and understanding on a wide array of issues. Chapter 2 presents an excellent history of how research on program quality has unfolded with respect to program quality, summarizes what we have learned from this line of inquiry, and outlines several promising new research directions that we need to address in the future. At the same time, the incremental nature of scientific inquiry means that it is difficult for research to match the pace in which new questions or issues emerge in practice; in fact, practice often precedes research in many fields. And this is no less true with respect to program quality. Further, some of the research evidence is inconsistent or contradictory, and much of it has little direct relevance for what needs to change right now in practice. For example, much of the research showing that key dimensions of program quality (e.g., process and structural factors) are related to positive child outcomes in general does not translate directly to the specific changes that an individual teacher needs to make to improve the quality of her educational program to benefit the children in her classroom. With respect to future efforts to improving program quality, research in this area needs to evolve to help the field predict with more precision which innovations improve early childhood programs, and under what conditions. Stated another way, this means that the research agenda to advance program quality needs to shift from observing, measuring, and showing associations to demonstrating causal linkages. The focus on a chain of causal evidence can be used to advance understanding, not just on what works on average, but, as suggested in Chapter 2, for specific subgroups of children (e.g., children from diverse cultural, linguistic, racial, and ability groups).

APPLYING DISRUPTIVE INNOVATIONS TO PROGRAM QUALITY IMPROVEMENT EFFORTS

This chapter presented ideas related to improving program quality in early childhood through the lens of disruptive innovation theory. We offered several innovations that would disrupt the current program quality infrastructure as well as fundamentally change and improve the quality of services and supports provided to young children and families. These included the notions that early education must be customized and matched to the learning needs of every child, that early childhood teachers would need new technologies and skill sets to manage this new instructional approach, and that the current fragmented infrastructure to support program quality be transformed into an integrated, cross-sector system. We conclude by sharing two scenarios: The first offers a view of how the field traditionally has approached program quality improvements—primarily, by tinkering around the edges of the program quality system (i.e., making slow, steady improvements to existing structures); the second sets the stage for how the field might create disruptive innovations to achieve dramatic improvements in program quality in the future.

Scenario #1: A Traditional Approach to Program Quality Improvement

The director of a state child care division and her staff are discussing the state's new QRIS for child care. Because the current licensing system reflects minimum standards of quality, they are looking for ways to make the most of the opportunities that QRIS provides for improving quality. With limited resources, the team decides to focus their efforts on rolling out the new program. The group plans a variety of strategies for getting the word out about the new QRIS, including the launch of a new presence on the state child care division's web site, a session at a statewide annual child care conference, and regional trainings conducted by resource and referral agencies that are mandatory for participating child care programs. Because they learned that this strategy was successful in a neighboring state, the team has decided to offer financial incentives to programs that improve their quality ratings. Finally, they have revised their program quality accountability system by adding a new measure related to language and literacy to address the importance of ensuring children's readiness for kindergarten. They are hopeful that all of these efforts will pay off and that next year they will be able to point to significant improvements in the quality of child care in their state.

Scenario #2: Disruptive Innovation Related to Program Quality

The governor in one state appointed a state-level, cross-sector planning team to create innovations related to program quality in early childhood. Their charge was to think about ways to improve early education experiences and outcomes for young children from low-resource communities. After carefully considering their options and their resources, the team decided to focus their efforts on one county in which Head Start programs were facing tremendous obstacles in meeting the needs of a growing population of Latino dual language learners. The problem was that almost all of the teachers were monolingual English speakers, whereas the children primarily spoke Spanish but were at various stages in developing English as their second language. The team decided that a tiered approach might offer teachers a framework for how to differentiate instruction for these children, primarily because it built on a component of RTI/R&R that teachers were already using—screening and progress monitoring—and it addressed the need for more targeted interventions in language and literacy that would complement their core curriculum. To find the specific tiered interventions in language and literacy, the team turned to the emerging knowledge base on tiered models in early childhood as well as specific accommodations for dual language learners from the research literature (e.g., making print materials available in both English and Spanish, repetition of interactive storybook reading to reinforce important concepts, the use of visual cues and props to introduce new vocabulary, the dramatization of story narratives, assistance in supporting the home language from bilingual teaching staff or volunteers). They summarized in writing the most promising practices that they could find in the literature for scaffolding learning for these children, organizing these by level of intensity and including the materials and steps for implementing them in early childhood classrooms. The team realized that their decision to implement this new approach with a new group of children in one type of setting would have many implications for what happened next, not the least of which was determining how to work with Head Start teachers, administrators, and families to introduce these ideas and gain their trust and cooperation. In addition, the team was already thinking about ways to help teachers acquire new skills and the technology needed to implement these new teaching strategies through intensive, professional development and ongoing support; the need to purchase new curricula and web-based assessment tools; and other components of the program quality infrastructure, such as the QRIS measures and accountability system that would need to be modified to ensure consistency with the new teaching practices they were planning to introduce. To harvest all of the energies of the innovation they were planning to introduce, they considered creating a virtual community of practice in which teachers, parents, and administrators could exchange ideas and share new insights about what they had learned about practices to support dual language learners in Head Start classrooms. Finally, the team recognized that the innovation they were creating could not be expected to improve program quality in early childhood overnight. However, they were hopeful that the investments they were making to customize teaching and learning for one group of children in one community would ultimately and fundamentally change the definition of program quality as well as the standards, accountability, and professional development systems to support the development and learning of all children, including those from diverse cultural, racial, linguistic, and ability groups.

SUMMARY

This is a defining moment in the early childhood field's efforts to improve program quality. The choice we face as a field is either to continue down a sustainability pathway in which we make slow, steady progress to improve what is currently in place, or we move in the direction of innovation to produce more dramatic results and fundamental changes in how we conceptualize and support program quality. Adopting an innovation orientation will entail a willingness to take risks and to think in ways that disrupt, rather than reinforce, current models and structures. We acknowledge that the second scenario involving innovation presents different challenges than those associated with more traditional improvement efforts. In addition, it likely raises more questions than it answers. For example, how would a team know where to look for innovative practices to implement? What steps will the state planning team take to integrate a community-level innovation with the existing program quality infrastructure? If the new practices for dual language learners are shown to be effective in Head Start programs in one community, how will the team share this information and promote the adoption of these practices in other early childhood sectors in other parts of the state? How long will it take before the innovation catches on and yields positive results for other children in other programs? Although the answers to these and other questions are not known at this time, we offer several take-home messages to guide future decisions about whether to adopt an innovation approach to improve program quality.

The first is that program quality efforts cannot remain at the systems level as viewed from 5,000 feet aboveground. Our efforts to improve program quality must begin to connect clearly defined educational practices that respond to pressing needs with the broader systems-level supports (e.g., QRISs, early learning standards, professional competencies) that serve as the foundation for these practices. As we begin to innovate, we can turn our thinking around by beginning with the identification of specific practices—for example, instructional supports for dual language learners—and introduce these in a noncompeting context as opposed to focusing all of our efforts on developing or revising program quality standards, as illustrated in the disruptive innovation scenario. Other principles from disruptive innovation theory, such as modularity, can help us look for points of interdependency within existing structures (e.g., differentiated teaching strategies and QRIS standards that reflect these practices) and seek ways to move toward a better interface between program quality components. In the end, every successful innovation will depend ultimately on the field's willingness to change. Many would say that the field has reached consensus on what we mean by *program quality* and how to get there; the literature suggests that the most fertile ground for innovation can be found in places where teachers work and children learn.

REFERENCES

Bowman, B.T., Donovan, S.M., & Burns, M.S. (Eds.). (2000). *Eager to learn: Educating our preschoolers.* Washington, DC: National Research Council. National Academies Press. Committee on Early Childhood Pedagogy.

Buysse, V., & Hollingsworth, H. (2009). Program quality and early childhood inclusion: Recommendations for professional development. *Topics in Early Childhood Special Education, 29*(2), 119–128.

Buysse, V., & Peisner-Feinberg, E. (Manuscript in preparation). *Recognition & response—R&R: Response to intervention (RTI) for pre-K.*

Buysse, V., & Wesley, P.W. (Eds.). (2006). *Evidence-based practice in the early childhood field.* Washington, DC: ZERO TO THREE: National Center for Infants, Toddlers, and Families.

Buysse, V., Winton, P.J., & Rous, B. (2009). Reaching consensus on a definition of professional development for the early childhood field. *Topics in Early Childhood Special Education, 28*(4), 235–243.

Castro, D., Páez, M.M., Dickinson, D.K., & Frede, E. (in press). Promoting language and literacy in young dual language learners: Research, practice, and policy. *Child Development Perspectives: Journal of the Society for Research on Child Development.*

Christensen, C.M., Horn, M.B., & Johnson, C.W. (2008). *Disrupting class: How disruptive innovation will change the way the world learns.* New York: McGraw-Hill.

Cochran-Smith, M., & Zeichner, K.M. (Eds.). (2005). *Studying teacher education: The report of the AERA Panel on Research and Teacher Education.* Mahwah, NJ: Lawrence Erlbaum Associates.

Cost, Quality, & Child Outcomes Study Team. (1995). *Cost, quality, and child outcomes in child care centers: Final report.* Denver: University of Colorado.

Dahlberg, G., & Moss, P. (2008). Beyond quality in early childhood education and care: Languages of evaluation. *CESifo DICE Report.* Retrieved on August 30, 2009, from http://www.cesifo.de/DocCIDL/dicereport208-forum4.pdf

DEC/NAEYC. (2009). *Early childhood inclusion: A joint position statement of the Division for Early Childhood (DEC) and the National Association for the Education of Young Children (NAEYC).* Chapel Hill: University of North Carolina, FPG Child Development Institute.

Hemmeter, M.L., Ostrosky, M., & Fox, L. (2006). Social and emotional foundations for early learning: A conceptual model for intervention. *School Psychology Review, 35*(4), 583–601.

National Professional Development Center on Inclusion. (2008). *What do we mean by professional development in the early childhood field?* Chapel Hill: University of North Carolina, FPG Child Development Institute.

No Child Left Behind Act of 2001, PL 107-110, 115 Stat. 1425. (2002). Retrieved August 15, 2009, from http://www.nochildleftbehind.gov/next/overview/index.html

Peisner-Feinberg, E., Buysse, V., Ayers, L., & Soukakou, E. (in press). Recognition & Response: Response to intervention for pre-kindergarten. In C. Groass & S.M. Maude (Eds.), *Early childhood programs and policies for special needs children.* Santa Barbara, CA: ABC-CL10.

Sandall, S.R., & Schwartz, I.S., (2008). *Building blocks for teaching preschoolers with special needs* (2nd ed.). Baltimore: Paul H. Brookes Publishing Co.

Shavelson, R.J., & Towne, L. (Eds.). (2002). *Scientific research in education.* Washington, DC: Committee on Scientific Principles for Education Research. Center for Education. Division of Behavioral and Social Sciences and Education. National Academies Press. National Research Council.

Shonkoff, J., & Phillips, D.A. (Eds.). (2000). *From neurons to neighborhoods: The science of early childhood development.* Washington, DC: National Academies Press, National Research Council and Institute of Medicine.

U.S. Department of Education. (1983). *A nation at risk.* Retrieved August 14, 2009, from www.ed.gov/pubs/NatAtRisk/intro.html

Wesley, P.W., & Buysse, V. (2006). Building the evidence base through communities of practice. In V. Buysse & P.W. Wesley (Eds.), *Evidence-based practice in the early childhood field* (pp. 161–193). Washington, DC: ZERO TO THREE: National Center for Infants, Toddlers, and Families.

Index

Abecedarian Study, 27
Accreditation
   National Association for the Education of Young Children (NAEYC), 23–24, 26, 48, 58, 120–121, 170–171
   overview, 3–4
   professional development, 119–122
ACF, see Administration for Children and Families
Administration for Children, Youth and Families, 167
Administration for Children and Families (ACF), 137–138
American Academy of Pediatrics, 48, 171
American Public Health Association, 171
American Recovery and Reinvestment Act (ARRA), 5–6, 7, 13, 132, 168
Assessment Profiles, 26, 56
At-risk children, 35, 36–37, 75, 105
Attrition, 12, 144

Balanced Budget Act of 1997 (PL 105-33), 137
Behavioral problems, 27, 35
"Brain Under Construction Zones," 169
BrightStars Child Care and Preschool Framework, 96
BUILD Initiative, 104, 107

Career Lattices, 99
Caregiver Interaction Scale (CIS), 23, 26
Caregiver training, 48–49
   see also Professional development
CCDBG, see Child Care and Development Block Grant
CCDF, see Child Care and Development Fund
CCR&R services, see Child Care Resource and Referral Services
CEC/DEC, see Council for Exceptional Children, Division for Early Childhood
Center for National Policy, 173
Charter schools, 190–191
Chicago Child-Parent Centers Study, 27
Child Care and Development Block Grant (CCDBG), 137, 168
Child Care and Development Fund (CCDF), 6, 13–14, 132, 137–138
Child Care Bureau, 137–138, 171
Child Care Quality Rating System Assessment project, 107
Child care resource and referral (CCR&R) services, 101, 137, 140–141, 144
Children, Schools, and Families of England, Department for, 80
CIS, see Caregiver Interaction Scale
Classroom Assessment Scoring System (CLASS), 56, 58, 60–61, 94
Coaches, 150
Committee on Education and Labor, 14
Competencies for Early Childhood Professionals, 72–73, 82–83, 87
CONNECT, see National Center to Mobilize Early Childhood Knowledge
Consultation, 150, 153–154
Contexts, noncompeting, 190–191
Cooperative Extension System, 137
Cost, Quality, and Outcomes in Child Care Centers (CQO) Study, 26–27, 30, 31–32, 34–35, 36
Costs, operational, 33–35
Council for Exceptional Children, Division for Early Childhood (CEC/DEC), 5–6, 120–121, 125, 170
Council of Chief State School Officers (CCSSO) survey, 73, 77
CQO Study, see Cost, Quality, and Outcomes in Child Care Centers Study
Curricula, 59–60, 75–76, 80–81
Curriculum Guidance for the Foundation Stage, 80

DAP, see Developmentally Appropriate Practice
Data collection, quality measurement, 56–59
DEC/CEC, see Division for Early Childhood of the Council for Exceptional Children
Department of Education, 104, 124, 136, 167
Developmentally appropriate practice (DAP), 4–5, 23, 24

Developmentally Appropriate Practice in Early Childhood Programs (NAEYC), 4–5, 23
Disabilities, children with, *see* Inclusion programs
Disruptive innovation theory
  application of, 195–197
  consensus for, 193–194
  features of, 189–193
  meaning of, 185–189
  overview, 183–185, 197
  professional development and, 124–127
Division for Early Childhood of the Council for Exceptional Children (DEC/CEC), 5–6, 120–121, 125, 170
Dual language learners (DLL), 3–4, 10, 60–61, 115–116, 188, 196–197

Eager to Learn (Bowman, Donovan, Burns), 186–187
Early Childhood Classroom Observation Scale, 26
Early Childhood Education Endowment Grant Program, Nebraska, 169
Early Childhood Education Professional Competencies (ECEPC), 72–73, 82–83, 87
Early Childhood Environment Rating Scale (ECERS), 26, 56, 57–58, 61
Early Childhood Environment Rating Scale–England (ECERS-E), 81, 94
Early Childhood Environment Rating Scale–Revised (ECERS-R), 32, 56, 140, 145
Early Childhood Higher Education Training Committee, 74
Early Childhood Longitudinal Study–Birth Cohort (ECLS-B), 32
Early Childhood Program Standards, NAEYC, 23–24
Early Head Start programs, 24, 32, 167
Early Head Start Research and Evaluation Project (EHSRE), 27, 32
Early Intervention, 104
Early Language and Literacy Classroom Observation Pre-K (ELLCO Pre-K), 23, 56
Early Learning Challenge grants, 107
Early Learning Guidelines, 71
Early learning standards (ELS), 9–10, 69–77
Early learning standards (ELS) and QRISs, alignment approaches, 86–87
  Early Childhood Education Professional Competencies (ECEPC), 82–83
  licensing and program standards, 80–81
  overview, 77–79, 87–88
  systems-level challenges, 84–86
Early Reading First, 53
EBP, *see* Evidence-based practice
ECEPC, *see* Early Childhood Education Professional Competencies
ECERS, *see* Early Childhood Environment Rating Scale
ECERS-E, *see* Early Childhood Environment Rating Scale–England
ECERS-R, *see* Early Childhood Environment Rating Scale–Revised
ECLS-B, *see* Early Childhood Longitudinal Study–Birth Cohort
Educational Resources Information Center (ERIC), 30
Education for All Handicapped Children Act of 1975 (PL 94-142), 136
Education of the Handicapped Act Amendments of 1986 (PL 99-457), 167
Education/training, *see* Professional development
Educators, 2–3, 4–5, 26, 31–34
  see also Professional development; Technical assistance
EHSRE, *see* Early Head Start Research and Evaluation Project
ELLCO Pre-K, *see* Early Language and Literacy Classroom Observation Pre-K
ELS, *see entries for* Early learning standards
Environment rating scales
  Family Child Care Environment Rating System (FCCERS), 140
  Infant Toddler Environment Rating System (ITERS), 26, 32, 56, 57–58
  preschool classroom quality, 32
  quality rating and improvement system (QRIS)
  use of, 8, 94
  see also entries for Early Childhood Environment Rating Scales
ERIC, *see* Educational Resources Information Center
Evidence-based practice (EBP), 124–126, 177–178, 187, 193
Evidence-Based Practice in the Early Childhood Field, 187
Extension agencies, 137

FACES, *see* Family and Child Experiences Survey, Head Start
Faculty Initiative Project (FIP), 74

Family and Child Experiences Survey
    (FACES), Head Start, 27, 31–32, 35
Family Child Care Environment Rating
    Scale (FCCERS), 140
Family Child Care Rating Scale (FCCRS), 26
FCCERS, *see* Family Child Care
    Environment Rating Scale
FCCRS, *see* Family Child Care Rating Scale
Finances
    incentives, 55–56, 167–168
    operational costs, 13–14, 33–35, 107
    quality rating and improvement system
        (QRIS), 92, 93
    state-funded programs, 36–37, 169
    teacher wages, 26, 33–34
    technical assistance, 132, 137–138
    see also Low-income families
FIP, *see* Faculty Initiative Project
Foundations, 73
From Neurons to Neighborhoods (Shonkoff,
    Philips), 187

General Accounting Office (GAO) report,
    9, 30
Good Start, Grow Smart (GSGS), 7, 9,
    170–171, 172
Government Performance and Results Act
    (GPRA), 170
GSGS, *see* Good Start, Grow Smart

Handicapped Children's Early Education
    Assistance Act of 1968 (PL 90-538), 136
Head Start
    development of, 167
    outcomes, 27, 31–32, 35
    policy action for, 13–14
    providers, 132, 172
    standards, 24
    see also Early Head Start Programs
Heads Up Reading, 56
Higher education, *see* Professional
    development
Higher Education Opportunity Act of 2008
    (PL 110-315), 13
Home-based care, 48–49, 59

IDEA, *see* Individuals with Disabilities
    Education Improvement Act (IDEA)
    of 2004 (PL 108-446)
IEPs, *see* Individualized education programs

Improving Head Start for School Readiness
    Act, 132
Inclusion programs
    disruptive innovations, 188
    early learning standards, 10, 77
    evidence-based practice, 124
    measurement of, 2, 3–4, 16, 33
    policies, 167, 170, 177
    professional development and, 11–12,
        115–116, 120–121, 125
    recommended practices for, 5–6
    technical assistance and, 136
Individualized education programs
    (IEPs), 77
Individuals with Disabilities Education Act
    (IDEA), 167, 175
Infant/Toddler Environment Rating Scale
    (ITERS), 26, 32, 56, 57–58
Infant-toddler programs, 23, 32–33, 71
INQUIRE, *see* Quality Initiatives Research
    and Evaluation Consortium
In-service professional development, 74–75
Institute of Education Sciences, 172
Institutions of higher education,
    see Professional development
Integration, system, 7, 12, 13, 189
Internet usage, 102
ITERS, *see* Infant Toddler Environment
    Rating Scale

Kindergarten, 82, 166

Leadership, 175–176
Legislation, *see* Policies, quality improvement
Licenses, 3, 80–81
    see also Standards, early childhood
        program
Low-income families, 27, 32, 101, 102
    see also Head Start

Maternal and Child Health's Early
    Childhood Comprehensive
    Systems, 104
Mathematics, 53
Measurements, program quality
    data collection, 56–59
    future development of, 171–172, 177–178
    improving, 59–61
    key issues, 54–59
    links to outcomes, 2–3, 48–49, 52–54
    overview, 47–48

Measurements, program quality—*continued*
  in quality rating and improvement systems (QRISs), 94–98
  research, 21–24
  for technical assistance, 144–146
  tools, 26
  types of, 48–52
  see also Accreditation; Process features, as quality measures; Structural features, as quality measures
Mental health agency as partner, 104
Mentors, 150
Milestones of Early Childhood Development, 73
Minnesota Indicators of Progress, 76
Mississippi Power, 169
Mississippi State University Early Childhood Institute, 169
Models, tiered, 39–40, 188, 192, 196–197
Modularity, 189–190
More at Four prekindergarten program, 35, 36–37, 75, 105
Mothers, 25, 165
Multicultural classrooms, *see* Dual language learners

NACCRRA, *see* National Association of Child Care Resource and Referral Agencies
National Association for the Education of Young Children (NAEYC)
  accreditation, 3–4, 26, 48, 58, 120–121, 170, 171
  inclusion, 6, 125
  practice statements, 10, 23–24, 94
National Association of Child Care Resource and Referral Agencies (NACCRRA), 103, 144
National Campaign for Child Day Care for Working Families, 167
National Center for Early Development and Learning (NCEDL), 31–32, 35, 37
National Center to Mobilize Early Childhood Knowledge (CONNECT), 124–126
National Child Care Information and Technical Assistance Center (NCCIC), 12–13, 78, 107
National Child Care Staffing Study (NCCSS), 26, 31–32, 33
National Commission on Manpower Policy, 165
National Conference of State Legislators, 173

National Council for Accreditation of Teacher Education (NCATE), 120–121, 170–171
National Day Care Study, 25
National Early Childhood Technical Assistance Center (NECTAC), 175
National Early Reading First Evaluation, 49
National Goals and Research for People with Intellectual and Developmental Disabilities (Lakin, Turnbull), 177
National Institute for Early Education Research (NIEER), 171
National Institute of Child Health and Human Development (NICHD), 27, 31–33, 35, 52, 53
National Professional Development Center on Inclusion (NPDCI), 11–12, 115–116
National QRIS Learning Network, 107
National Technical Assistance Center, 107
Nation at Risk report (1983), 185
Native Americans, 7
NCATE, *see* National Council for Accreditation of Teacher Education
NCCIC, *see* National Child Care Information and Technical Assistance Center
NCCSS, *see* National Child Care Staffing Study
NCEDL, *see* National Center for Early Development and Learning
NCLB, *see* No Child Left Behind Act of 2001 (PL 107-110)
NECTAC, *see* National Early Childhood Technical Assistance Center
Networks, user, 192–193
NICHD, *see* National Institute of Child Health and Human Development
NIEER, *see* National Institute for Early Education Research
No Child Left Behind (NCLB) Act of 2001 (PL 107-110), 170–171, 172, 185
NPDCI, *see* National Professional Development Center on Inclusion

Obama, Barack, administration, 13, 168
Observational Record of the Caregiving Environment (ORCE), 52–53, 59
Office of Budget and Management, 170
Office of Child Development, 167
Office of Planning, Research and Evaluation, 98, 107
Office of Special Education Programs, 124, 170
OECD, *see* Organisation for Economic Co-operation and Development

Opening the Door to Quality:
  Centers, 132
ORCE, *see* Observational Record of the
  Caregiving Environment
Organisation for Economic Co-operation
  and Development (OECD), 173
Outcomes
  Head Start, 27, 31–32, 35
  inclusion programs, 170
  measurements, 2–3, 27, 48–49,
    52–54
  program quality and, 34–40
  quality rating and improvement systems
    (QRISs) and, 103
  see also Cost, Quality, and Outcomes in
    Child Care Centers Study

PAF, *see* Preschool Assessment Framework
Parent Aware, 76
Parents Speak Out, 126
PART, *see* Program Assessment Review Tool
Patient Intervention Comparison Outcome
  (PICO), 125
PCERC, *see* Preschool Curriculum
  Evaluation Research Consortium
PCF, *see* Preschool Curriculum Framework
PD, *see* Professional development
Peer interactions, 60
Perry Preschool Project, 27
Personal Responsibility and Work
  Opportunity Reconciliation Act
  (PRWORA) of 1996 (PL 104-193), 137
PICO, *see* Patient Intervention Comparison
  Outcome
PKKTPAI, *see* Pre-Kindergarten and
  Kindergarten Teacher Performance
  Appraisal Instrument
PL 90-538, *see* Handicapped Children's
  Early Education Assistance Act of
  1968 (PL 90-538)
PL 94-142, *see* Education for All Handicapped
  Children Act of 1975 (PL 94-142)
PL 99-457, *see* Education of the
  Handicapped Act Amendments of
  1986 (PL 99-457)
PL 104-193, *see* Personal Responsibility and
  Work Opportunity Reconciliation Act
  (PRWORA) of 1996 (PL 104-193)
PL 105-33, *see* Balanced Budget Act of
  1997 (PL 105-33)
PL 108-446, *see* Individuals with Disabilities
  Education Improvement Act (IDEA)
  of 2004

PL 110-315, *see* Higher Education
  Opportunity Act of 2008 (PL 110-315)
Policies, quality improvement
  current, 169–173
  future, 173–178
  history of, 167–169
  overview, 165–166, 178
  quality improvement movement and,
    13–15
Position Statement on Inclusion
  (DEC/NAEYC), 125
Pre-Kindergarten and Kindergarten
  Teacher Performance Appraisal
  Instrument (PKKTPAI), 82
Preschool Assessment Framework (PAF), 76
Preschool classroom quality, 31–32
Preschool classrooms, 33
Preschool Curriculum Evaluation Research
  Consortium (PCERC), 59
Preschool Curriculum Framework (PCF), 76
Preschool Incentive Grants program, 167
Preservice professional development,
  73–74
Process features, as quality measures
  defined, 48
  history of, 25–26
  outcomes, 35
  overview, 50–52
  program standards, 36, 37
  in research and practice, 21–23
  specific versus global measurements, 39
Professional development (PD)
  accreditation, 119–122
  for caregivers, 48–49
  data collection, 56–57
  as disruptive innovation, 187–188
  early learning standards, 72, 73–75,
    76–77
  measures, 3, 59–60
  overview, 113–117, 132–133
  quality ratings and improvement
    systems (QRISs) and, 82–83, 86–87,
    99, 105, 122–123
  quality improvement movement and,
    10–13, 16
  recommendations for, 123–127
  research on, 31, 37, 117–119,
    172–173
  support for, 176–177
  for technical assistance (TA) providers,
    143–144
Professional development providers, 77
Professional Development
  Registries, 99

Program Assessment Review Tool (PART), 170
Program evaluation studies, 22
PRWORA, *see* Personal Responsibility and Work Opportunity Reconciliation Act (PRWORA) of 1996 (PL 104-193)
Psychometric methods, 61

QRISs, *see* Quality rating and improvement systems
QRS Assessment Project, 98
Quality, dimensions of, 2–3, 15, 171–172
Quality improvement movement
 future directions for, 15–16
 government support for, 6–10
 meaning of, 2–6
 policy, 13–15
 professional development and, 10–13
Quality Initiatives Research and Evaluation Consortium (INQUIRE), 107
Quality rating and improvement systems (QRISs)
 child assessments, 81
 Cost, Quality, and Outcomes in Child Care Center Study (CQO) and, 36
 measures adopted by states for, 55–56, 169
 outcome links, 52, 53, 54
 overview, 91–92, 107–108
 for parents and children, 100–104
 professional development, 122–123
 for programs, 95–100
 quality improvement movement and, 7–9, 16
 scenarios, 195–197
 service system building and, 104–107
 structure of, 92–95
 technical assistance and, 139, 140–141
 see also Early learning standards and QRISs
Quantity of care, 27

Rainbow Child Care example, 139–141, 156–158
RAND study, 8, 94
Ratings, *see specific entries, e.g.,* Quality rating and improvement systems (QRISs)
Ratios, child–caregiver, 9, 35, 48–49
 see also technical assistance
Recognition and Response model, 39–40, 188, 192, 196–197
Recommended Practices (CEC/DEC), 5–6

Research, program quality
 assessment of, 31–33
 disruptive innovations and, 188–189
 future directions for, 38–40, 194–195
 history of, 25–30
 measuring, 21–24
 operational costs versus quality, 33–35
 predictors of quality in, 30–31, 33
 process of, 183–184
 program standards in relation to, 36–38
 for technical assistance (TA) services, 142–143
 trends, 31–33
 see also specific studies, e.g., Cost, Quality, and Outcomes in Child Centers Study
Response to intervention (RTI) principles, 39–40

School readiness skills, 37
Science, 187
Smart Start, 107, 142–143, 168
Social policy research, 30
Social Security Act, 168
Social Services Block Grant, 168
Special education, *see* inclusion programs
Standards, early childhood program
 accountability and, 170–171, 184
 alignment of, 2, 15–16
 research in relation to, 36–38
 state, 24
 see also Accreditation; Early learning standards (ELS); Quality rating and improvement systems (QRISs)
STARS for KIDS NOW, 96–97
Statewide Early Education Programs Study (SWEEP), 35
Structural features, as quality measures
 history of, 25–30
 licensing requirements and, 80
 outcomes, 35
 overview, 48–49
 predictors of quality and, 30–31
 program standards, 37
 in research and practice, 21–24
 specific versus global measurements, 39
Studying Teacher Education (AERA), 188
Supports, quality improvement, 98–99
SWEEP, *see* Statewide Early Education Programs Study
Systems for professional development, 116–117

TA, *see* technical assistance
Teachers, *see* Educators; Professional development; Technical assistance
Technical assistance (TA)
  challenges, 142–146, 175
  guiding principles for, 150–151
  history of, 135–138
  network, 146–150
  organizing services for, 151–158
  overview, 131–134
  professional development and, 16, 122–123, 172
  provider competencies, 158–162
  quality rating and improvement systems (QRISs) and, 9
  roles, 138–142
Technical Assistance Development System, 136

Temporary Assistance for Needy Families, 137
Tiered models, 39–40, 188, 192, 196–197
Tiers, technical assistance, 151–158
Title XX, 168
Training/education, *see* Professional development

U.S. Department of Health and Human Services, 98, 104, 137–138

Validation studies, QRISs, 97

Wages, teacher, 26, 33–34
Women/mothers, 25, 165